I08002335

IMAGES
of America

JEWISH DETROIT

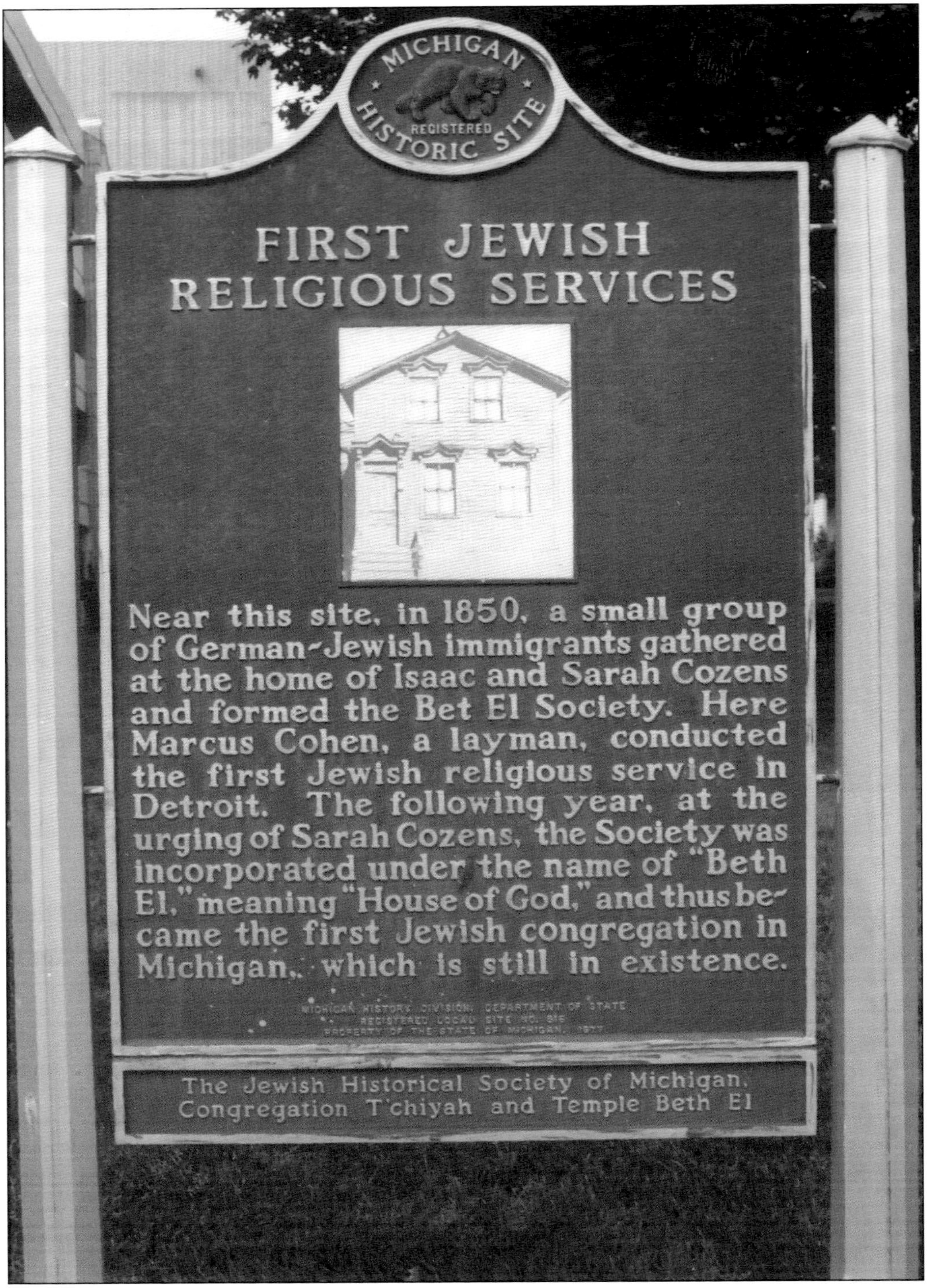

This plaque on East Congress and St. Antoine tells of the beginning of Detroit's Jewish community.

IMAGES of America

JEWISH DETROIT

Irwin J. Cohen

ARCADIA PUBLISHING

ISBN 978-0-7385-1996-8

Published by Arcadia Publishing
Charleston, South Carolina

Printed in the United States of America

Library of Congress Catalog Card Number: 2002106084

For all general information contact Arcadia Publishing at:
Telephone 843-853-2070
Fax 843-853-0044
E-mail sales@arcadiapublishing.com
For customer service and orders:
Toll-Free 1-888-313-2665

Visit us on the Internet at www.arcadiapublishing.com

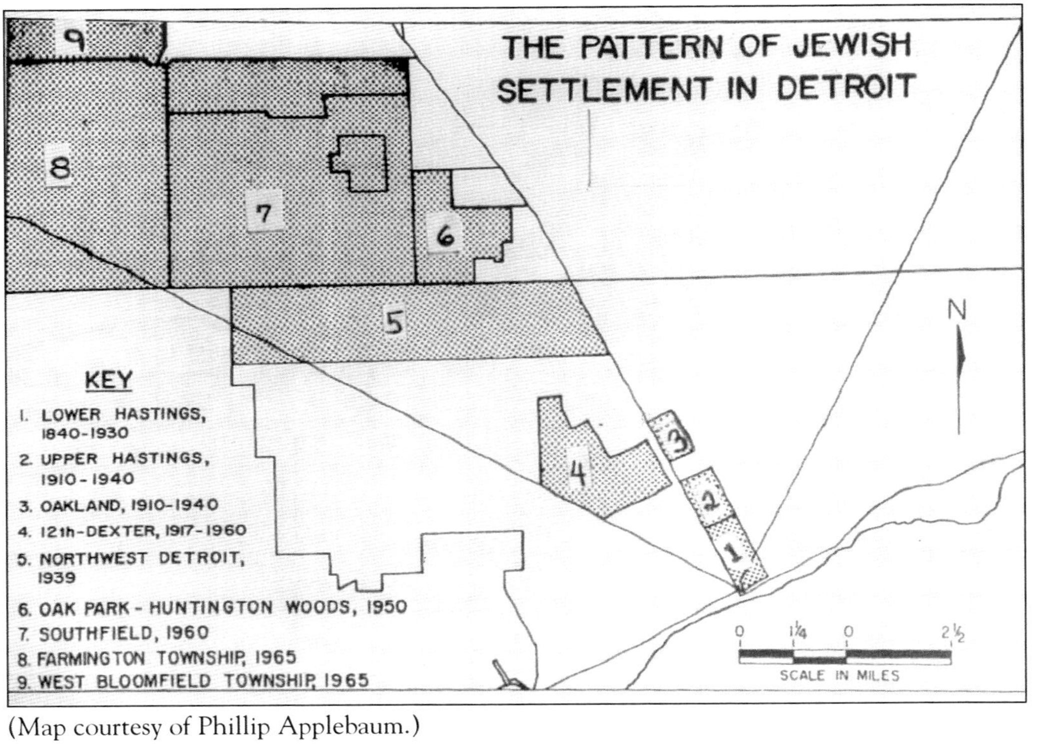

(Map courtesy of Phillip Applebaum.)

Contents

ACKNOWLEDGMENTS

You cannot complete any history of Detroit without spending an enormous amount of time at the Burton Historical Collection of the Detroit Public Library. There you will find a team of capable, professional, helpful people under the direction of author-historian David Lee Poremba.

Incidentally, on my frequent trips there to research this book, I always parked near the former B'nai Israel synagogue on Ferry Street. The building—now a church—is the oldest structure in Detroit to once be used as a synagogue and is a not too distant walk from the main library, which houses the Burton collection.

For a Jewish history, you must visit the Leo M. Franklin Archives of Temple Beth El, ably managed by archivist Holly Teasdale. Another recommended visit is the Leonard N. Simons Archives of the Jewish Federation of Metropolitan Detroit, where director Heidi Christein will give you the proper answers and guidance. And a special thank you to Loretta Crum of Boreal Press, who fine tunes all of my book projects.

It's great to have friends such as Jim Grey of the Jewish Historical Society, who offer great tips and leads. Most of all, though, it helps to be somewhat of a photographer, as you can't really borrow valuable pictures but must make copies of them, assuming you get permission, of course.

In my travels in the area, I have met Detroit historians who never experienced the city's neighborhoods, as they were either born in the suburbs or are from other states.

I consider myself lucky to have been born and bred in Detroit and had the chance to experience life in its Jewish neighborhoods. I spent my early years in the Twelfth Street area and my teen years in the Dexter section before moving to northwest Detroit, about a half mile east of the large Meyers-Curtis branch of the Jewish Community Center.

So, armed with a camera and firsthand experience, here is my story of Jewish Detroit

Introduction

Detroit was founded in 1701 by the dashing French explorer Antoine de la Mothe Cadillac. To control the rich fur trade, a fort was built near the narrowest part of the Detroit River, providing an excellent vantage point to view any river traffic coming from the east or west.

The British also wanted to control the lucrative fur trade. Natural rivalries existed as the French were Roman Catholic and the British Protestant. Skirmishes and Indian attacks often punctured the decades before the arrival of Detroit's first Jew.

Chapman Abraham, a trader from Montreal who dealt in the fur trade in the Upper Peninsula, became Detroit's first recorded Jew in 1762 when he ventured south along the Detroit River for trading purposes. Abraham maintained a residence in the small village of Detroit until his death in 1783.

Six years later, in 1789, Ezekial Solomon, a successful businessman in the Mackinac region, moved to Detroit to dabble in the fur trade. By the nineteenth century, Detroit still didn't have more than a few Jews in town at the same time.

The opening of the Erie Canal in 1825 shaved some seven weeks off what was previously a two-month trip from the eastern seaboard. In 1825 Detroit's population was under 2,000; less than twenty years later it was over 10,000.

By the mid 1840s, Jews began to settle in the Ann Arbor-Ypsilanti area, as it was the state's best land for farming purposes. The residents were mostly of German extraction, so language posed no problem for the Jews who came from Bavaria to escape persecution.

By 1845, Ann Arbor had the state's first Jewish religious service established by the three Weil brothers. Five years later, Detroit's population was 21,019 and included about sixty Jews.

Sarah and Isaac Cozens relocated from New York in 1850. Mrs. Cozens, a religious woman who attended services regularly in New York, urged her husband to seek out any interested Jewish males for the purpose of organizing a synagogue.

Mr. and Mrs. Cozens offered the use of their home for religious services, and twelve men established the Beth El Society. Exactly a hundred years later, Temple Beth El would claim a membership of 1,500.

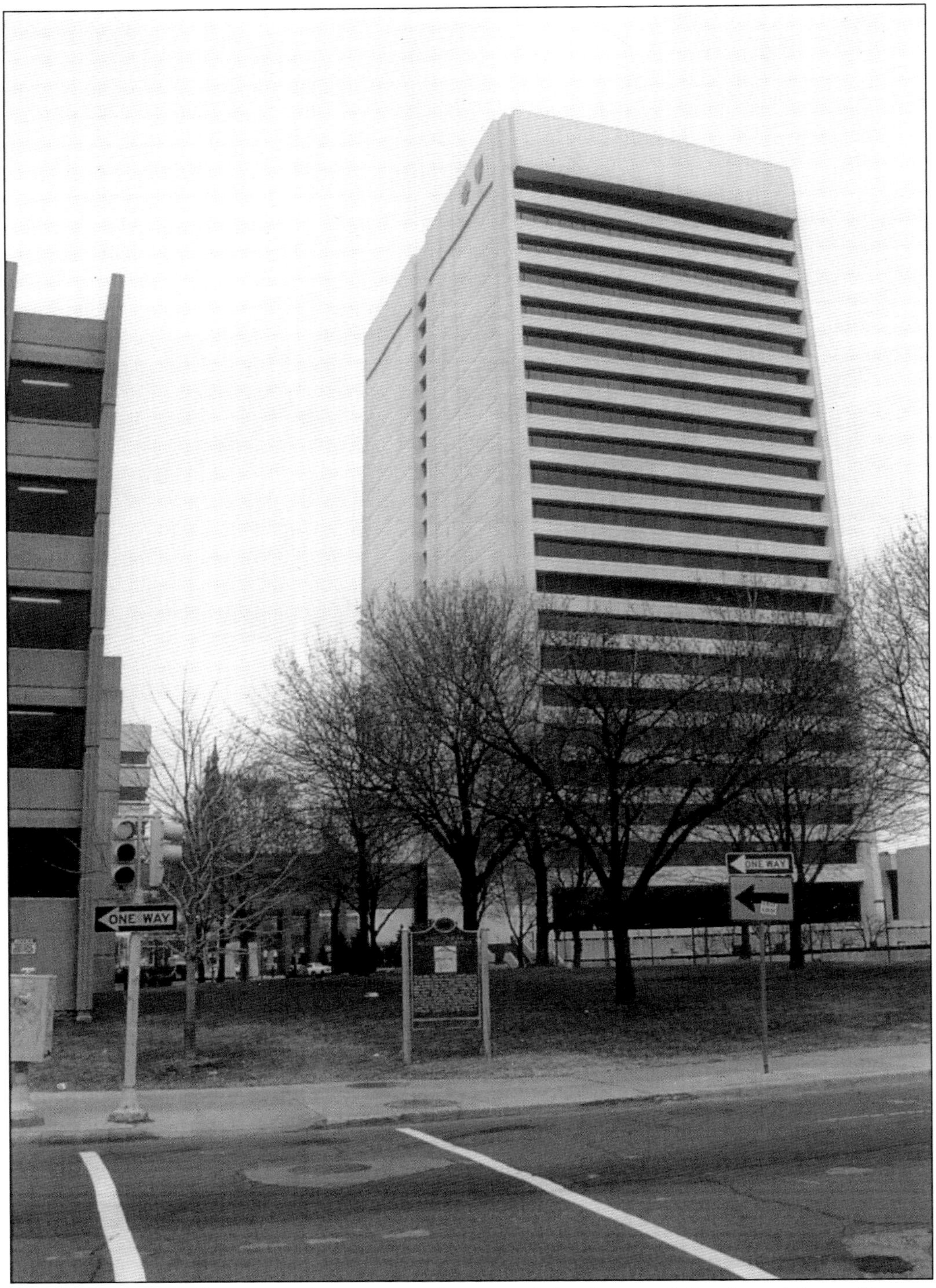

The Blue Cross office tower looms over the site of the home of Sarah and Isaac Cozens. The historical plaque—between the one-way signs—is a few feet north of the sidewalk on East Congress.

One

1850–1875

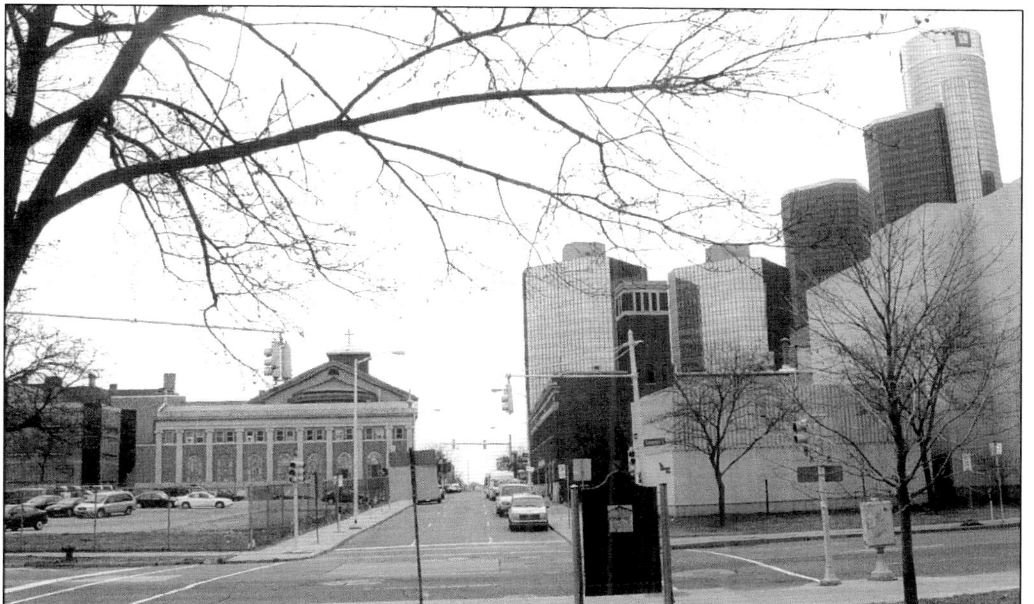

The grassy area under the tree and plaque marks the site of Detroit's first religious service in the Cozens home. Looking south down St. Antoine Street, the parking area to the left is where Congregation Shaarey Zedek built the city's first synagogue. The towers of the General Motors World Headquarters can be seen in the distance.

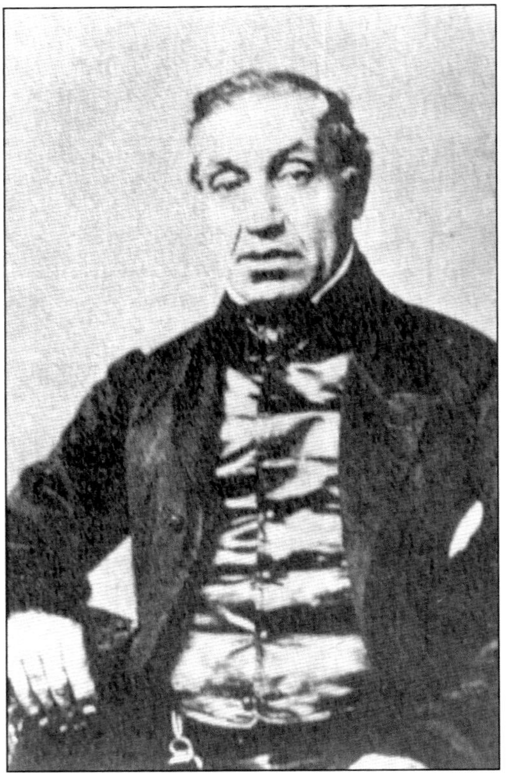

Isaac Cozens was born in Germany and came to New York in 1820. Thirty years later the Cozens family came to Detroit in search of new opportunities. Cozens eventually sold horses to the Union Army during the Civil War.

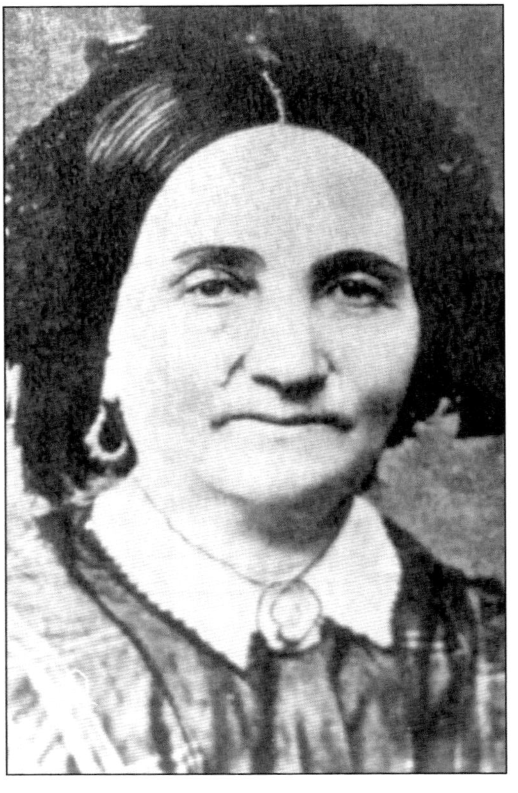

Sarah Cozens urged her husband to locate co-religionists in Detroit and form a congregation. Mrs. Cozens died in 1875 and was buried in Beth El's Section North F of Woodmere Cemetery.

September 22, 1850, marked the founding of the Beth El Society by twelve German Jews in the Cozens home. Rabbi Samuel Marcus eventually arrived from New York to serve as spiritual leader, cantor, ritual slaughterer, and circumciser at an annual stipend of $200.

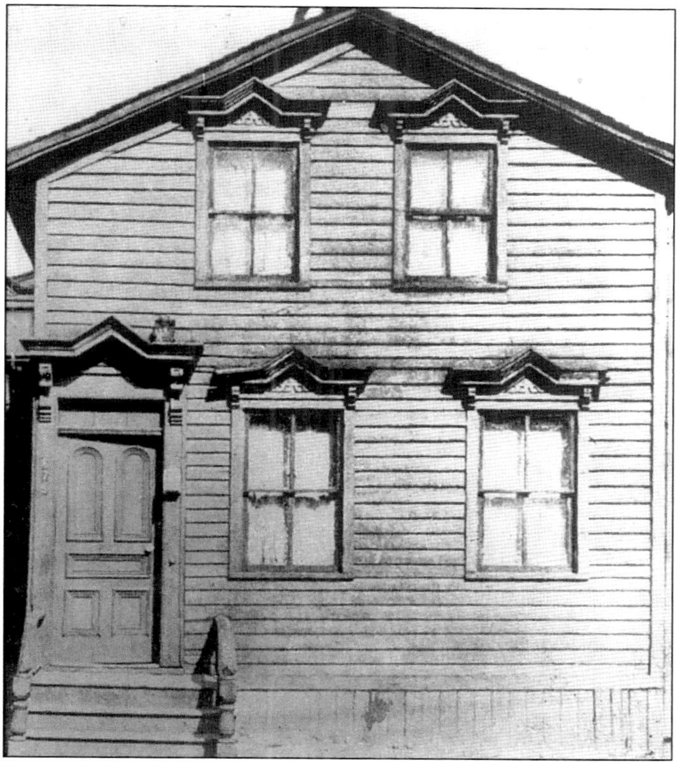

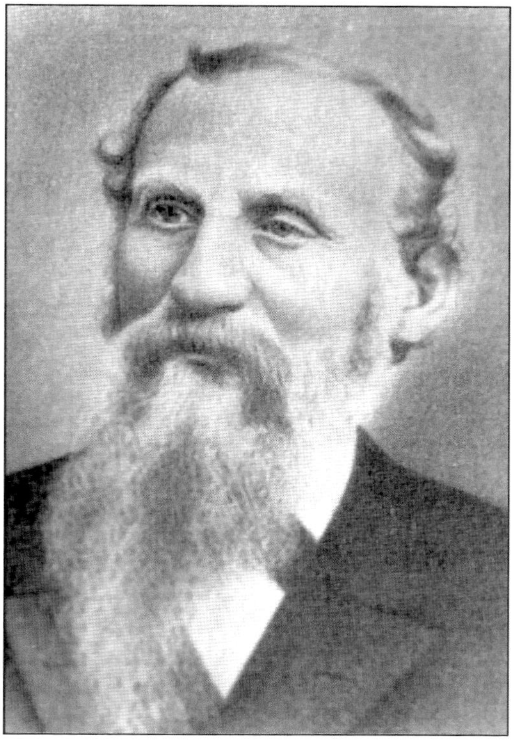

Jacob Silberman was the first president of the small Beth El congregation, which would move from the Cozens home in 1852 to a room above his store. (Courtesy Rabbi Leo M. Franklin Archives, Temple Beth El.)

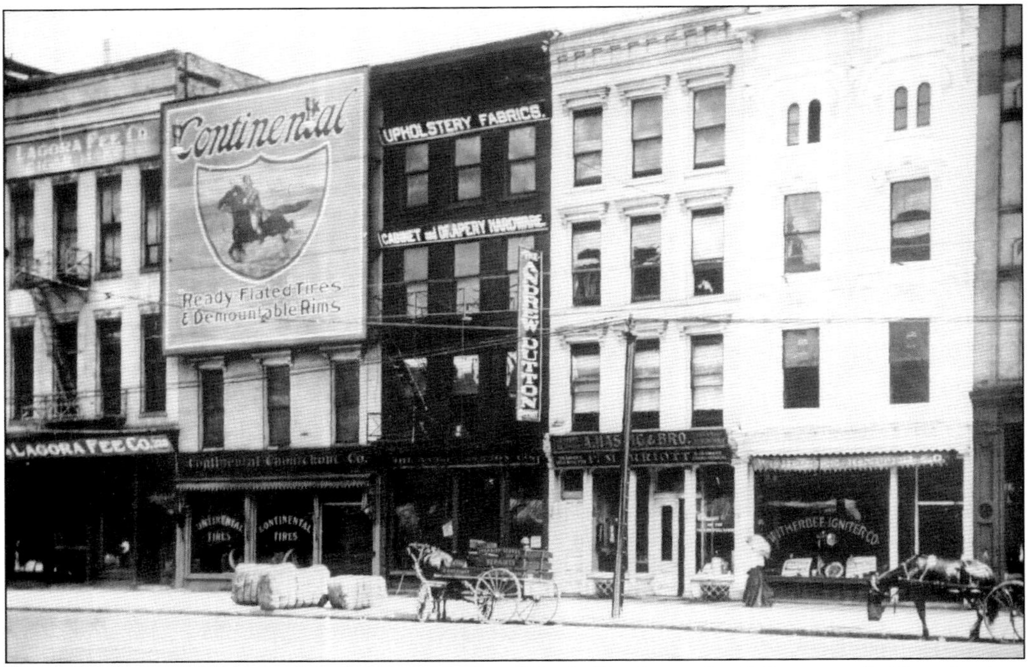

The building on the right was the second site of Beth El, above the Silberman & Hersch cigar and tobacco store on Jefferson east of Woodward. (Courtesy Rabbi Leo M. Franklin Archives, Temple Beth El.)

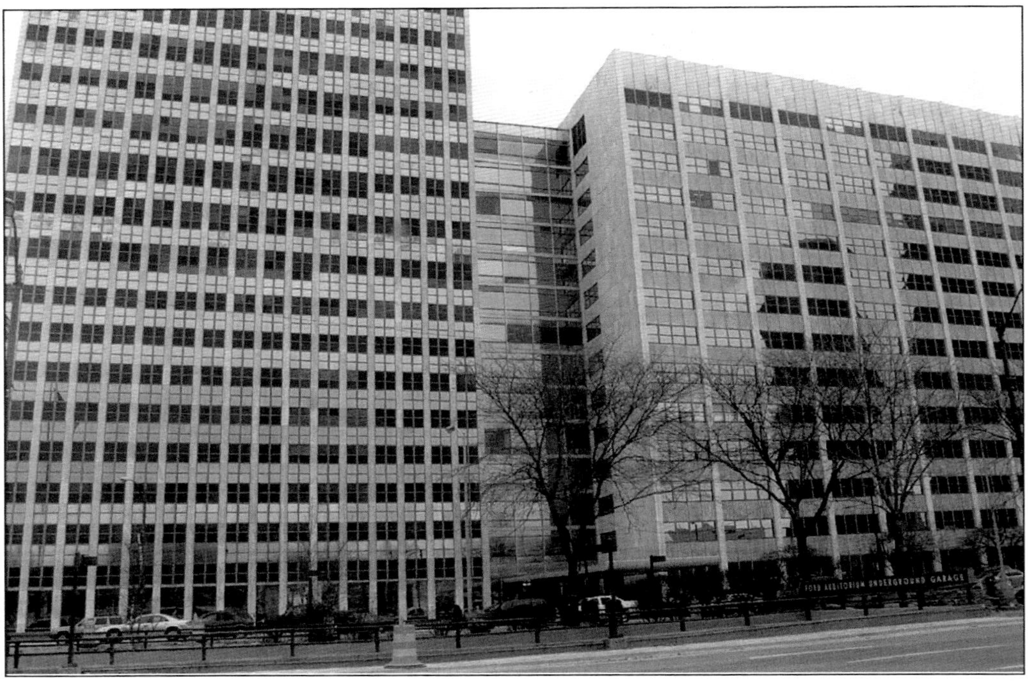

The Coleman A. Young Municipal Building—formerly the City County Building—sits on Beth El's Jefferson site today.

Half an acre in Elmwood Cemetery's southeast corner was purchased by Beth El as a separate cemetery.

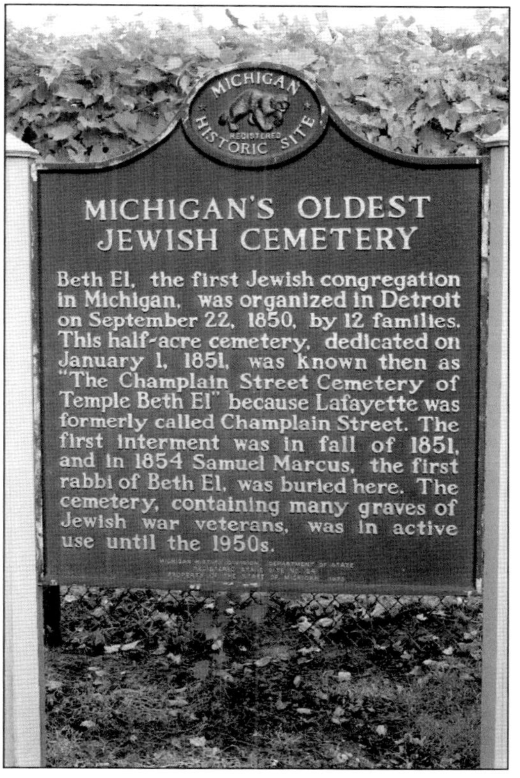

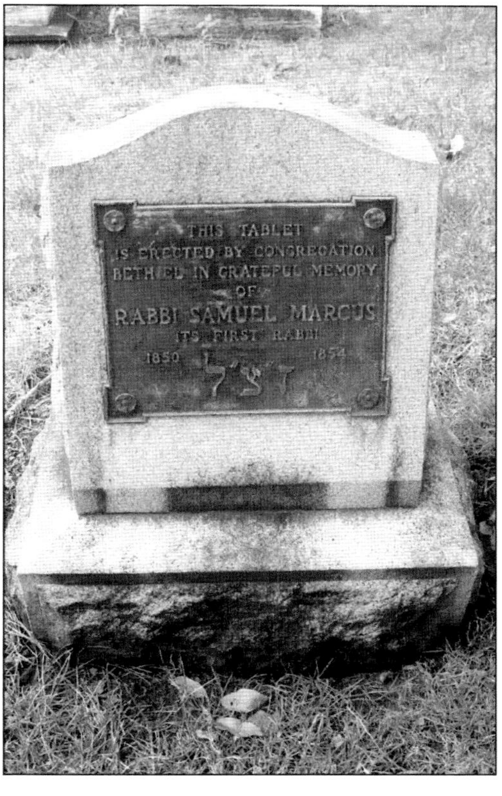

The cholera epidemic of 1854 claimed Rabbi Samuel Marcus, Detroit's first rabbi.

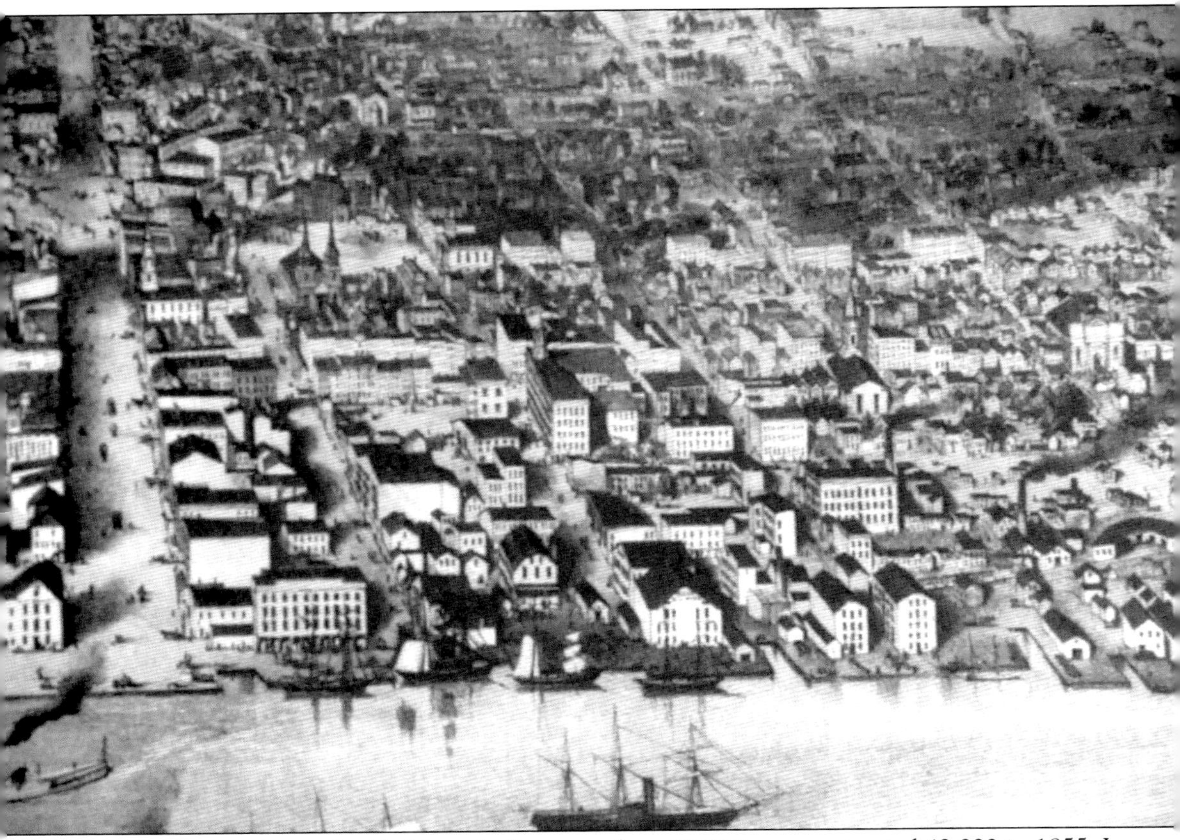

Detroit's population doubled in only five years from 21,019 to an estimated 42,000 in 1855. In the same period, Beth El's membership went from 12 to 25. Most of Detroit's Jewish residents lived east of Woodward—the street on the left—and north of Congress Street. (Courtesy of Burton Historical Collection of the Detroit Public Library.)

In the latter part of the 1850s, Beth El moved from traditional religious services to introducing more reform. In 1861, seventeen men renounced their membership and formed the Schaarey Zedeck Society, now Congregation Shaarey Zedek. They rented space above Scherer's Drug Store in Cadillac Square between Bates and Randolph streets. The site—in the center of the photo—previously was rented by Beth El in 1859 before it purchased its first building in 1861 on Rivard. (Courtesy Burton Historical Collection of the Detroit Public Library.)

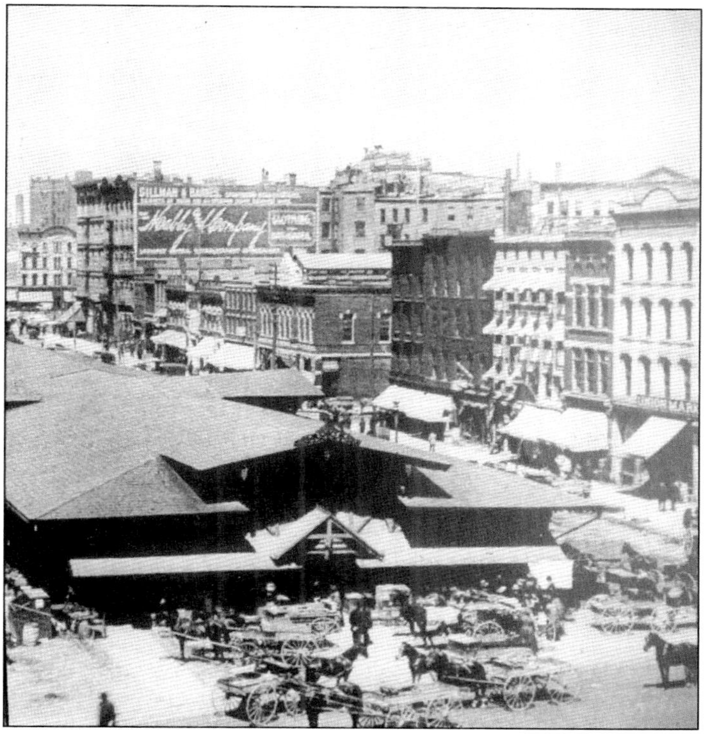

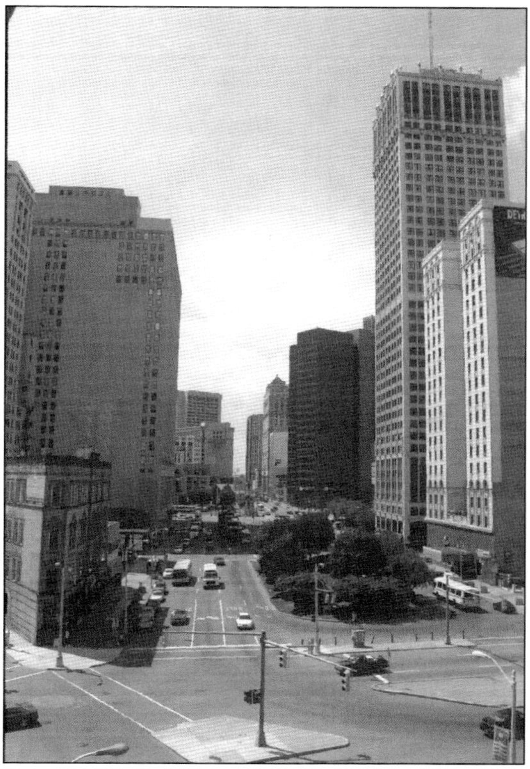

Today the 40-story Cadillac Square Tower sits on the site of Scherer's Drug Store. A tree-filled grassy island now occupies the area of the former market.

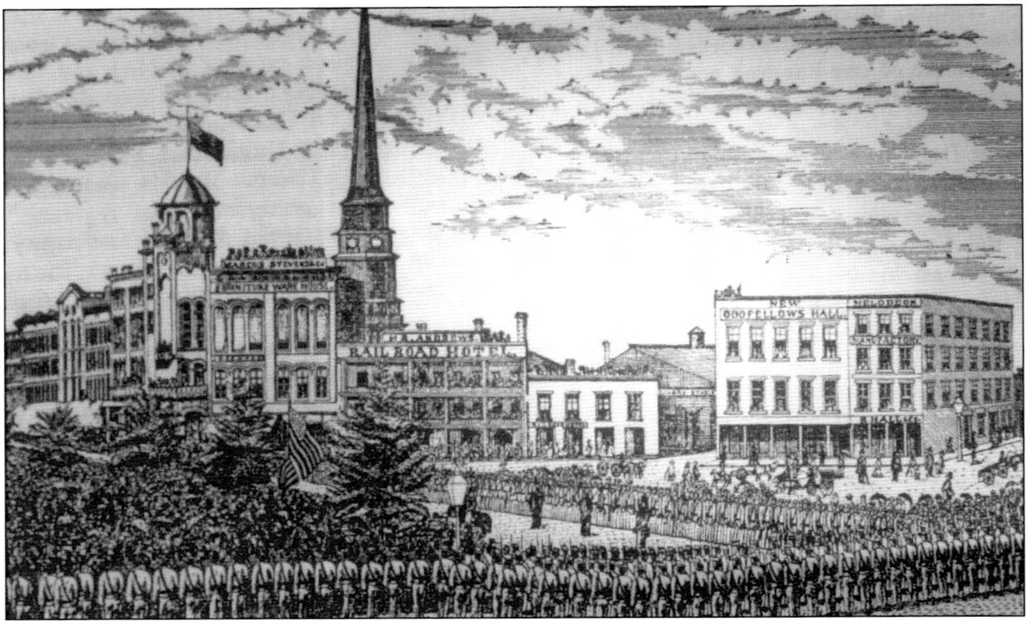

Detroit's population was 47,000 when President Abraham Lincoln proclaimed a state of war on April 17, 1861, and called for volunteers. 181 Jewish soldiers from Michigan—more than one per family—served. Well-wishers filled Campus Martius to see the soldiers march to the rail depot. (Courtesy Burton Historical Collection of the Detroit Public Library.)

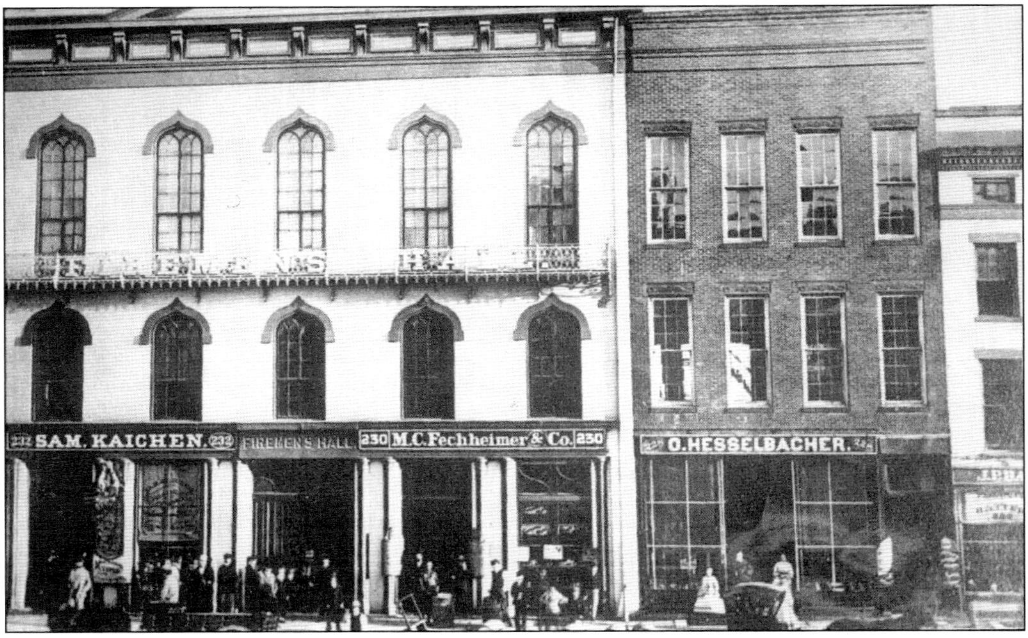

Morris Fechheimer was born in Bavaria and came to Detroit in 1851 at the age of 28. He entered the clothing business and became a liquor salesman before starting a wine and liquor business in 1861 on Jefferson between Woodward and Randolph. (Courtesy Rabbi Leo M. Franklin Archives, Temple Beth El.)

Simon Heavenrich, president of Beth El for six years, operated one of the biggest clothing establishments in the Midwest. (Courtesy Rabbi Leo M. Franklin Archives, Temple Beth El.)

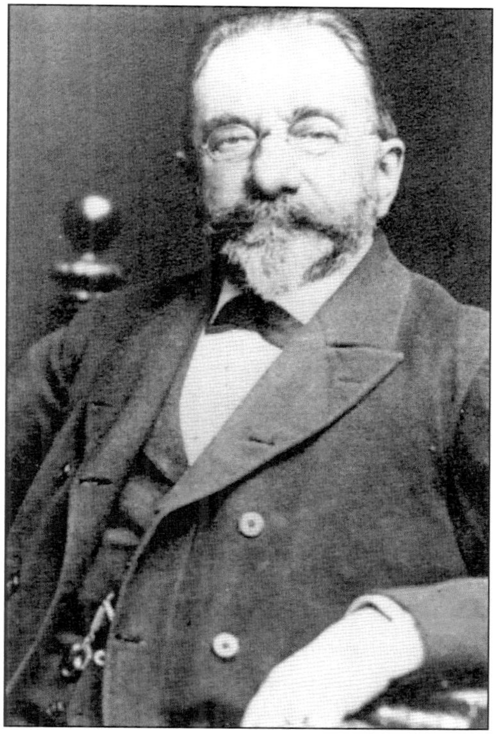

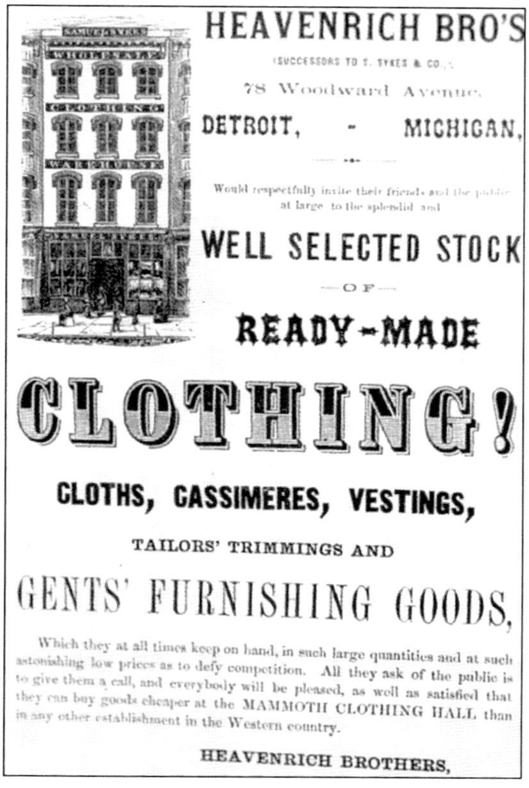

Advertisement from the 1862 Clark's City Directory. (Courtesy Burton Historical Collection of the Detroit Public Library.)

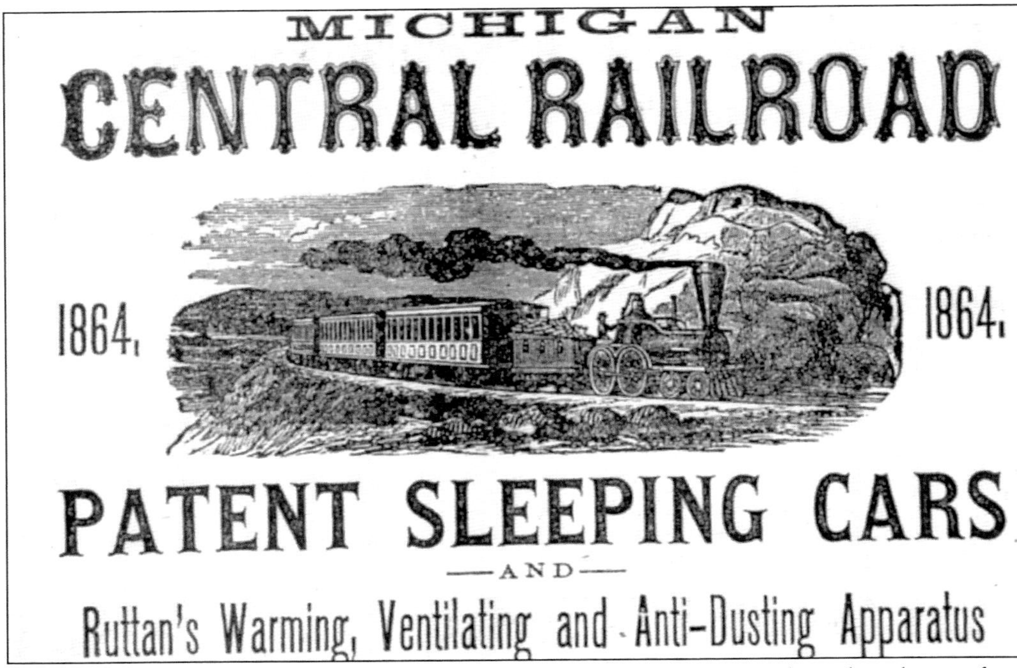

Detroit's population passed 53,000 in 1864 and many Jewish Detroiters brought relatives from the east via the Michigan Central Railroad. (Advertisement courtesy of Burton Historical Collection of the Detroit Public Library.)

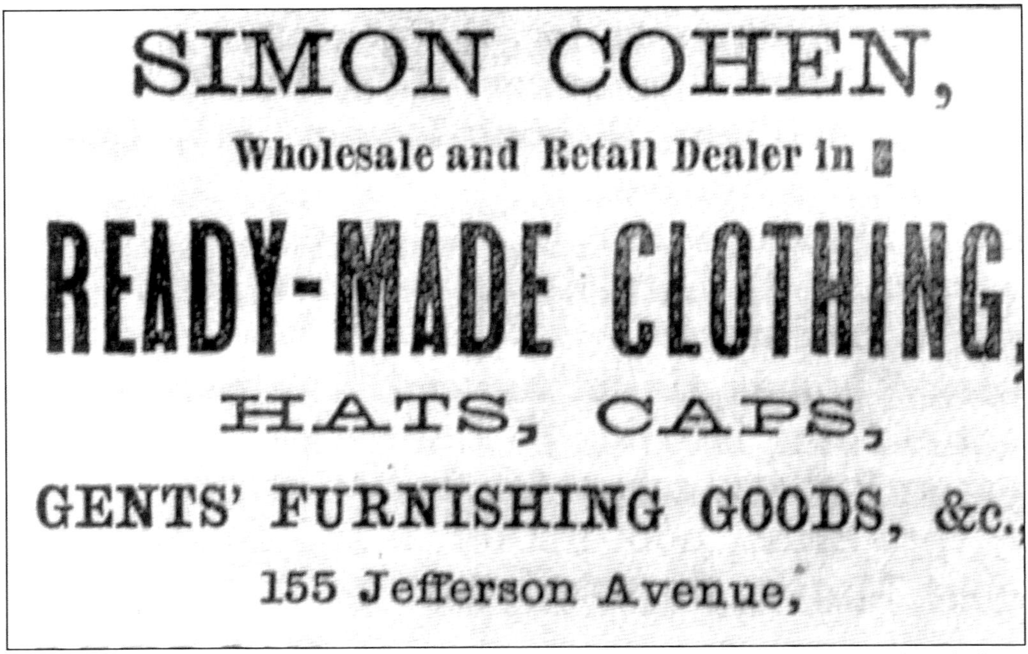

Besides Simon Cohen's Jefferson establishment, the 1864 *Detroit City Directory* listed these Jewish names in the clothing business located on Woodward: Nathan Marks, Abraham Heller, Isador Kaufman, the Heavenrich Brothers, and the E.S. Heineman Company.

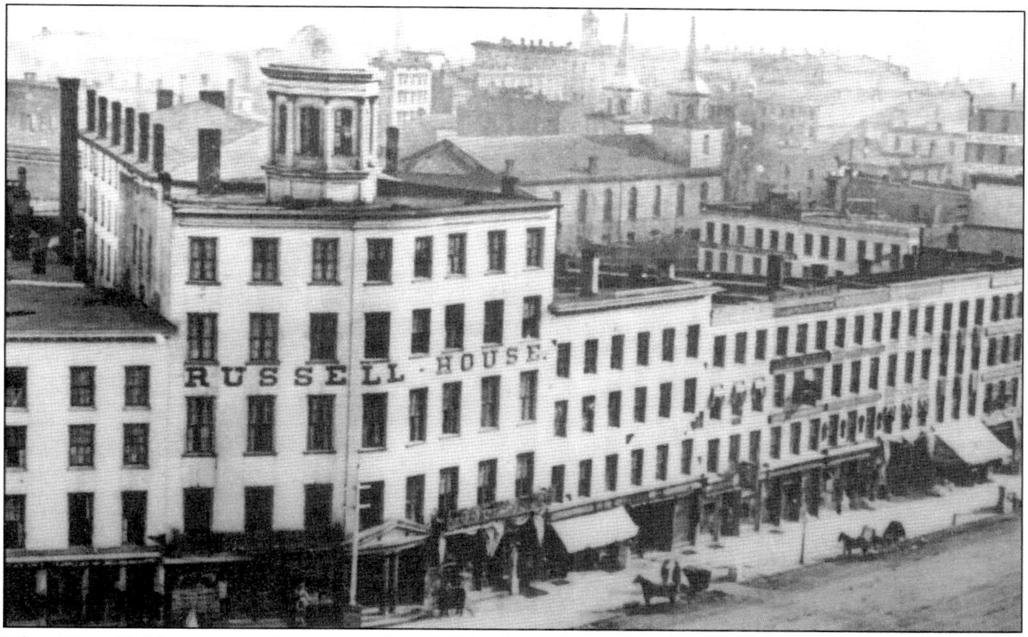

The Russell House on the east side of Woodward, south of Campus Martius, was Detroit's leading hotel. It opened in 1857 and would stand until 1907. The E.S. Heineman Company was located in the building north of the Russell House.

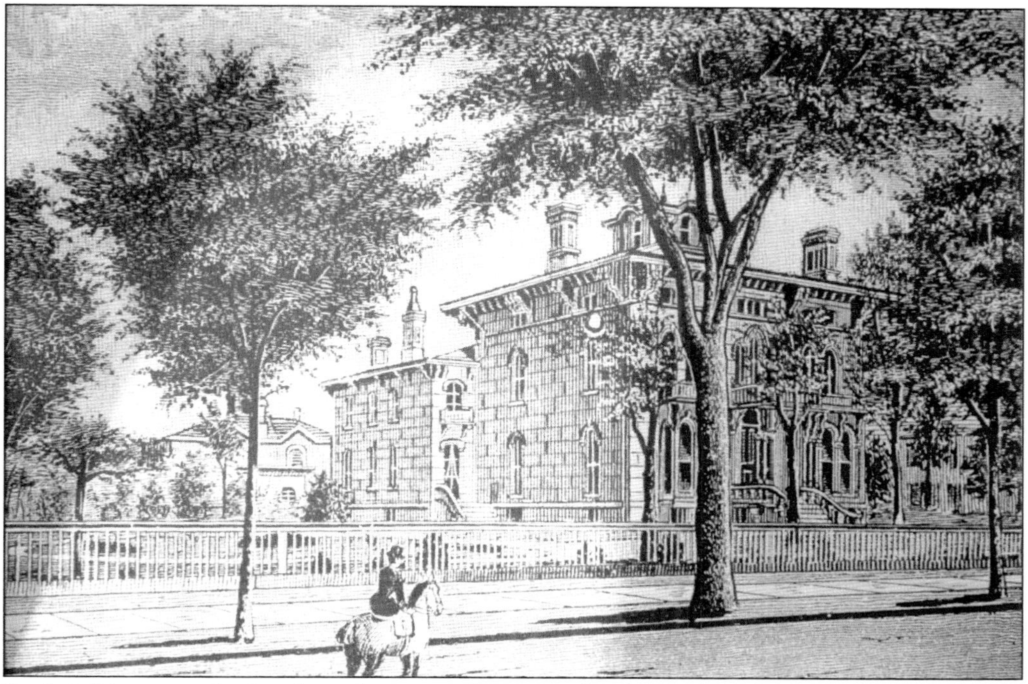

Emil S. Heineman built a large home on the east side of Woodward about a half mile north of Adams. Heineman's clothing company employed 300 people in 1864. (Drawing courtesy of Burton Historical Collection of the Detroit Public Library.)

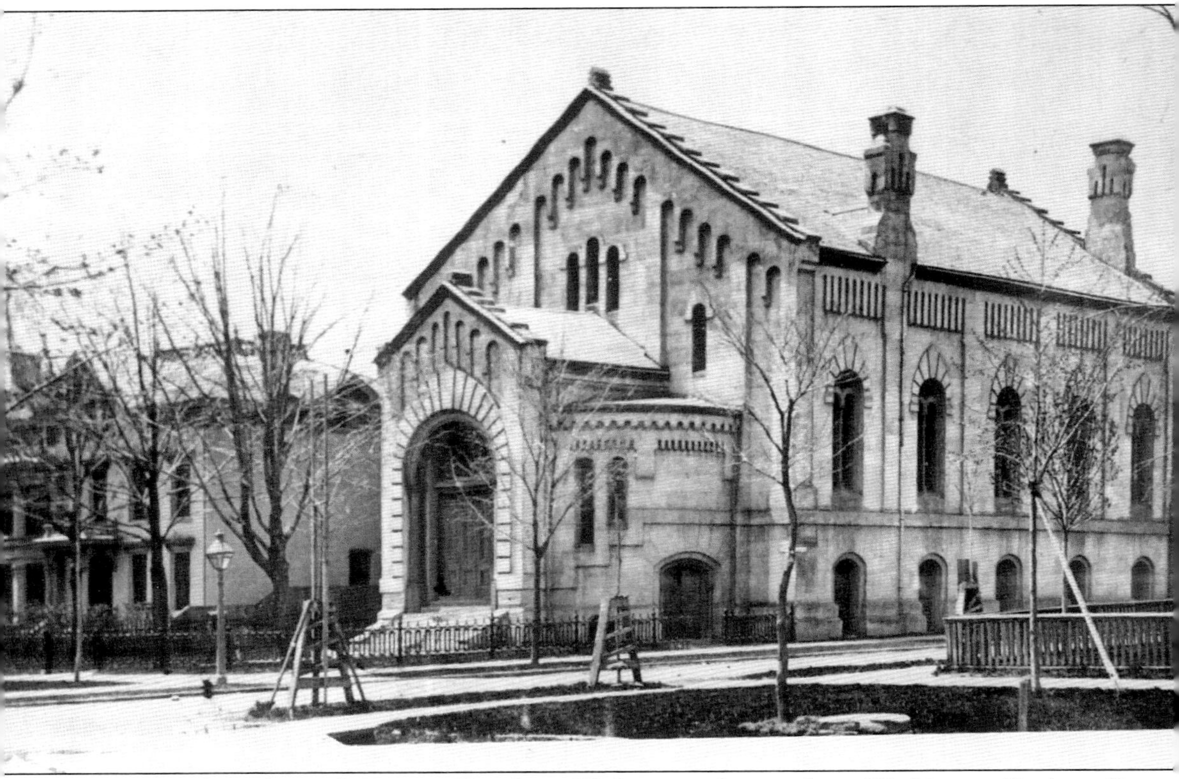

In 1867 the Tabernacle Baptist Church on Washington Avenue (now Washington Boulevard) and Clifford Street was purchased by Beth E1 for $17,000. Less than 70 families belonged to the temple at its dedication. (Courtesy Rabbi Leo M. Franklin Archives, Temple Beth E1.)

The City Hall on Woodward between Michigan Avenue and Fort Street was dedicated in 1871. Watchmen looking for fires in the city of 80,000 were stationed near the roof around the clock. (Courtesy Burton Historical Collection of the Detroit Public Library.)

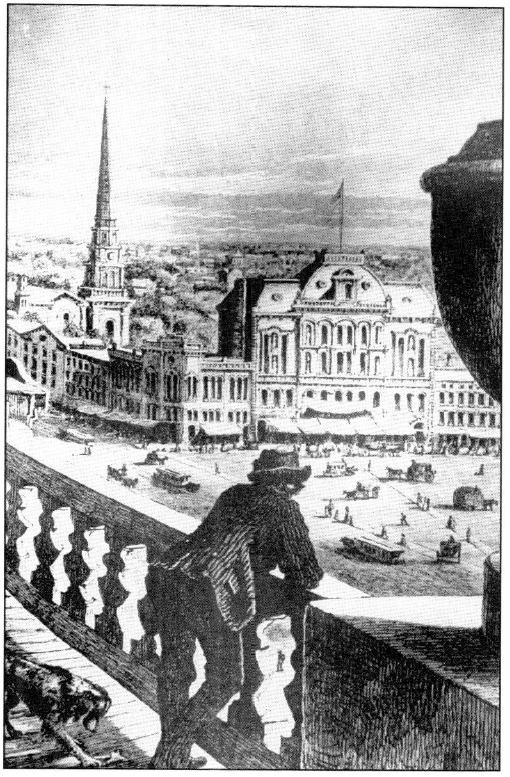

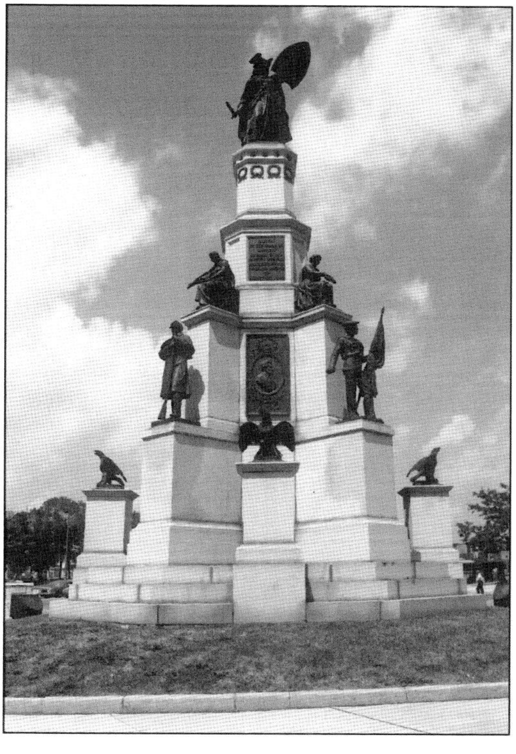

The Michigan Soldier and Sailors Monument was dedicated in Campus Martius in 1872. Jewish Civil War veterans beamed proudly at the monument honoring the sacrifices of Michiganders during the war.

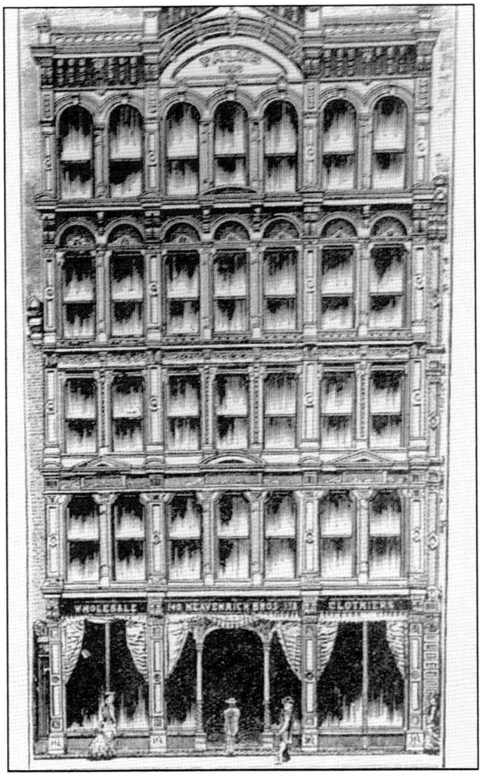

Simon Heavenrich's business interests kept expanding in the 1870s, and the Heavenrich Brothers' Clothing business moved into one of Detroit's tallest buildings.

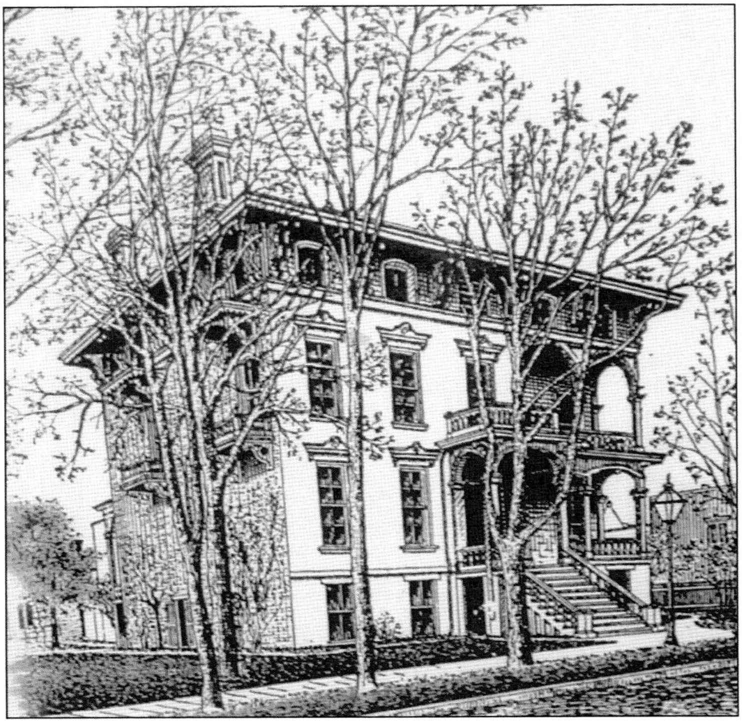

Heavenrich built a new home on Winder Street between Woodward and John R. (Drawing courtesy Burton Historical Collection of the Detroit Public Library.)

Two

1875–1900

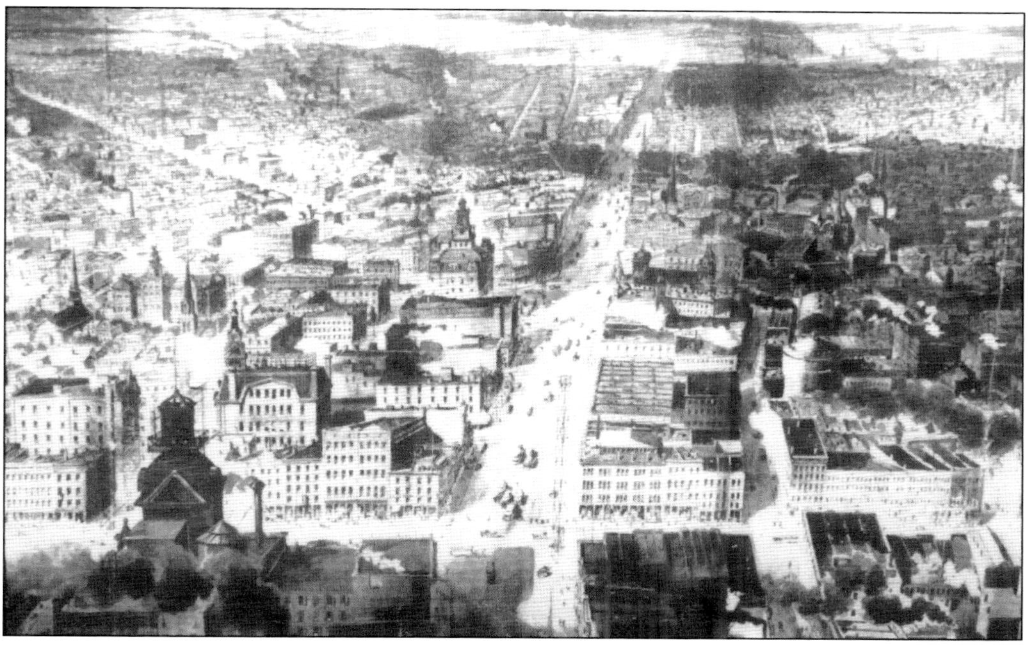

Detroit's population passed 102,000 in 1875. There were three congregations to serve the city's almost 600 Jewish residents. Beth El had 80 members in its reform temple, while Shaarey Zedek had over 50. The other, much smaller orthodox congregation was the four-year-old B'nai Israel, located today near the northeast entrance to Ford Field. (Courtesy Burton Historical Collection of the Detroit Public Library.)

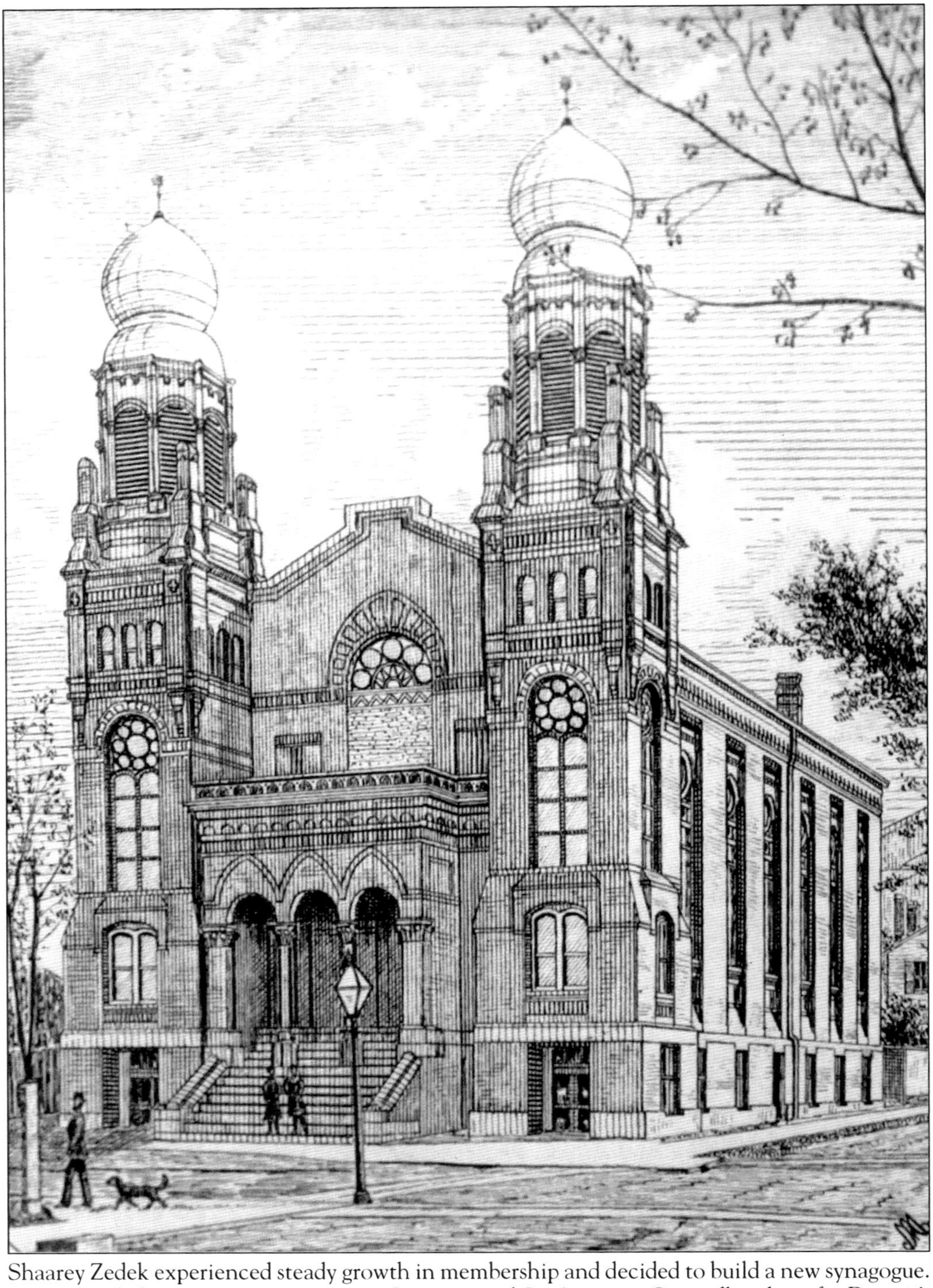

Shaarey Zedek experienced steady growth in membership and decided to build a new synagogue. It was decided to use its present site on Congress and St. Antoine. Groundbreaking for Detroit's first structure built for synagogue use was held on July 4, 1877. At the time Shaarey Zedek had 68 members. (Courtesy Archives of Shaarey Zedek.)

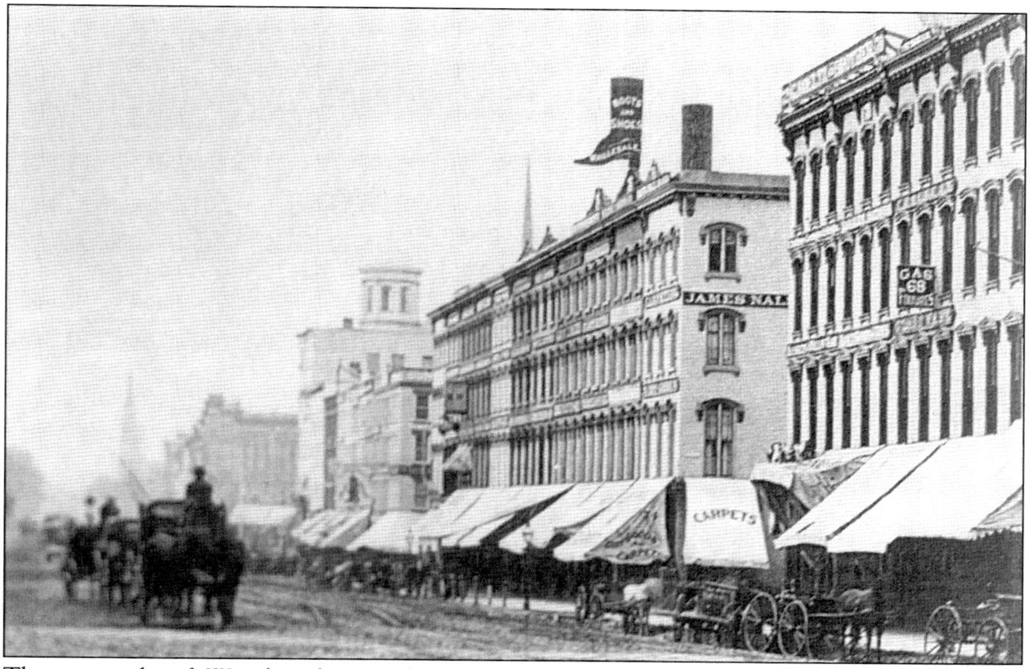

The east side of Woodward around Jefferson was where many of the biggest downtown businesses were located.

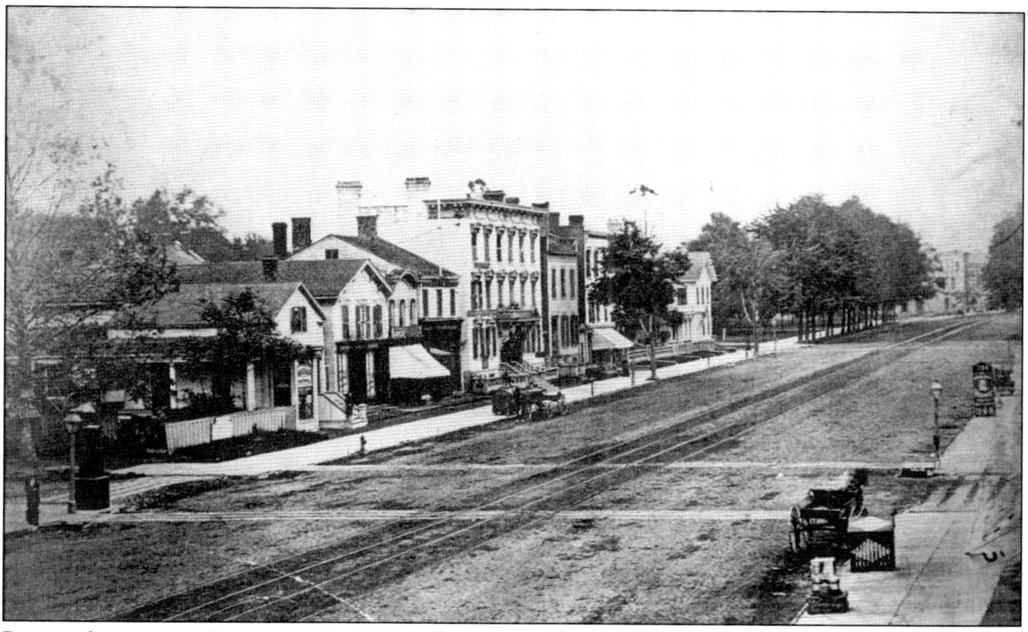

Private homes on the west side of Woodward south of Grand Circus Park were giving way to larger buildings. The last building near the park's trees is where the David Whitney Building stands today. (Courtesy Burton Historical Collection of the Detroit Public Library.)

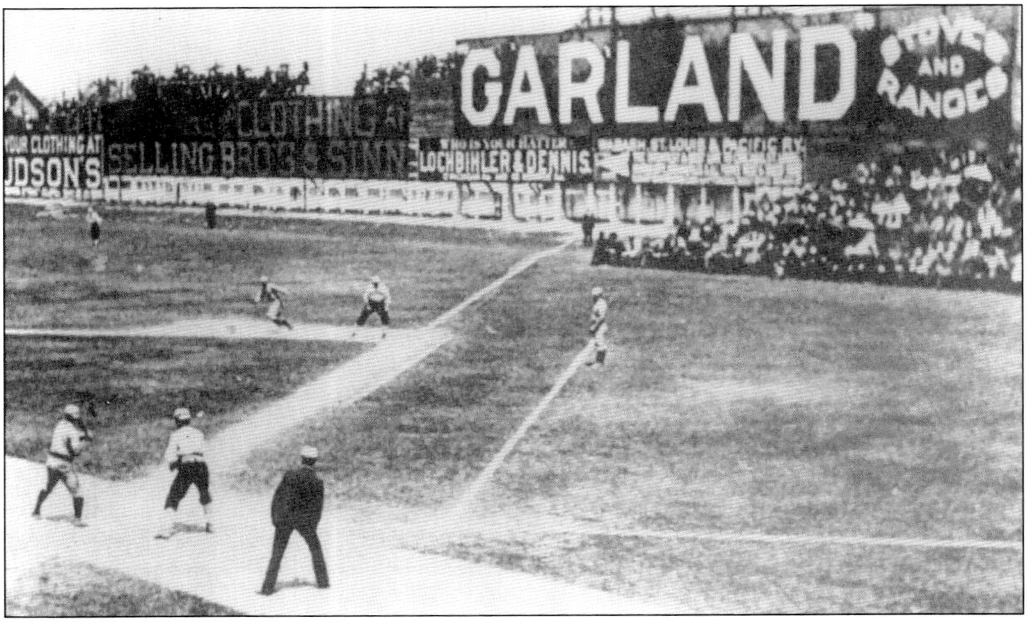

Pro baseball began in 1881 as Detroit became a member of the National League. The Detroits—as the team was called—played at Recreation Park on Brady between John R and Brush, where Harper Hospital stands today. The team had a Jewish first baseman, Dan Stearns, popular with Jewish youngsters who often walked to the games. The Garland Stove sign in the right field corner was one of many stoves Detroit turned out in its stove factories along Jefferson.

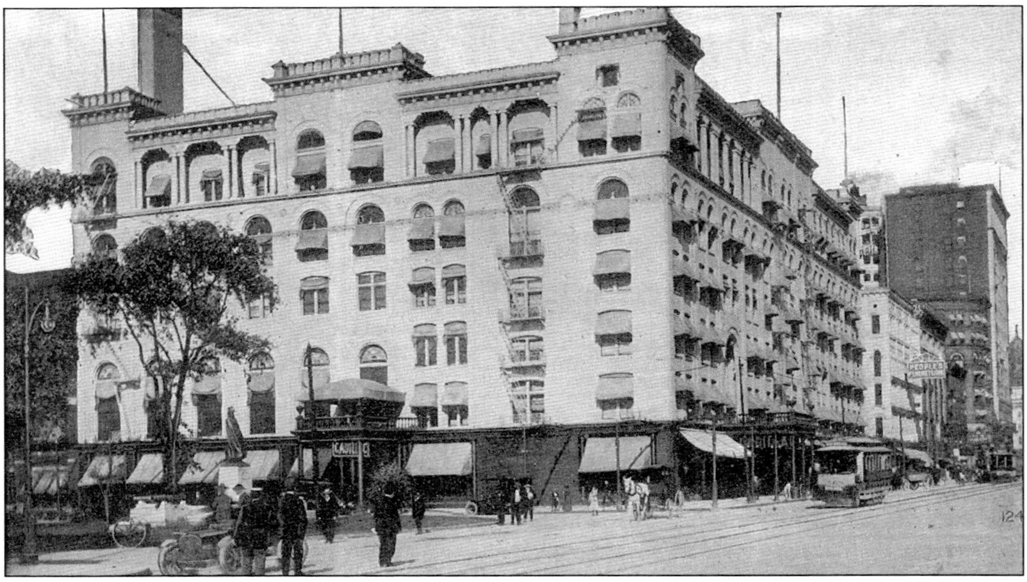

While Detroit's fanciest hotel—the 200-room Cadillac Hotel—was going up on Washington Boulevard at the corner of Michigan Avenue, the local Jewish population was rising. The city directory listed 33 Cohens, 23 Levys, and 14 Cohns. Mrs. Emil S. Heineman was president of the 169-member "Ladies' Society for the Support of Hebrew Widows and Orphans." It was the city's first Jewish philanthropic society, formed 25 years earlier.

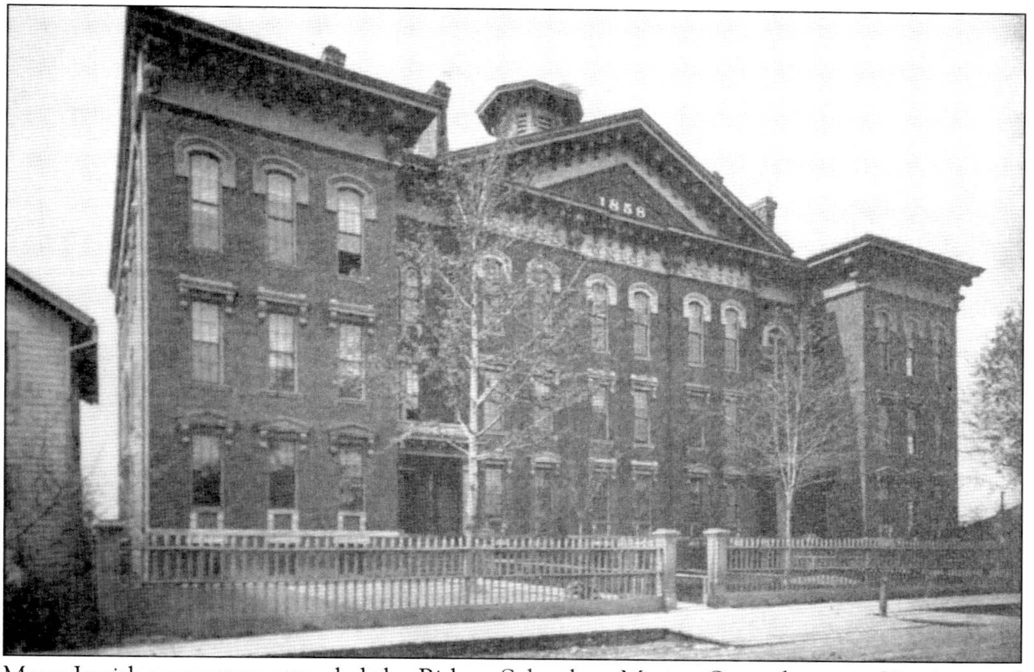

Many Jewish youngsters attended the Bishop School on Marion Street between Hastings and Prospect. (Courtesy Burton Historical Collection of the Detroit Public Library.)

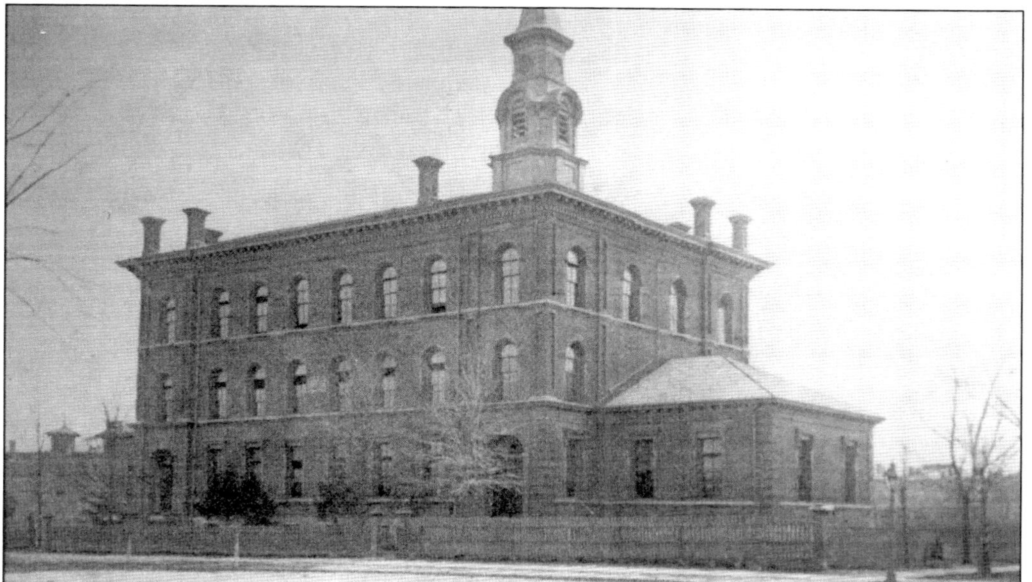

The original Cass School on Grand River between Second and High had an excellent reputation and many Jewish students. (Courtesy Burton Historical Collection of the Detroit Public Library.)

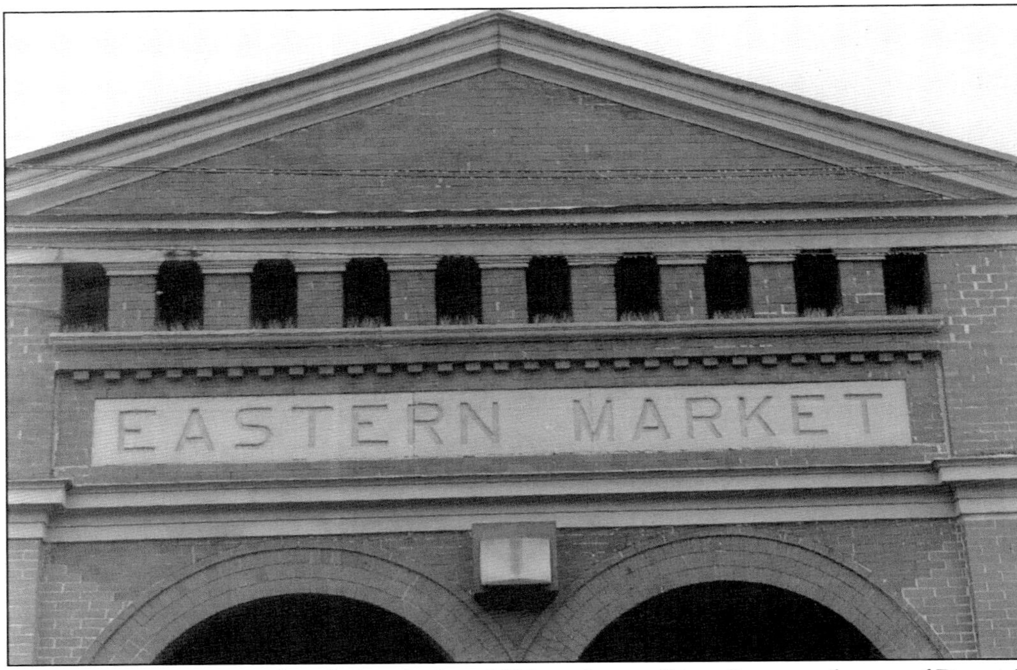

The Eastern Market was founded in the late 1880s within walking distance of many of Detroit's Jewish residents.

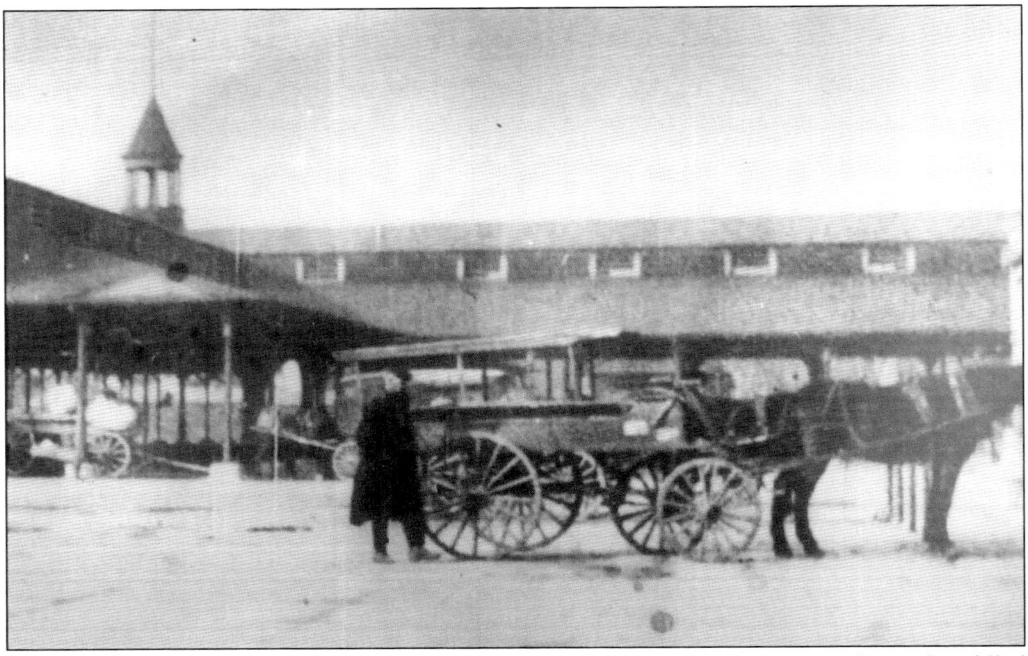

Many new immigrants bought fruits and vegetables, loaded the goods into sacks, and peddled in certain districts carrying the weight on their backs. Others saved or borrowed enough to buy a horse and wagon to carry more and cover more territory. (Courtesy Burton Historical Collection of the Detroit Public Library.)

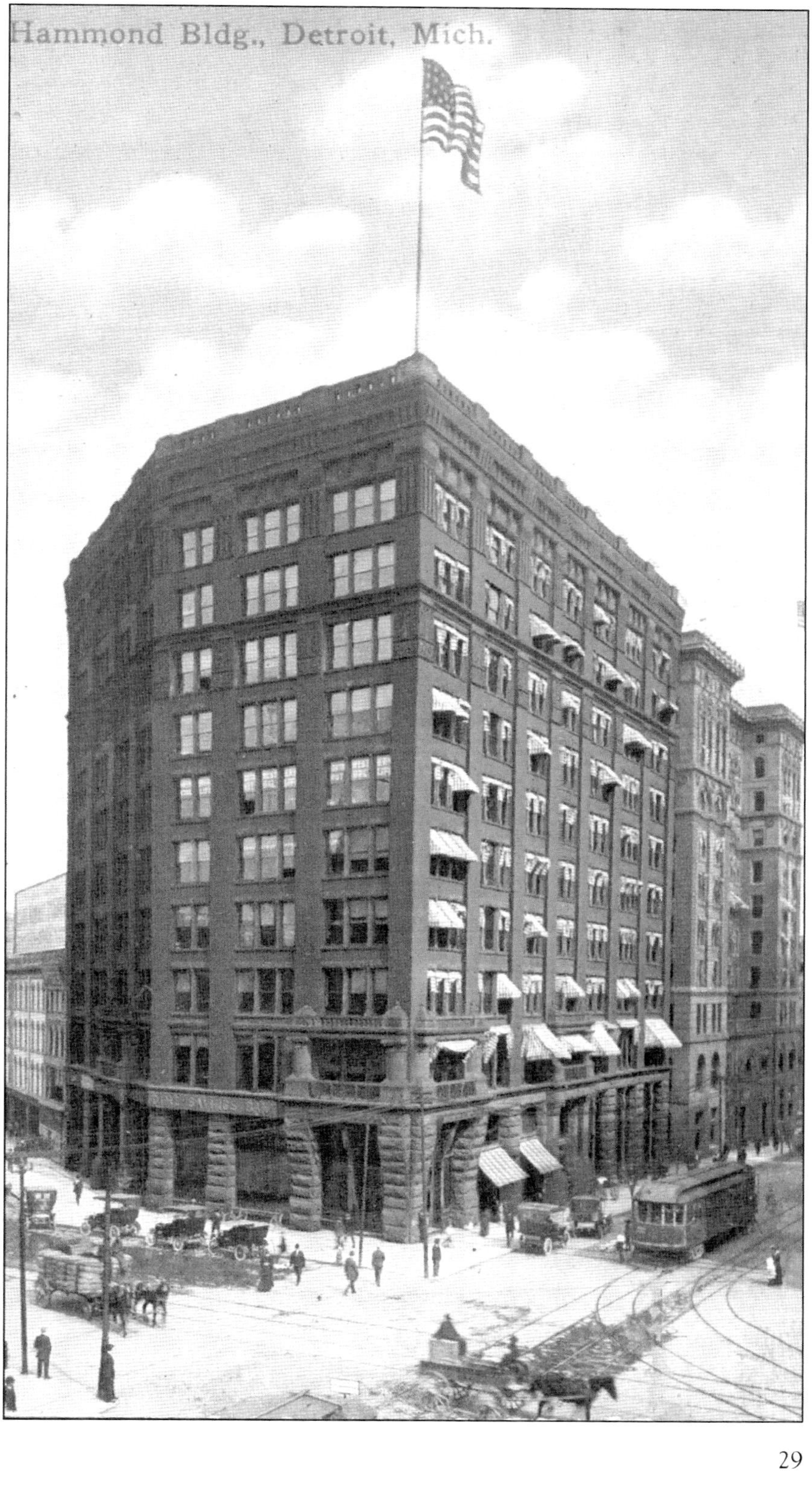

The 10-story Hammond Building, on the corner of West Fort and Griswold, was Detroit's tallest when it opened in 1889. To celebrate the opening, the public was invited to see a highwire performer successfully complete a cable walk stretched high above Fort Street from the Hammond Building to the City Hall tower.

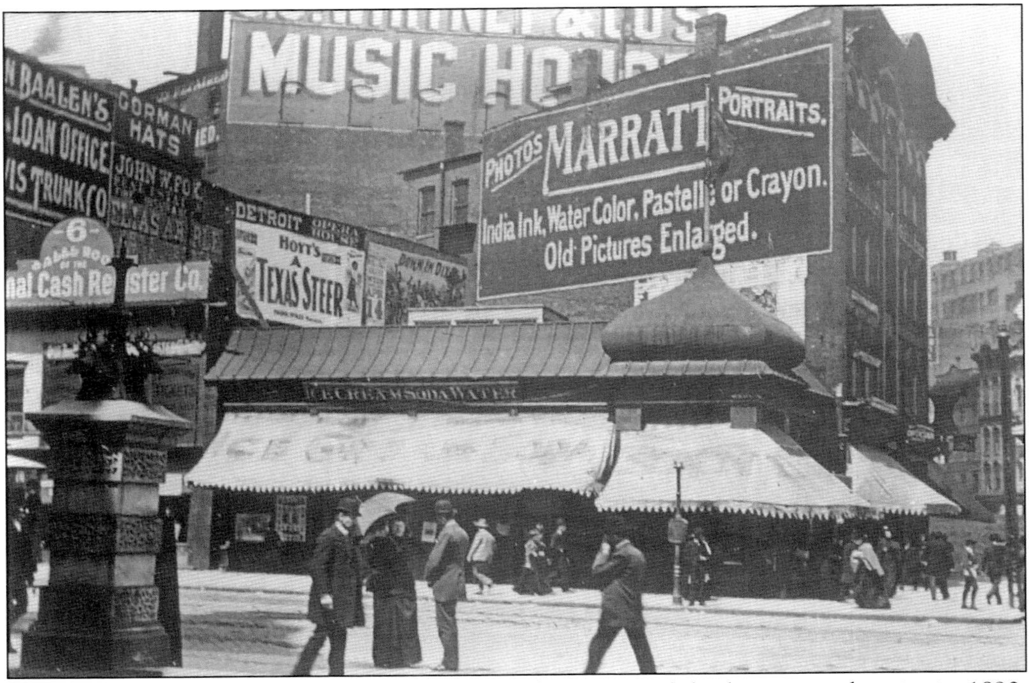

The corner of Michigan Avenue and Woodward was one of the busiest in the city in 1890. Detroit's population of 205,876 included an estimated 1,200 Jews. (Courtesy Burton Historical Collection of the Detroit Public Library.)

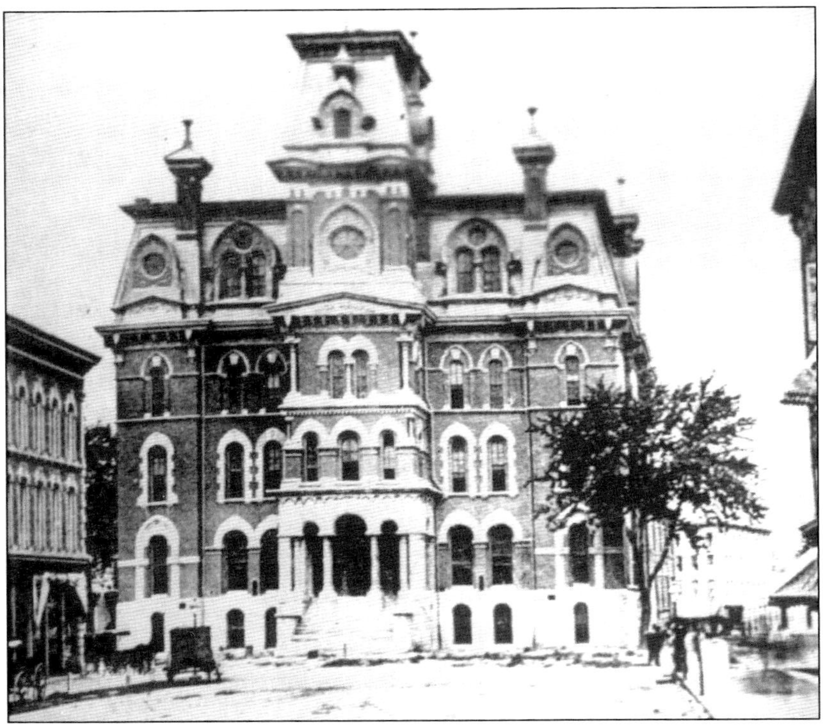

The old Capitol Building at the head of Griswold was enlarged to accommodate a Detroit public high school. A fire destroyed the building in 1893, and Beth El allowed the city to use its facilities on Washington Boulevard. (Courtesy Burton Historical Collection of the Detroit Public Library.)

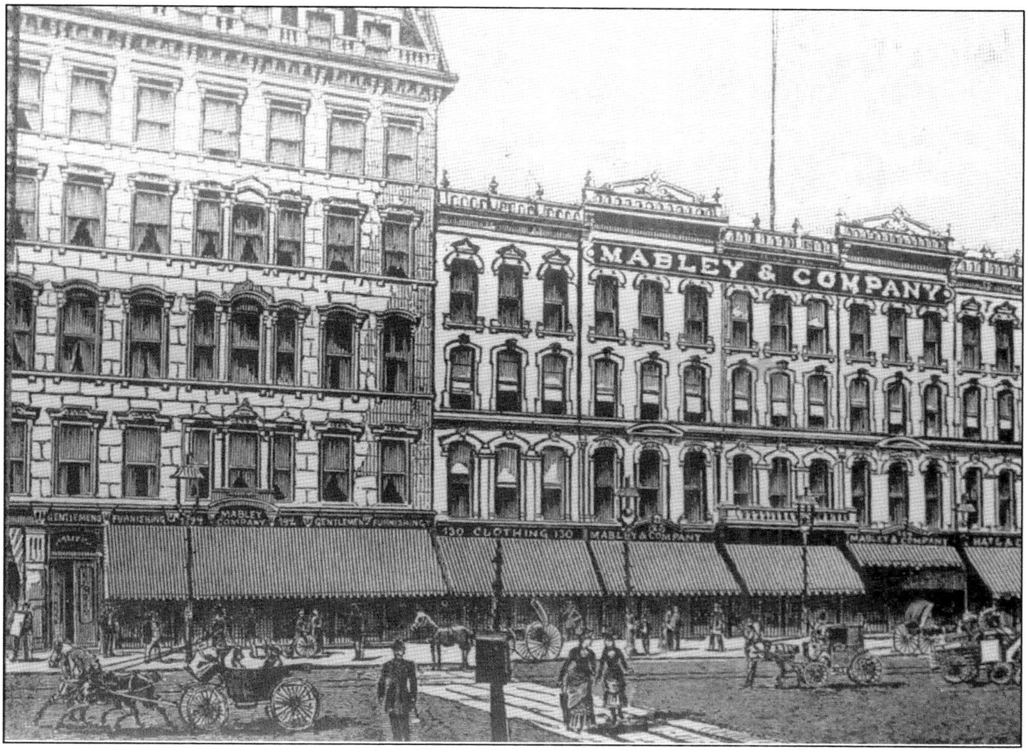

Lavish stagecoaches brought well-dressed women to Detroit's classy store, Mabley & Company, on the east side of Woodward south of Campus Martius.

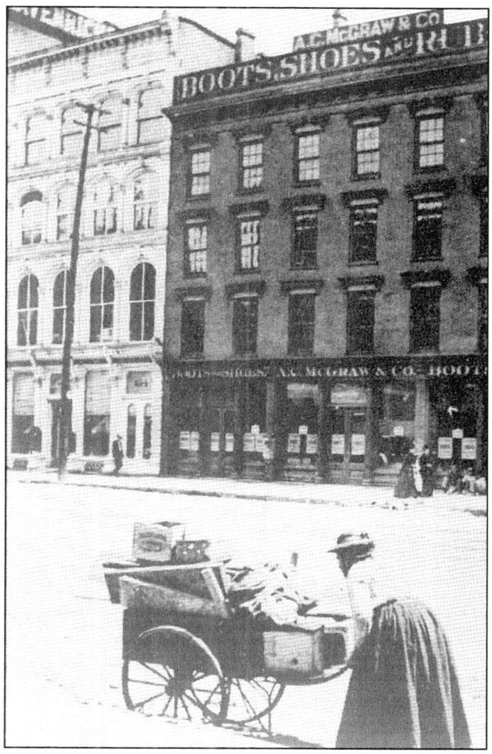

A short walk away, it wasn't an uncommon sight to see women peddlers. Some were widows, while others helped while their husbands were in ill health. (Courtesy Burton Historical Collection of the Detroit Public Library.)

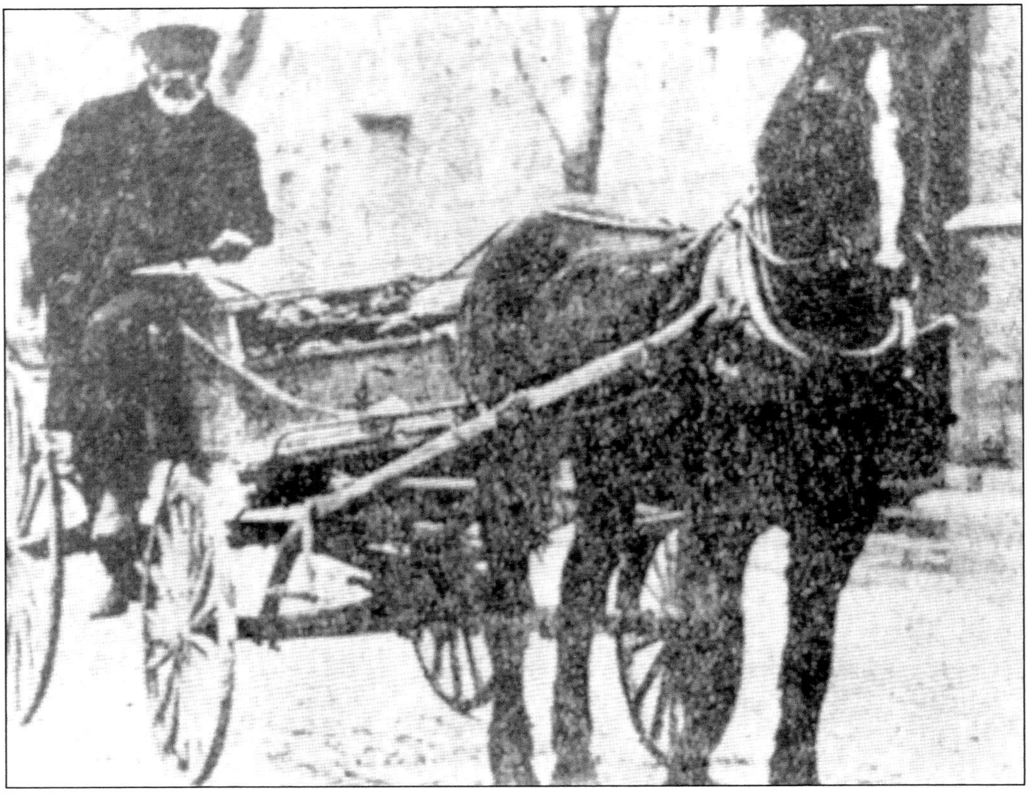

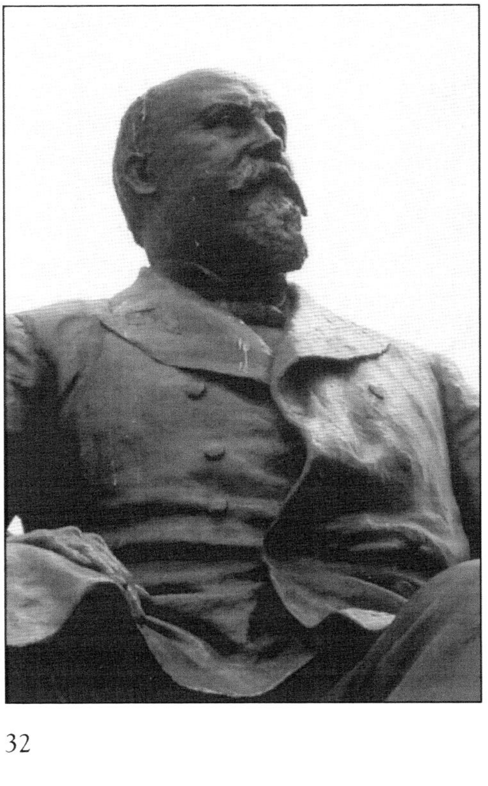

There were more peddlers on the streets in 1894 as the national economic crisis worsened. Railroads went broke and 500 banks around the country failed. The depression hit Detroit hard, as the city had 25,000 jobless citizens. (Courtesy Burton Historical Collection of the Detroit Public Library.)

Detroit's Mayor Hazen Pingree, popular with Jewish voters, urged real estate speculators holding vacant land to use their properties for the growing of vegetables and potatoes. Pingree also appealed for funds to purchase gardening tools. He set an example by selling his favorite horse and using the funds to buy seeds and tools. Soon Pingree's ideas were picked up by newspapers in other cities. New York papers dubbed Detroit's mayor "Potato Patch Pingree."

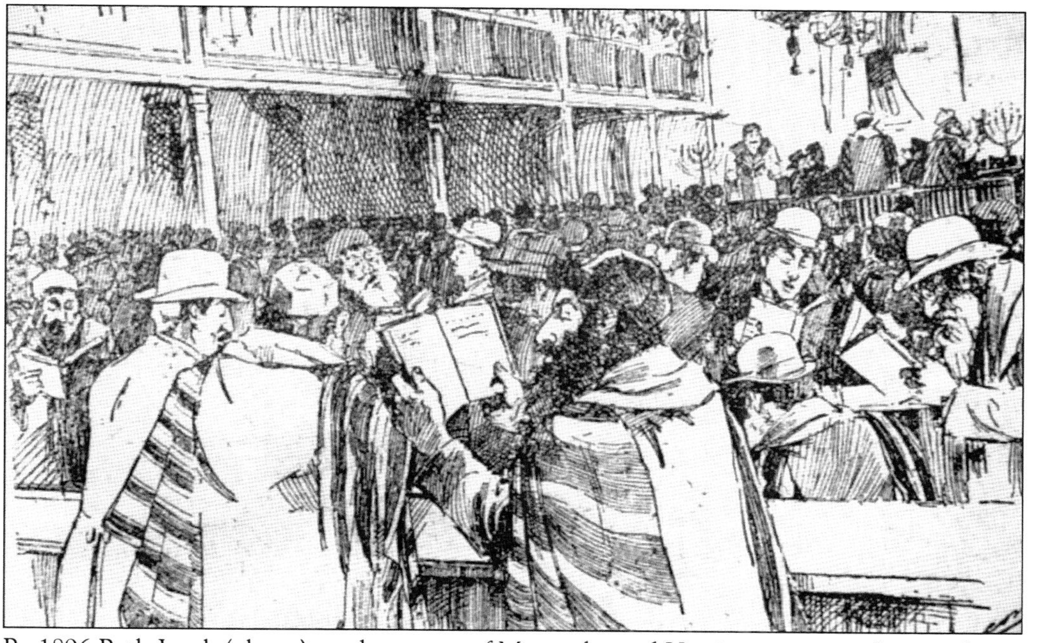

By 1896 Beth Jacob (above) on the corner of Montcalm and Hastings was considering a larger building next to its present site. Four years earlier, eleven Russian Jews founded Beth David, now B'nai David, in a hall on the northwest corner of Gratiot and Hastings. A day later, Beth Abraham became Detroit's fifth orthodox congregation when it was established on the second floor of a private home on Hastings and Winder.

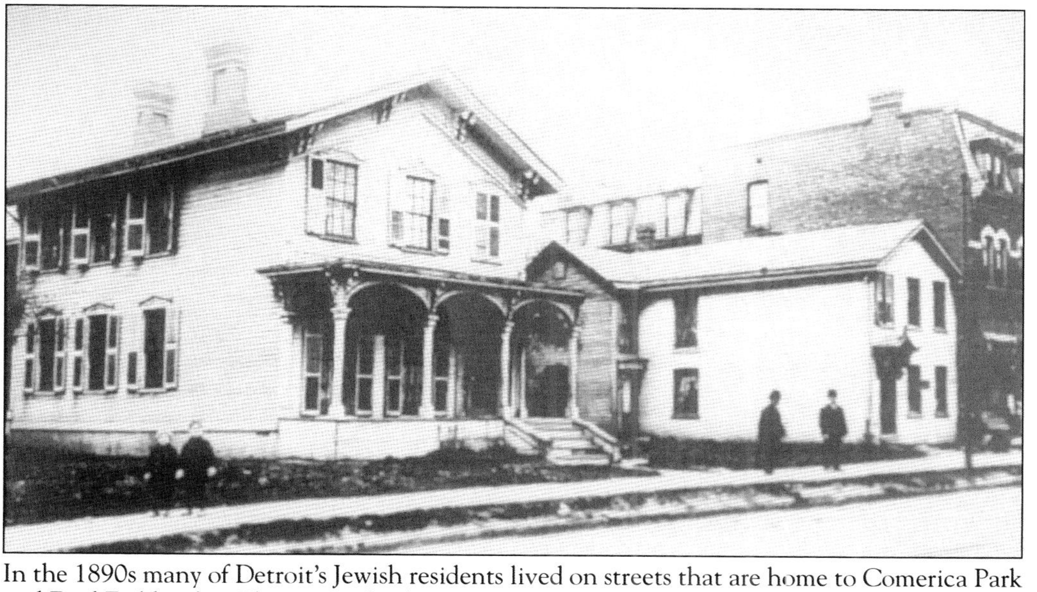

In the 1890s many of Detroit's Jewish residents lived on streets that are home to Comerica Park and Ford Field today. This view of Adams Street looking east was two blocks south of the Beth Jacob Synagogue. All five of the orthodox congregations were east of Woodward, a short walk from Hastings Street—now the Chrysler Freeway. (Courtesy Burton Historical Collection of the Detroit Public Library.)

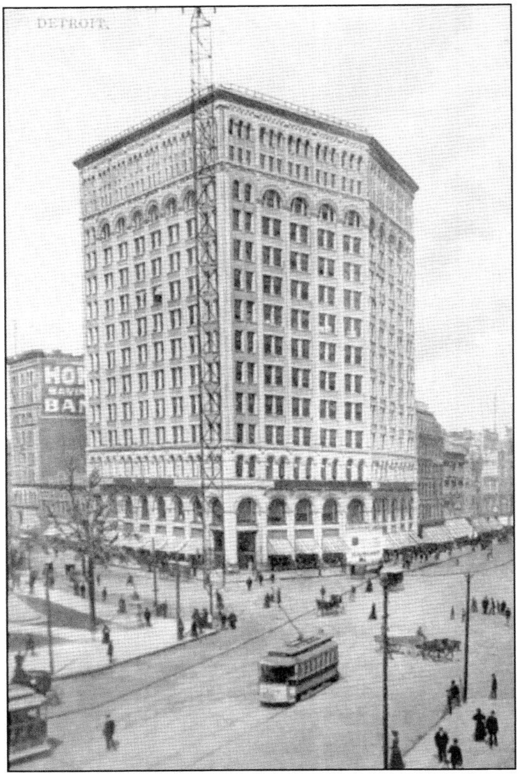

The Majestic Building on Woodward at Michigan Avenue was Detroit's tallest when it opened in 1896, eclipsing the Hammond Building by four floors. Sightseers went to the fourteenth story and for ten cents could climb a flight of stairs to the observatory on the roof to view the growing city. Many Jewish community leaders had offices in the building.

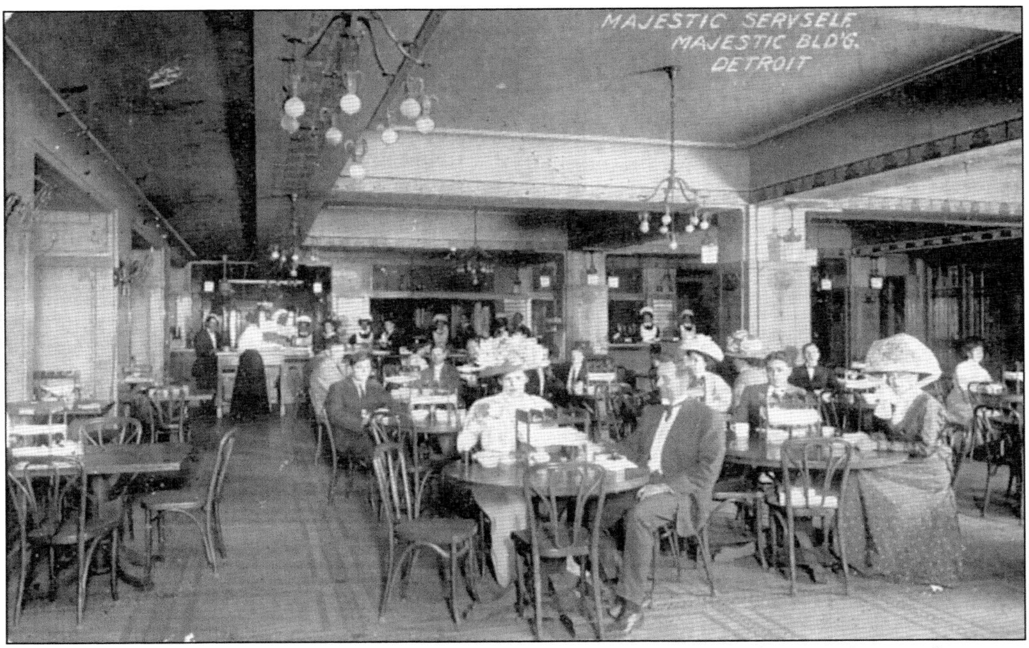

The ground level Majestic Servself Cafeteria had a serving capacity of over a thousand persons an hour and attracted all types of Detroiters and out of town visitors.

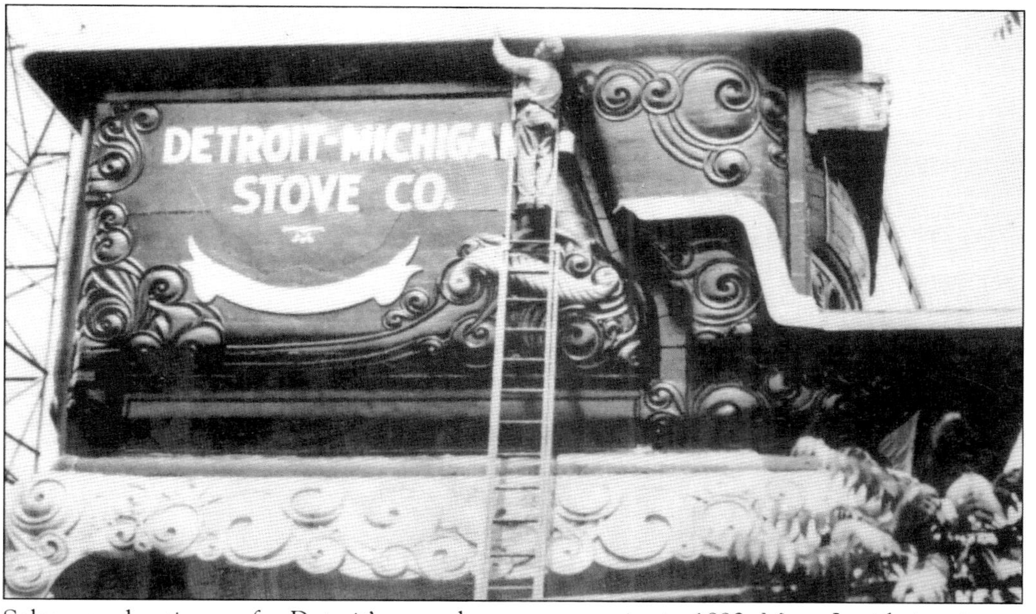

Sales were heating up for Detroit's several stove companies in 1893. Many Jewish immigrant workers were among the 3,000 employees who produced 165,000 stoves. This huge stove was on permanent display for decades on Jefferson near the Belle Isle Bridge. Today it can be seen at the State Fairgrounds on Woodward south of Eight Mile Road. (Courtesy Burton Historical Collection of the Detroit Public Library.)

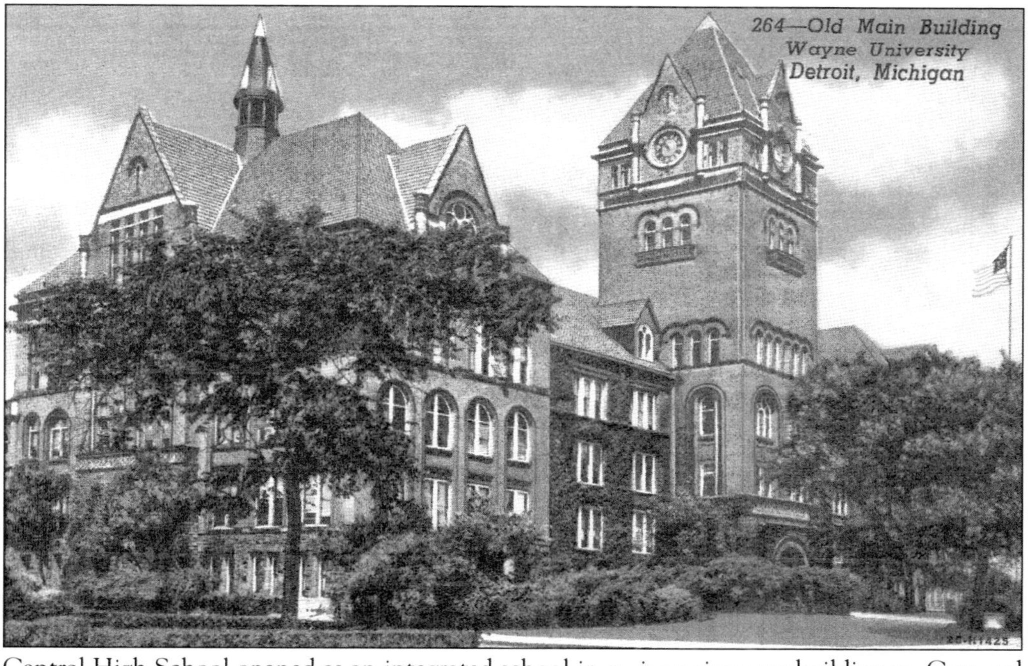

Central High School opened as an integrated school in an imposing new building on Cass and Warren. Many Jewish students would attend high school there. Decades later, the structure would be known as "Old Main" in the Wayne State University complex.

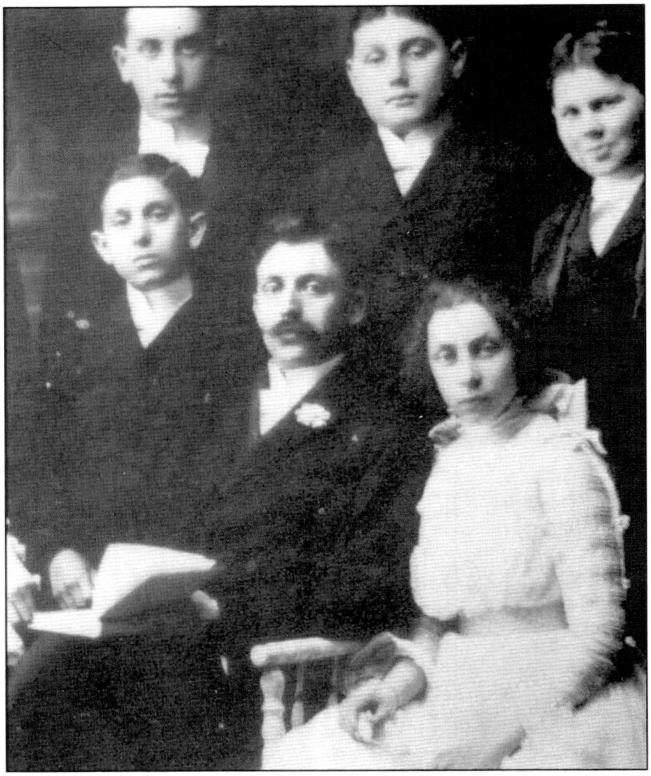

Rabbi Leo M. Franklin arrived in 1899 and became the eleventh spiritual leader of Beth El's 136-member temple. Besides overseeing his first confirmation class, Franklin quickly became involved with community leaders and oversaw the organization of the United Jewish Charities, Detroit's first central philanthropic organization. (Courtesy Rabbi Leo M. Franklin Archives, Temple Beth El.)

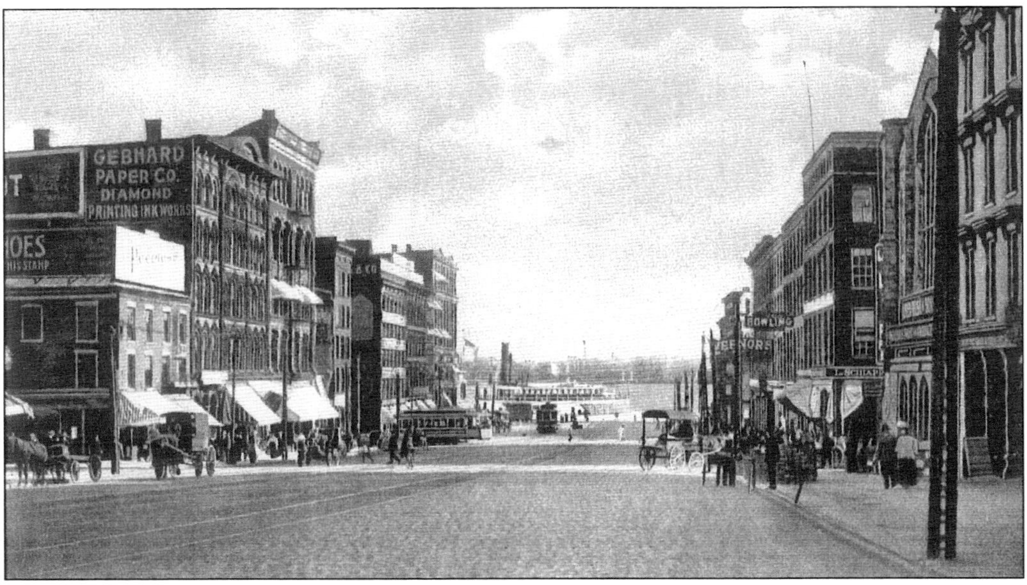

As the nineteenth century ended, Detroit city officials talked about removing many of the older buildings on lower Woodward between Jefferson and the river for a Civic Center Park, as the city sorely lacked a downtown riverfront park.

Three

1900–1925

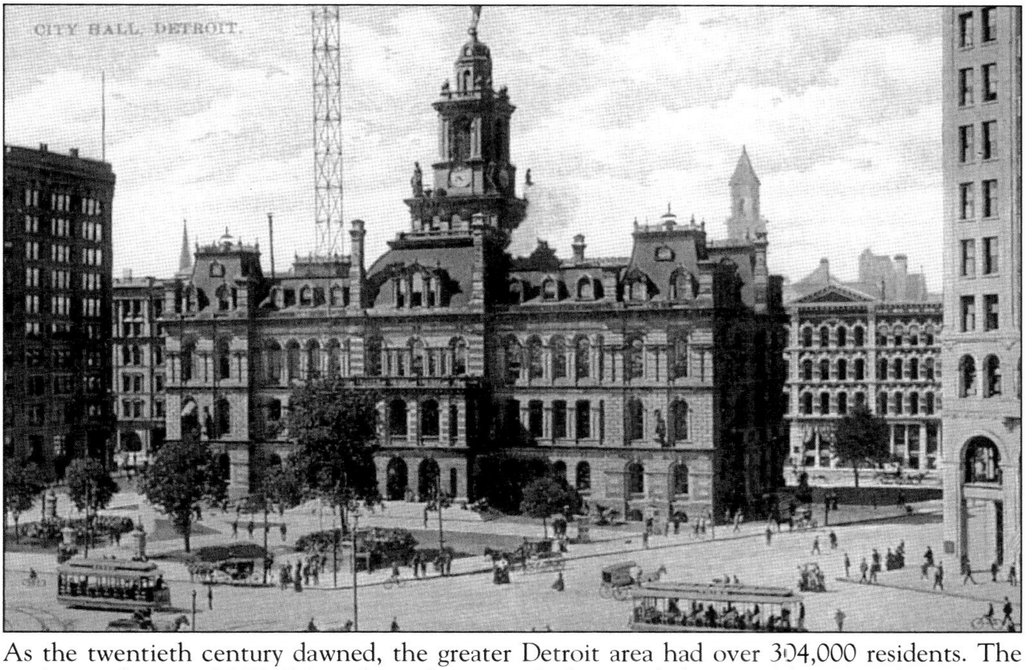

As the twentieth century dawned, the greater Detroit area had over 304,000 residents. The city's population of 285,704 made it the nation's thirteenth largest. Almost twelve percent couldn't speak English, and many Jewish residents were employed in Detroit's stove factories and breweries. All of the city's streetcar lines were united into one system: the Detroit United Railway, or DUR.

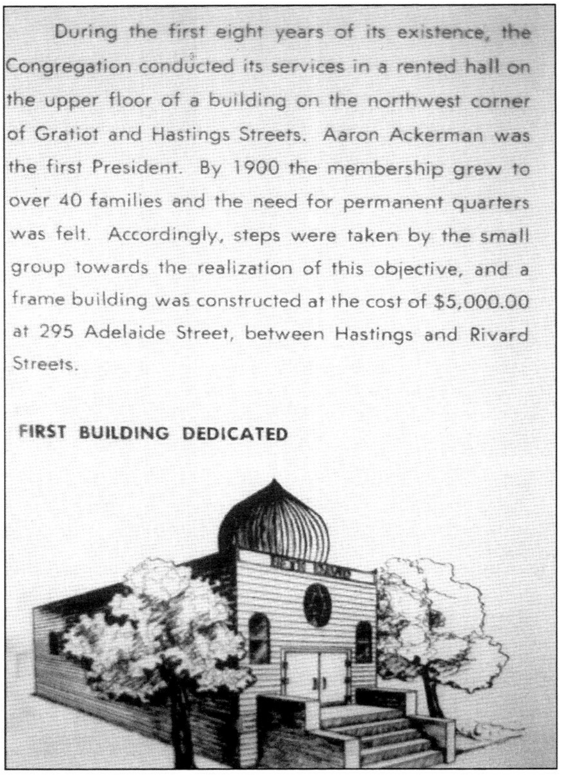

During the first eight years of its existence, the Congregation conducted its services in a rented hall on the upper floor of a building on the northwest corner of Gratiot and Hastings Streets. Aaron Ackerman was the first President. By 1900 the membership grew to over 40 families and the need for permanent quarters was felt. Accordingly, steps were taken by the small group towards the realization of this objective, and a frame building was constructed at the cost of $5,000.00 at 295 Adelaide Street, between Hastings and Rivard Streets.

FIRST BUILDING DEDICATED

Beth David—now B'nai David—dedicated its first building on Sunday, September 9, 1900. Mayor Maybury and many city officials attended the ceremonies, walking behind a band of musicians heading the procession going north up Hastings. (Courtesy Congregation B'nai David.)

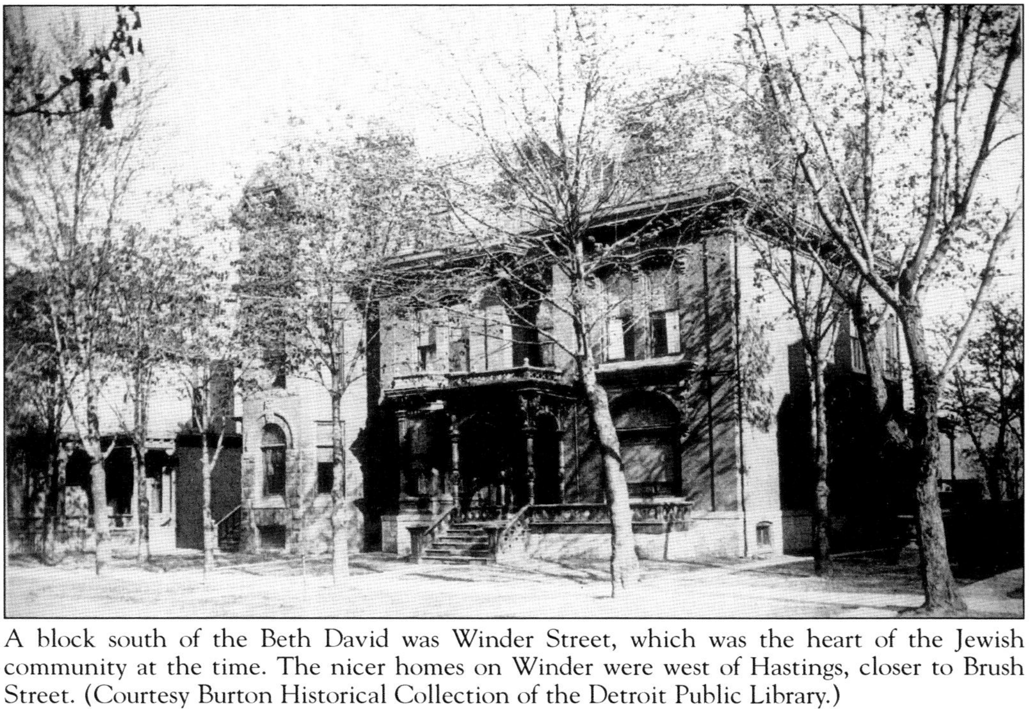

A block south of the Beth David was Winder Street, which was the heart of the Jewish community at the time. The nicer homes on Winder were west of Hastings, closer to Brush Street. (Courtesy Burton Historical Collection of the Detroit Public Library.)

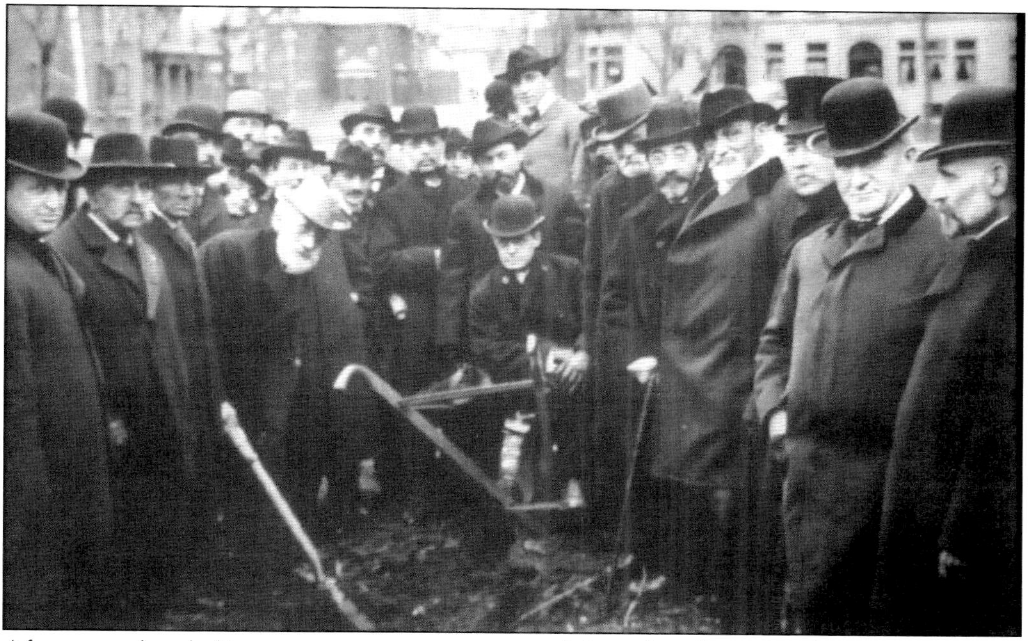

After more than half a century as a community, and three decades on Washington Boulevard, Beth El built its first temple. The groundbreaking took place in 1901 on Woodward and Eliot. (Courtesy Rabbi Leo M. Franklin Archives, Temple Beth El.)

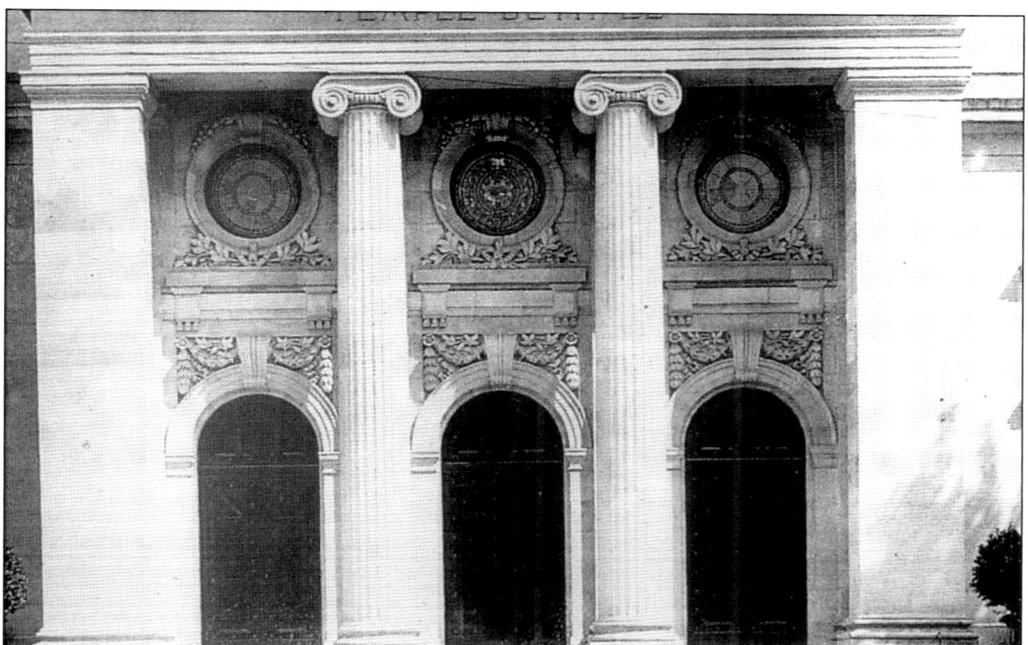

Famed architect Albert Kahn—a member of Beth El—designed the exterior with Louis XVI decoration. The domed and porticoed Roman Pantheon edifice quickly became a tourist attraction. (Courtesy Rabbi Leo M. Franklin Archives, Temple Beth El.)

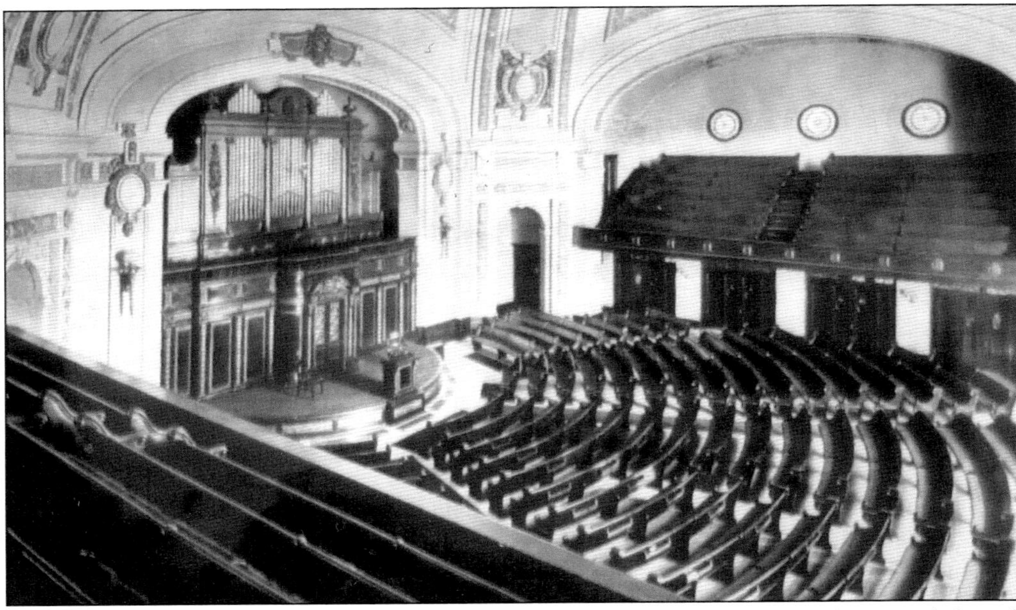

The ornate interior of Temple Beth El combined the best features of a theater while still maintaining intimacy. (Courtesy Rabbi Leo M. Franklin Archives, Temple Beth El.)

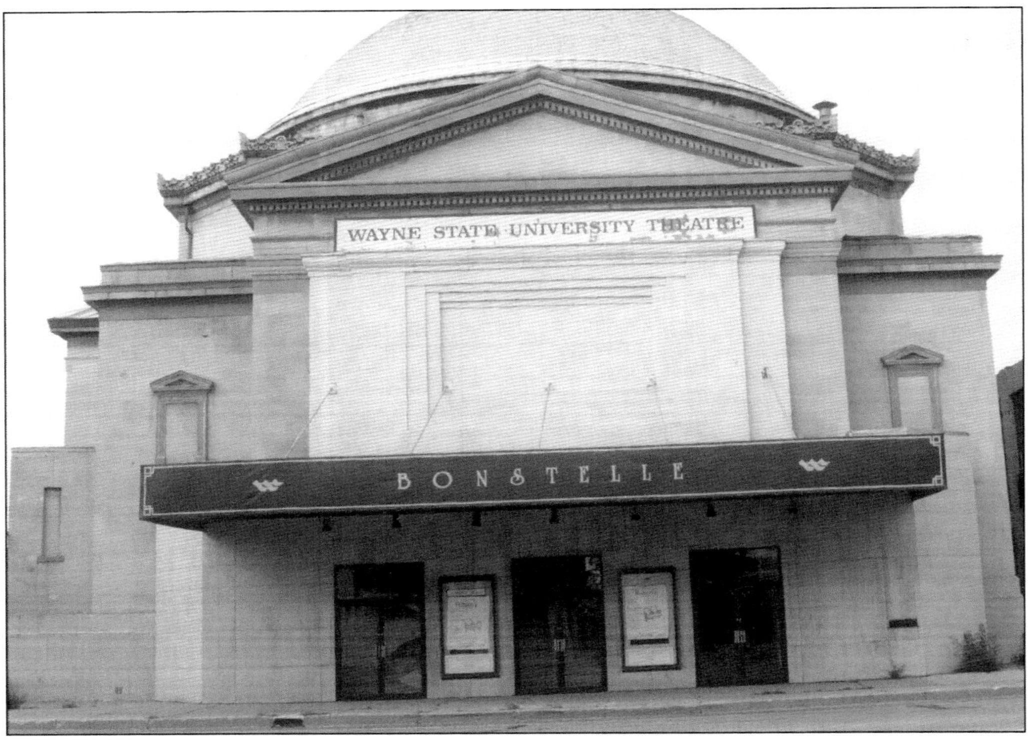

Beth El stayed at the Woodward-Eliot location for almost 20 years. Today much of the Romanesque exterior is gone and the building serves as the Bonstelle Theatre of Wayne State University.

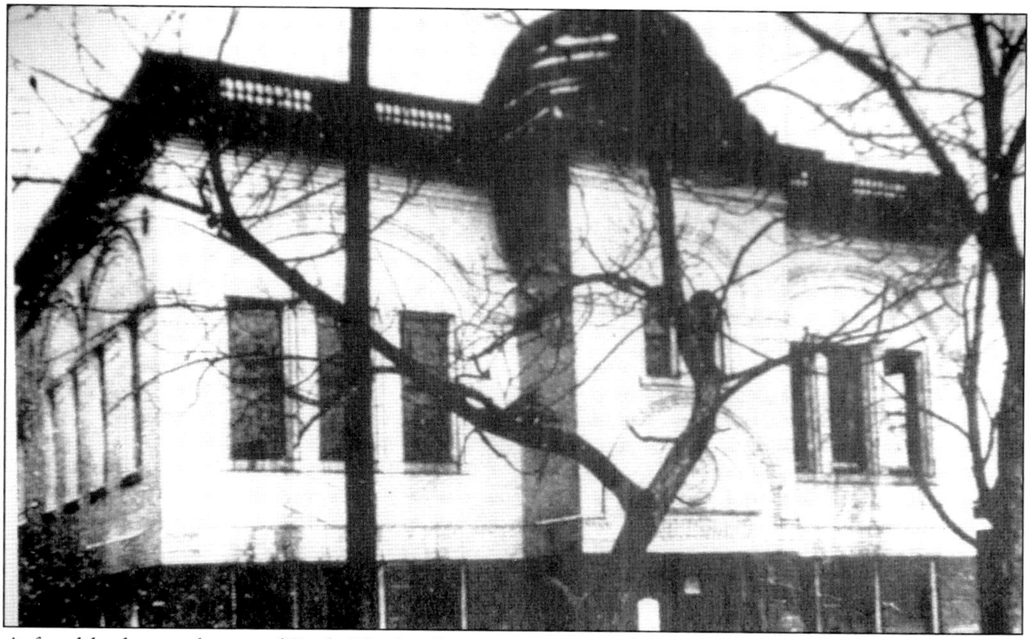

A few blocks southeast of Beth El, the Division Street Talmud Torah opened to give children religious study programs on Sunday mornings and weekday afternoons. (Courtesy Archives of Congregation Shaarey Zedek.)

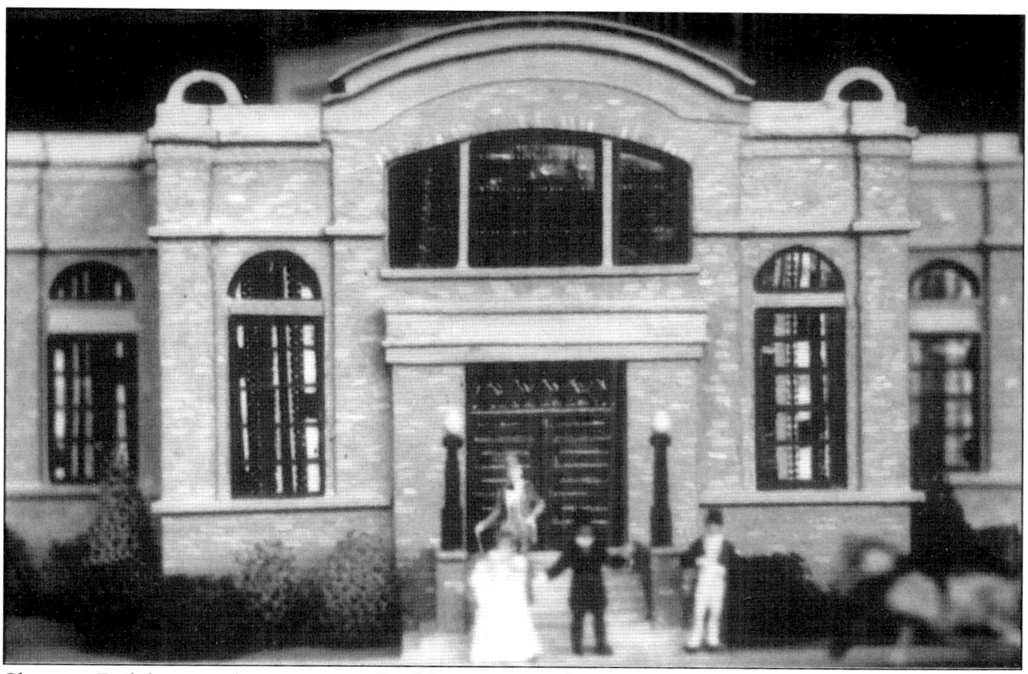

Shaarey Zedek moved into its new building on Winder Street in 1903. The main floor had 400 seats and there were an additional 300 in the balcony. (Courtesy Archives of Congregation Shaarey Zedek.)

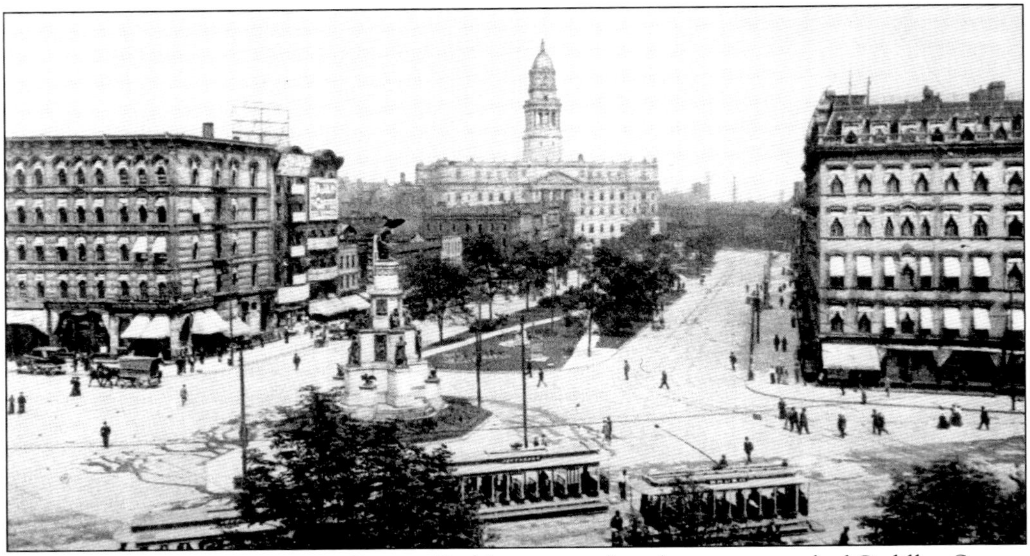

In 1902 the impressive Wayne County Building opened at the eastern end of Cadillac Square and Randolph. Detroit's first Jewish-founded bank—the German American Bank—was on the western end of Cadillac Square at Campus Martius.

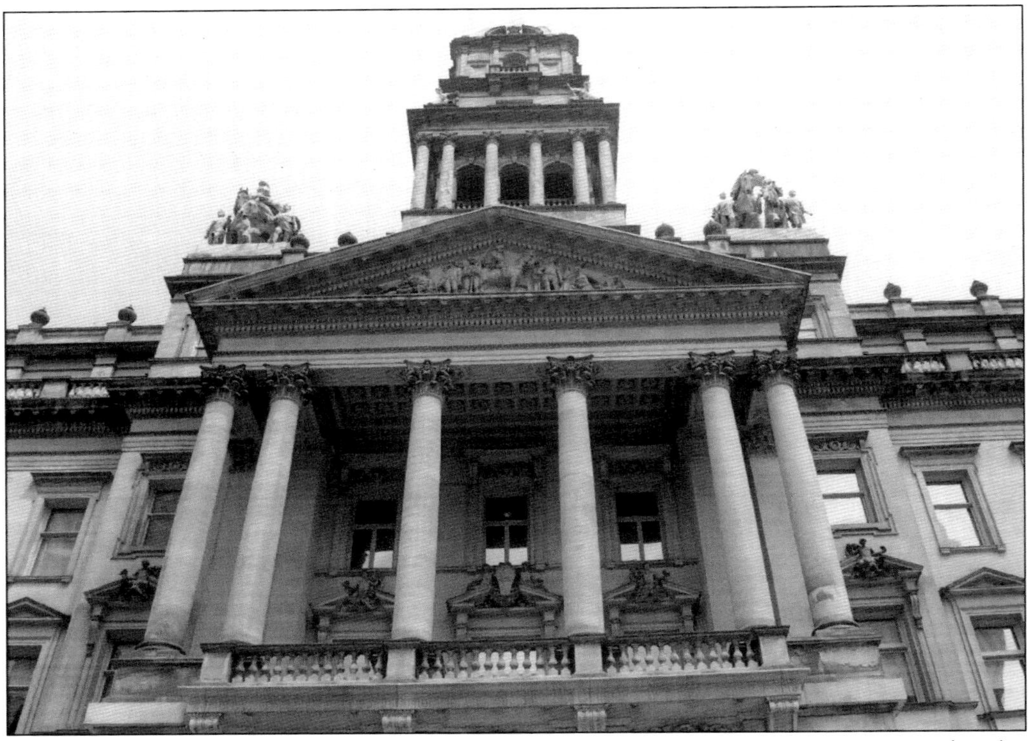

Detroiters craned upward at the County Building to gaze at the carved ornamentation, cherubs, and wreaths above the windows. The figures above the pillars on the Randolph Street side included General Anthony Wayne and Indians concluding a peace treaty. The bronze quadrigas on the roof represented Victory and Progress.

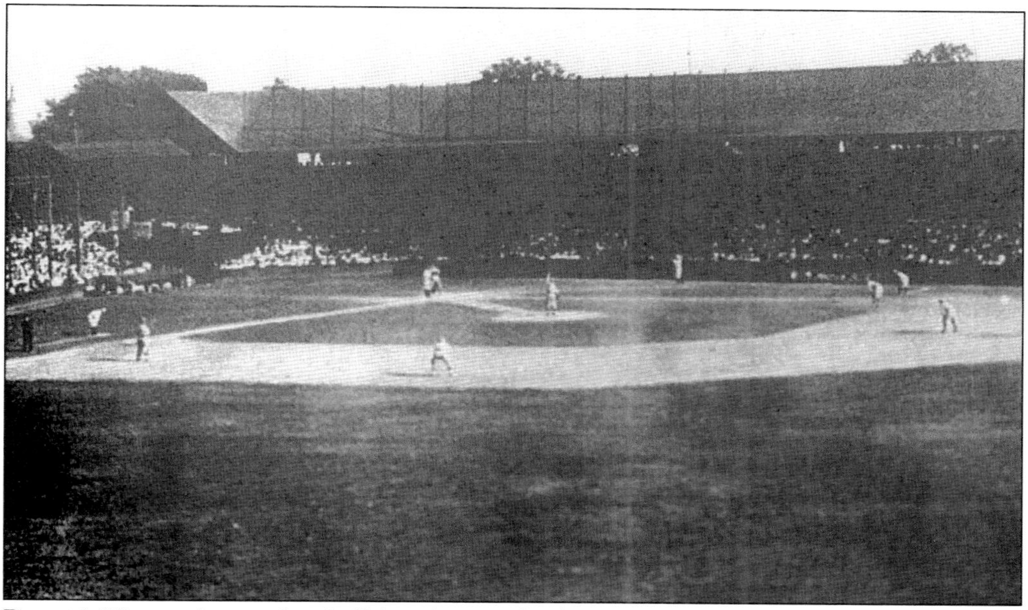

Detroit's Western League baseball franchise evolved into the American League Detroit Tigers, and the club played at Bennett Park at Michigan and Trumbull. In 1903 the Tigers had their first Jewish player, pitcher Harry Kane. Kane's real name was Cohen but anti-Semitism forced many Jewish players of that era to play under non-Jewish names. (Courtesy Burton Historical Collection of the Detroit Public Library.)

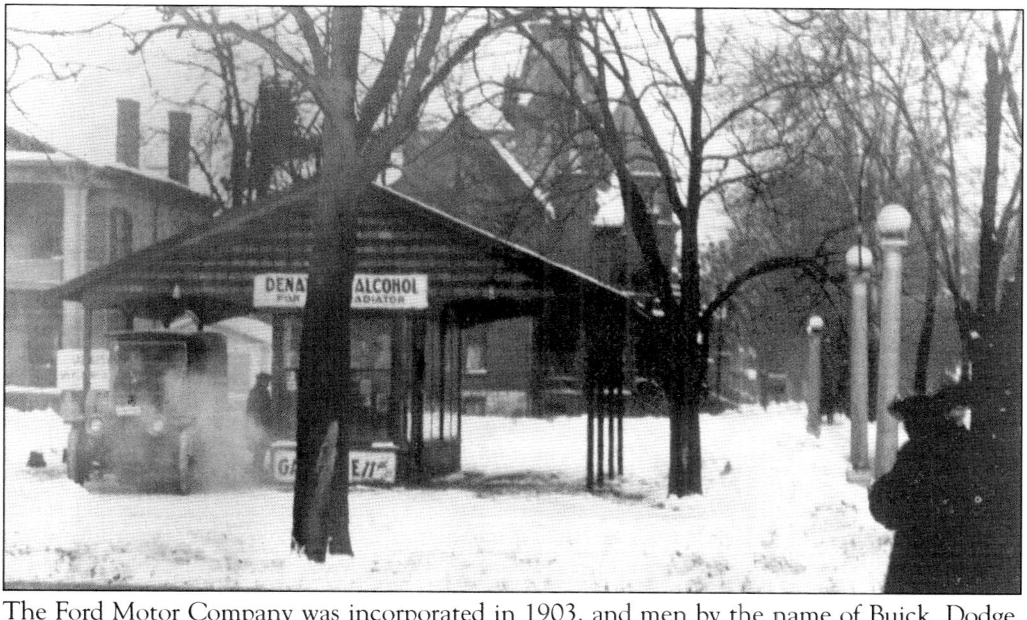

The Ford Motor Company was incorporated in 1903, and men by the name of Buick, Dodge, Maxwell, and Olds were becoming known through their automobile companies. Jefferson and Brush was the hub of automobile row, with four dealerships near the corner. The closest gas station to the Jewish community was this one on Woodward and High (later Vernor Highway). (Courtesy Burton Historical Collection of the Detroit Public Library.)

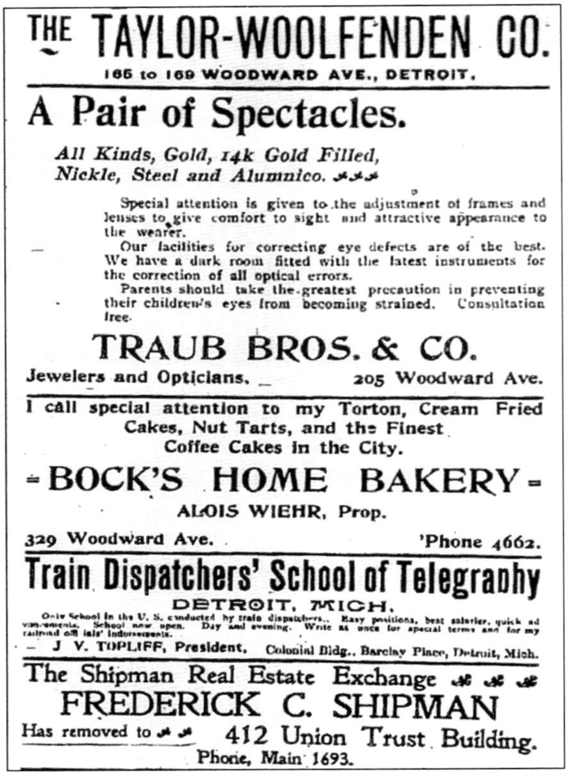

Regular advertisers in the weekly *Jewish American* in 1905.

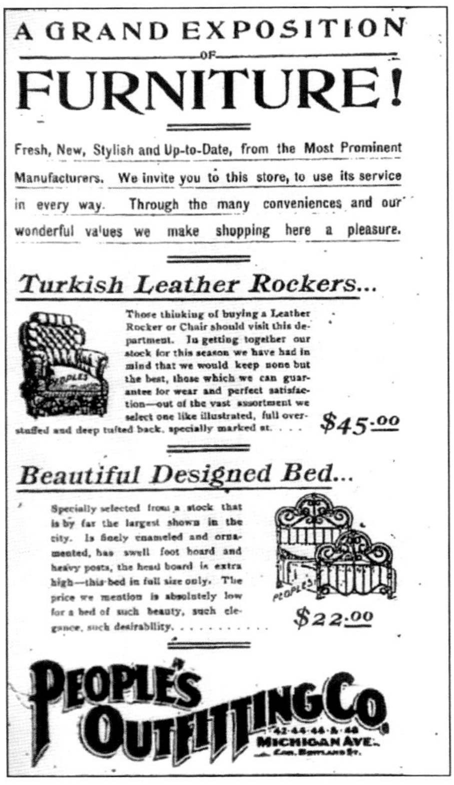

People's Outfitting Company on Michigan Avenue east of Washington Boulevard was a frequent advertiser in Detroit's *Jewish American*.

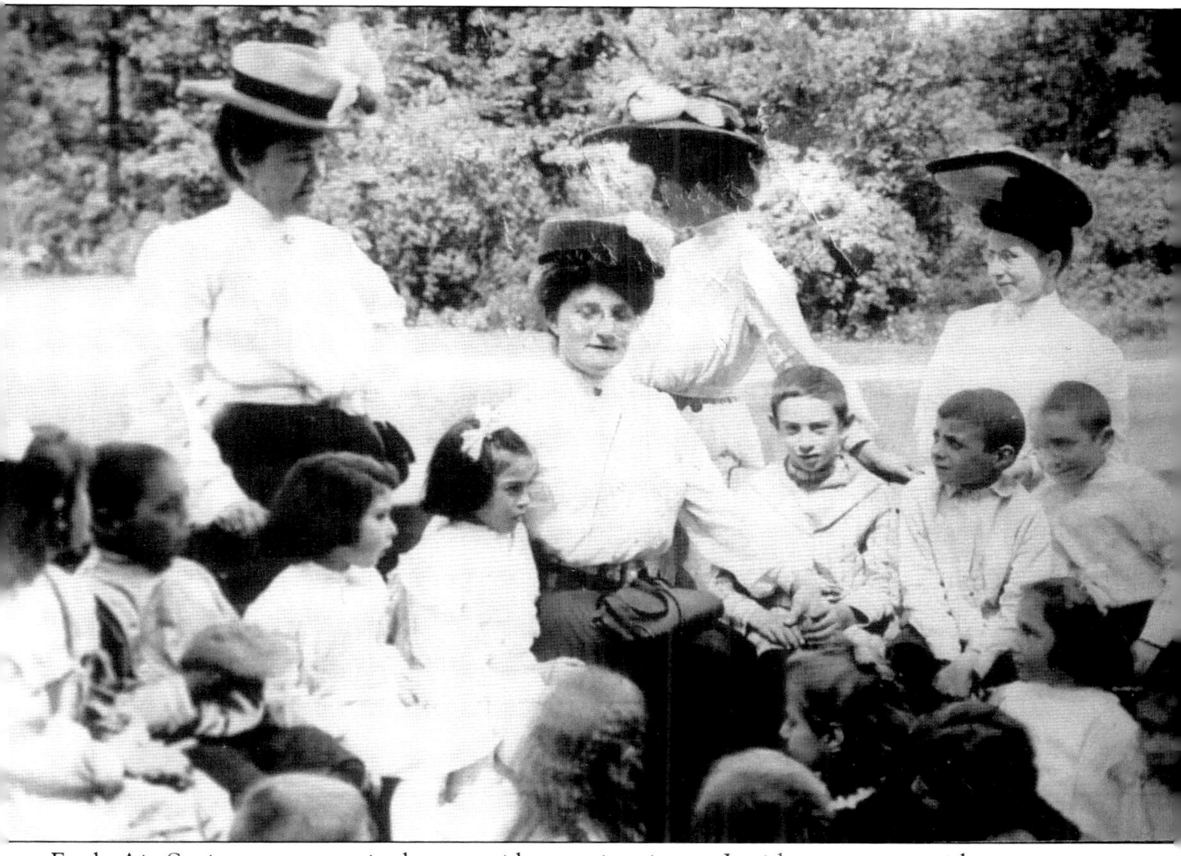

Fresh Air Society was organized to provide new immigrant Jewish youngsters with summer programs of fun and nourishment. Streetcars were chartered and baskets of food were prepared as volunteers accompanied youngsters on frequent outings for a day in the fresh air at Belle Isle. This Camp Tamarack trip to Belle Isle took place on August 2, 1905. (Courtesy Leonard N. Simons Jewish Community Archives.)

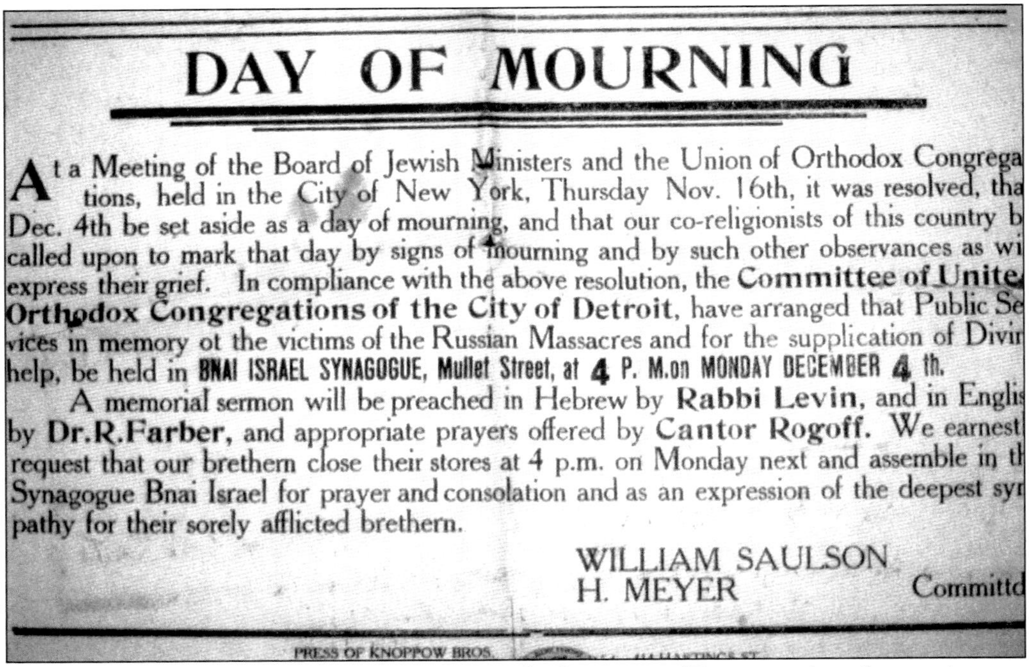

DAY OF MOURNING

At a Meeting of the Board of Jewish Ministers and the Union of Orthodox Congrega tions, held in the City of New York, Thursday Nov. 16th, it was resolved, tha Dec. 4th be set aside as a day of mourning, and that our co-religionists of this country b called upon to mark that day by signs of mourning and by such other observances as wi express their grief. In compliance with the above resolution, the **Committee of Unite Orthodox Congregations of the City of Detroit**, have arranged that Public Se vices in memory of the victims of the Russian Massacres and for the supplication of Divir help, be held in **BNAI ISRAEL SYNAGOGUE, Mullet Street, at 4 P. M. on MONDAY DECEMBER 4 th.**

A memorial sermon will be preached in Hebrew by **Rabbi Levin**, and in Englis by **Dr. R. Farber**, and appropriate prayers offered by **Cantor Rogoff.** We earnest request that our brethern close their stores at 4 p.m. on Monday next and assemble in th Synagogue Bnai Israel for prayer and consolation and as an expression of the deepest syr pathy for their sorely afflicted brethern.

WILLIAM SAULSON
H. MEYER
Committ

PRESS OF KNOPPOW BROS.

Because of violent attacks on Jews in Russia and other parts of Europe, a day of mourning was proclaimed. This sign was posted in store windows and other public places.

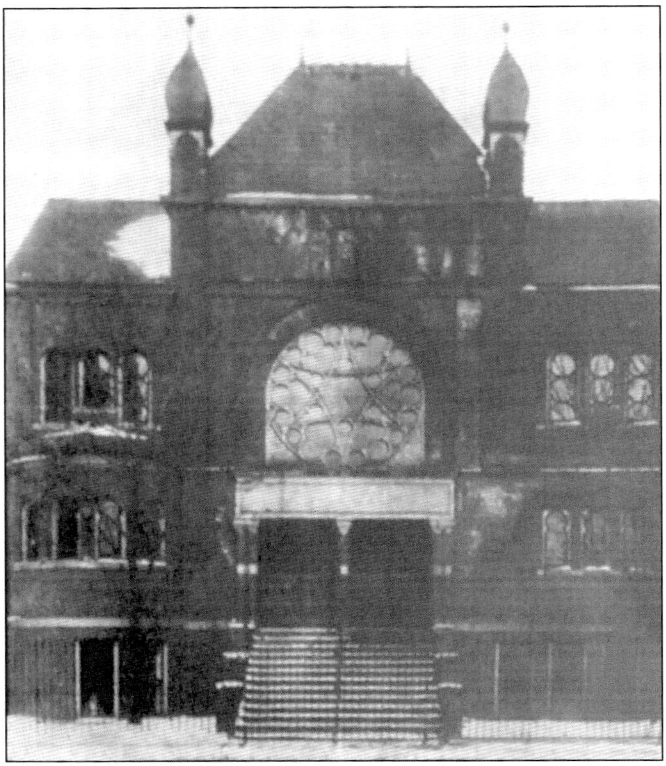

The B'nai Israel Synagogue on Mullett Street near Hastings was built in 1894 and was often the scene of community gatherings. (Courtesy Archives of Congregation Shaarey Zedek.)

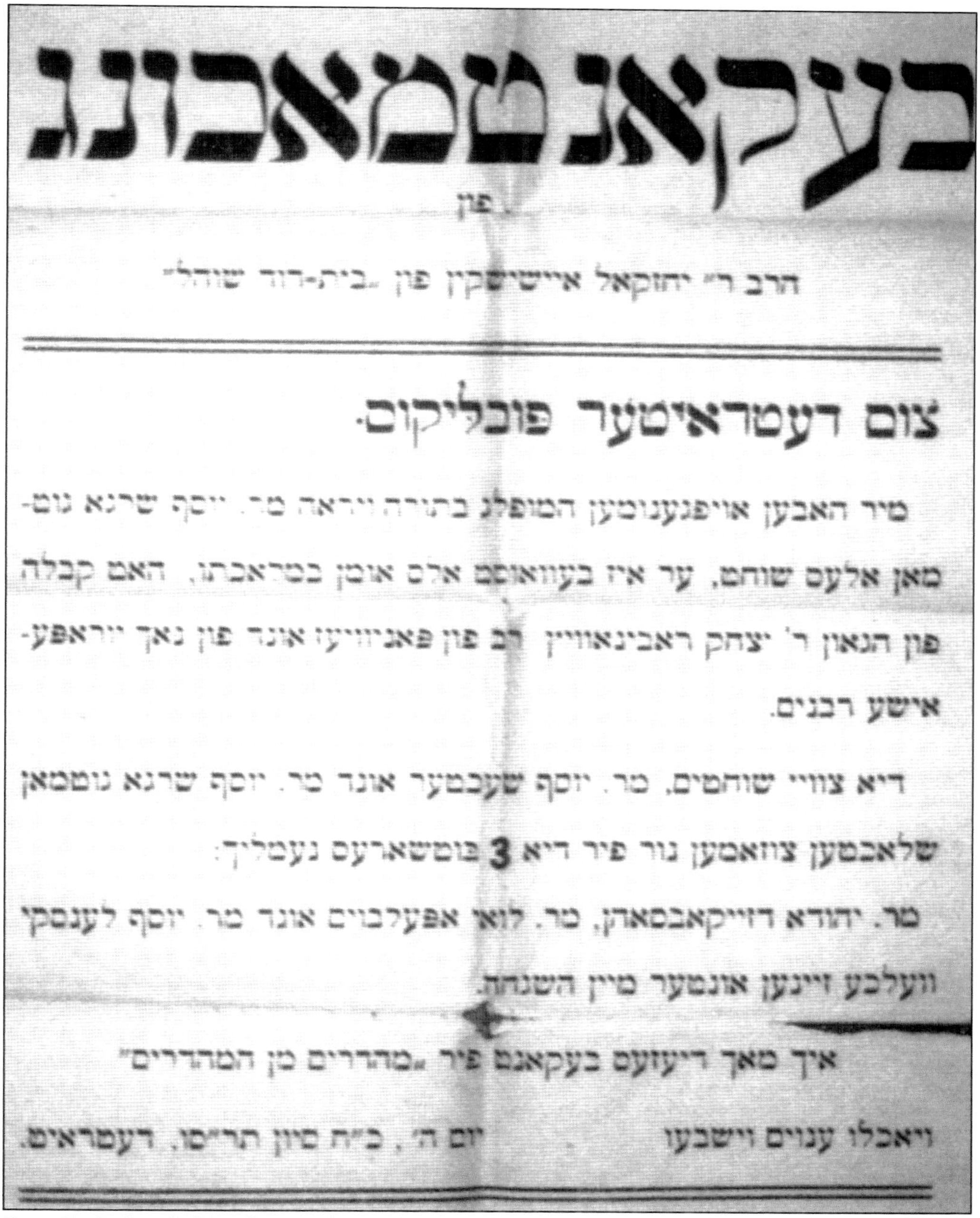

בעקאנטמאכונג

פון

הרב ר' יחזקאל אישישקן פון „בית-דוד שוהל"

צום דעטראיטער פובליקום.

מיר האבען אויפגענומען המופלג בתורה ויראה מר. יוסף שרגא גוט-מאן אלעס שוחט, ער איז בעוואוסט אלס אומן במלאכתו, האט קבלה פון הגאון ר' יצחק ראבינאוויץ רב פון פאניוועז אונד פון נאך יוראפע-אישע רבנים.

דיא צוויי שוחטים, מר. יוסף שעכטער אונד מר. יוסף שרגא גוטמאן שלאכטען צוזאמען נור פיר דיא 3 בוטשארס נעמליך:

מר. יהודא דזשייקאבסאן, מר. לואי אפעלבוים אונד מר. יוסף לענסקי וועלכע זיינען אונטער מיין השגחה.

איך מאך דיזעס בעקאנט פיר „מהדרים מן המהדרים"

ויאכלו ענוים וישבעו   יום ה', כ"ח סיון תרס"ו. דעטראיט.

From Ezekial Aishishkin from Beth David Shul:
For the Detroit public. I'm introducing an expert in Torah & a god-fearing Jew. Mr. Yosef Goodman as a shoichet (ritual slaughterer). He is well-known in his trade and has certification from Hagoan Yitzchak Rabinowitch, a rabbi from Ponevitch and from other European Rabbonim. The schochtim, Mr. Yosaif Schechter and Mr. Yosef Shragah Goodman are shechting together only for three butchers. Namely, Mr. Yehudah Jacobsen and Mr. Louis Applebaum and Mr. Yosef Lansky. They are all under my haschgacha. I'm making this known that it's Kosher to the strictest standards. Eat, Drink & Enjoy. Detroit, 5th day of Sivan, 1906.

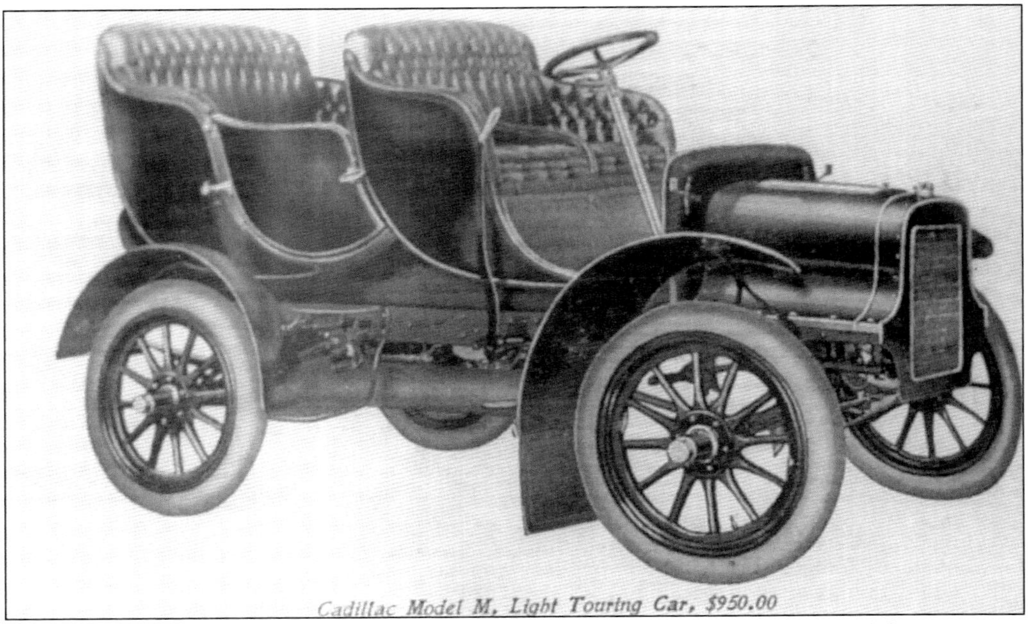

The 1906 Cadillac, priced at $950, was considered an American status symbol for European immigrants. (Courtesy Burton Historical Collection of the Detroit Public Library.)

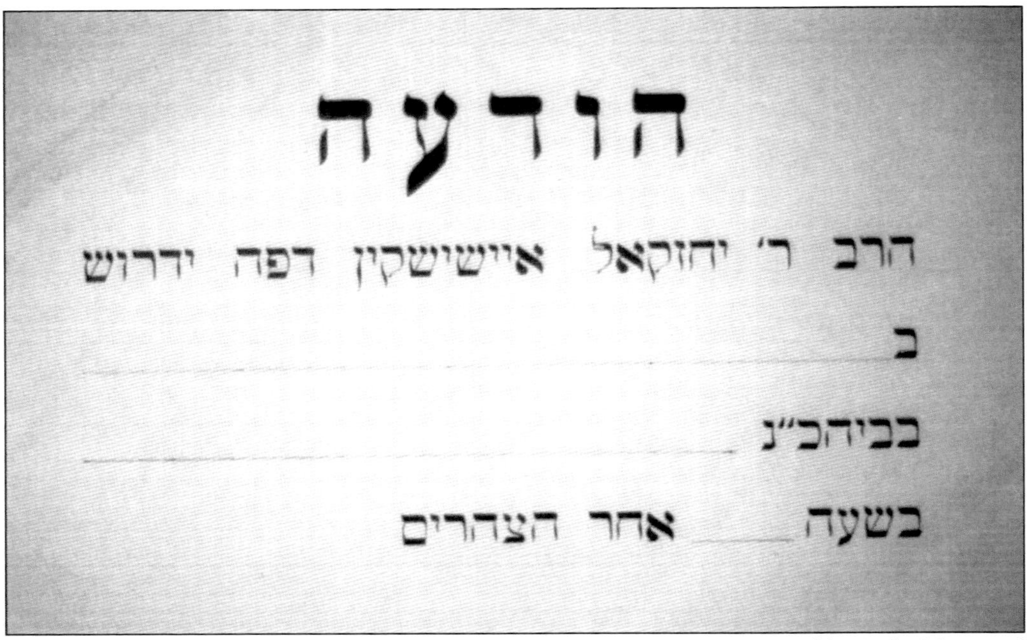

During this period, rabbis served several congregations at the same time. Rabbi Aishishkin used this sign, which was posted at synagogues, and filled in the blanks to tell worshippers which Friday evening and Saturday morning and afternoon services he would be at. (Courtesy Dr. Jack Belen.)

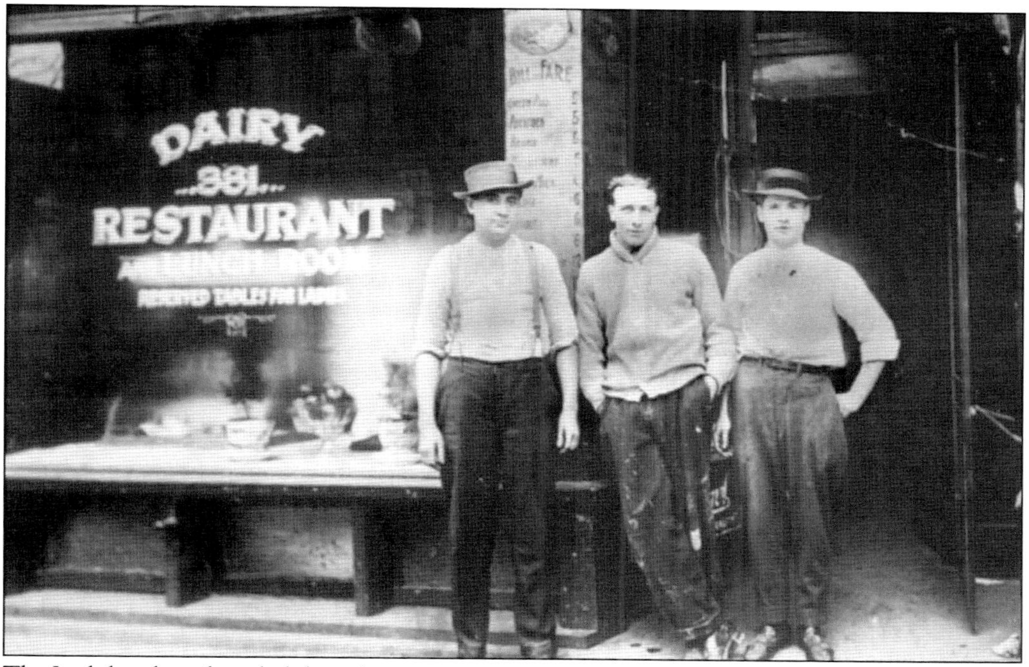

The Lash brothers founded their dairy restaurant on Hastings Street in 1900. (Courtesy Leonard N. Simons Jewish Community Archives.)

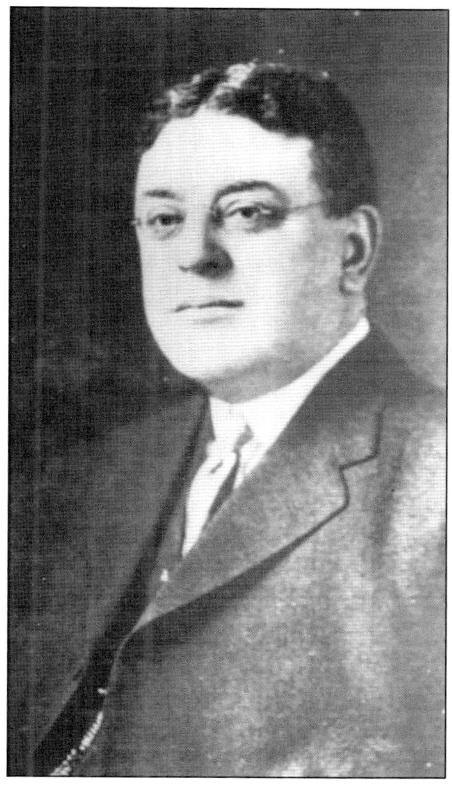

Bernard Ginsberg, a well-known community leader in the early 1900s, was president of the United Jewish Charities from 1904 to 1908. (Courtesy Rabbi Leo M. Franklin Archives of Temple Beth El.)

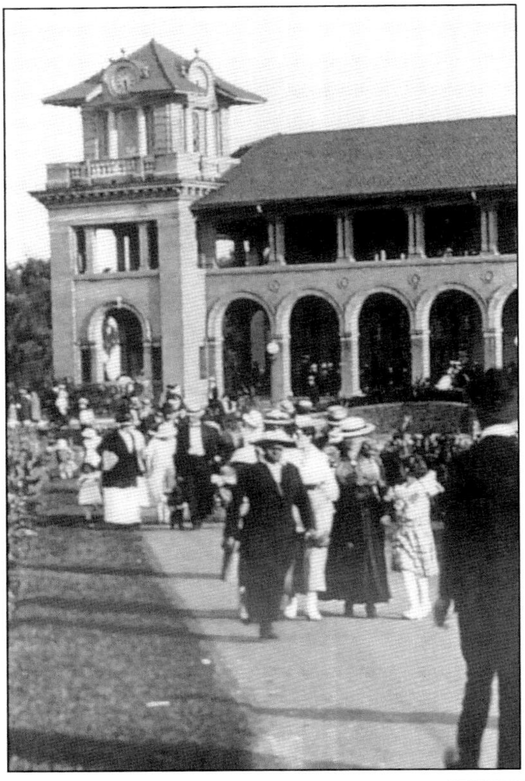

Sunday social outings at Belle Isle were part of the Jewish community in 1907. According to the *Detroit Jewish Directory*, published in Yiddish in 1907, 16 percent of the 2,145 working males listed were peddlers. Four were policemen and one was a fireman. (Courtesy Burton Historical Collection of the Detroit Public Library.)

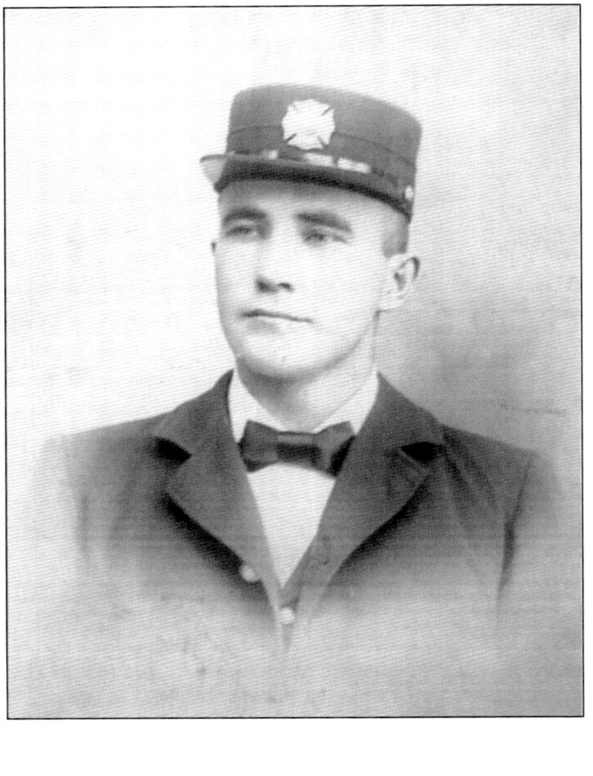

Detroit's lone Jewish fireman was Moses Weingarden. He would serve for 35 years and retire with the rank of Battalion Chief. (Courtesy Alan Bennett.)

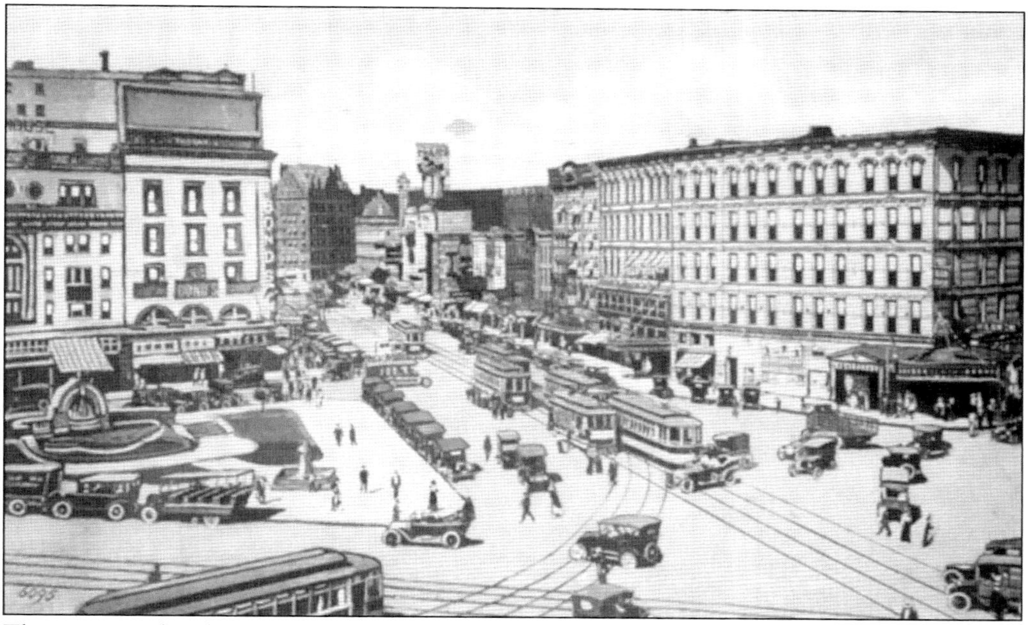

Theaters populated Monroe Avenue from Randolph to Campus Martius in 1910. Detroit had 157,334 foreign-born citizens out of a population of 465,766.

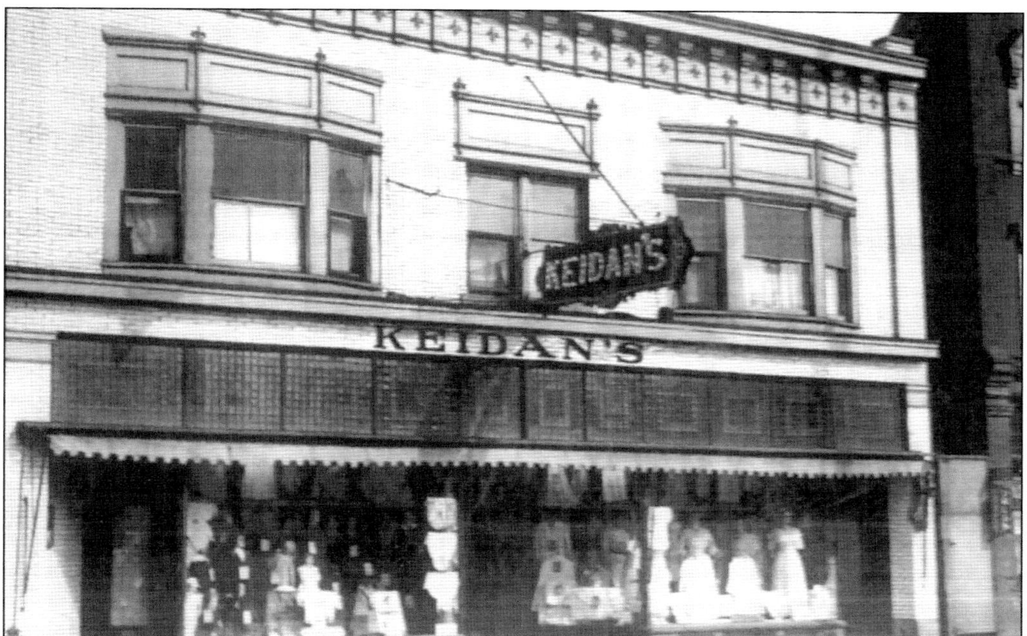

Not far from Monroe Avenue, on Gratiot near St. Antoine, was Keidan's, owned by Chana Fredl and Abba Keidan. (Courtesy of Judith Levin Cantor.)

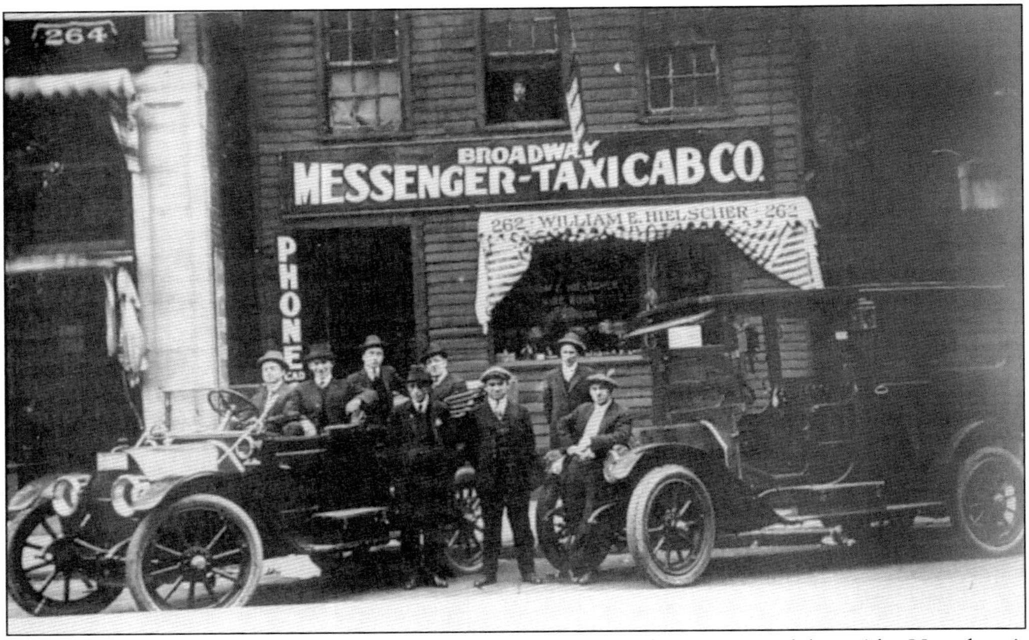

Four years after taxicabs with automatic fare registers made their Detroit debut, Abe Hertzberg's growing Messenger Taxicab Company was located on Broadway south of Grand Circus Park. (Courtesy Archives of Congregation Shaarey Zedek.)

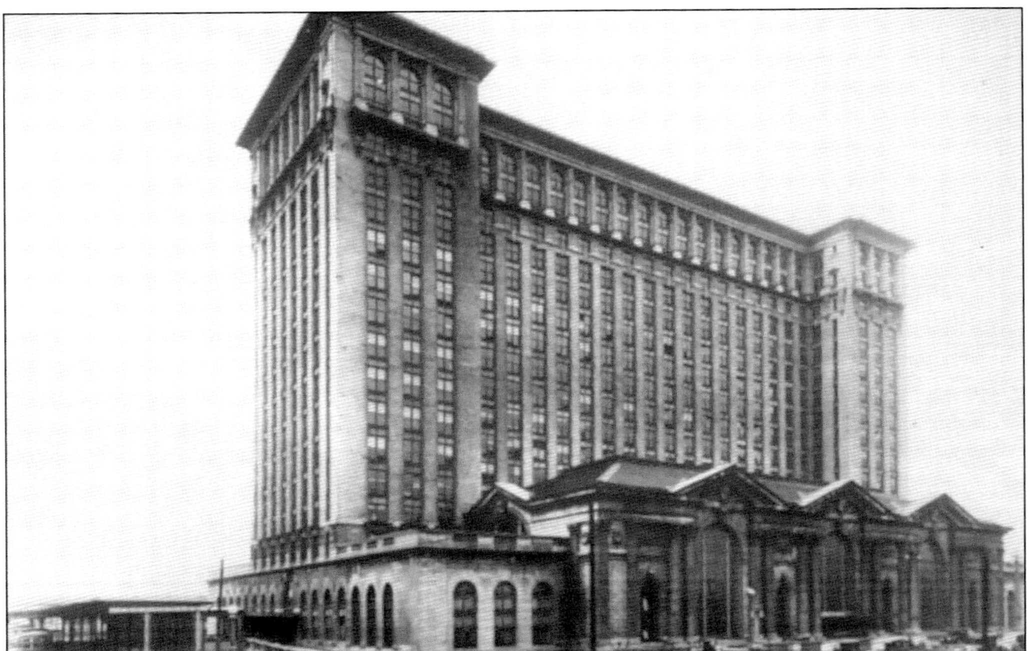

Many rabbinical and national Jewish leaders often came to Detroit and were met at the Michigan Central Depot by leading Detroiters, who gave them a motorcade to their destination. (Courtesy Burton Historical Collection of the Detroit Public Library.)

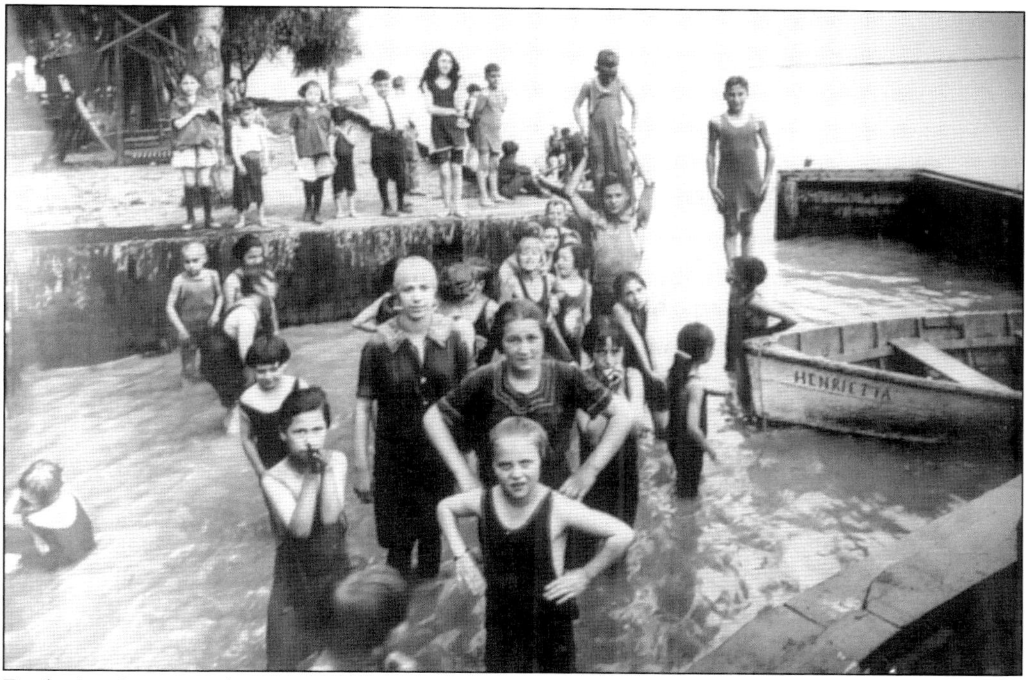

Fresh Air Camp used Venice Beach near Mt. Clemens in 1912. (Courtesy Leonard N. Simons Jewish Community Archives.)

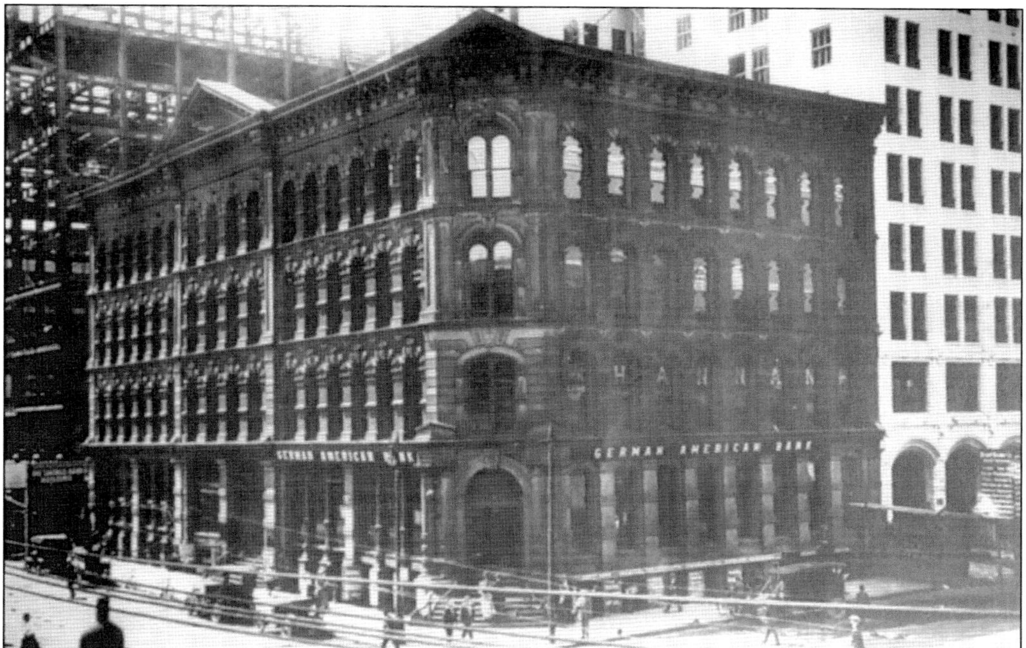

The Jewish-operated German American Bank moved from Campus Martius to Griswold near Fort. (Courtesy Burton Historical Collection of the Detroit Public Library.)

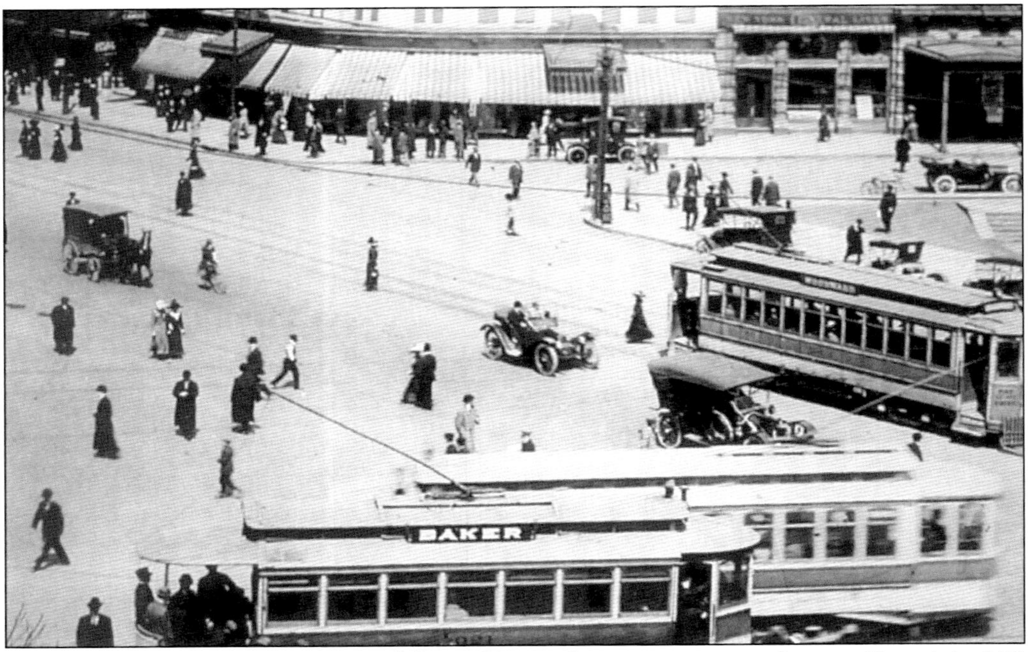

People traveled by streetcar, automobile, and horse-drawn carriage as a thriving Detroit had 70 moving picture houses and 14 variety theaters in 1913. (Courtesy Burton Historical Collection of the Detroit Public Library.)

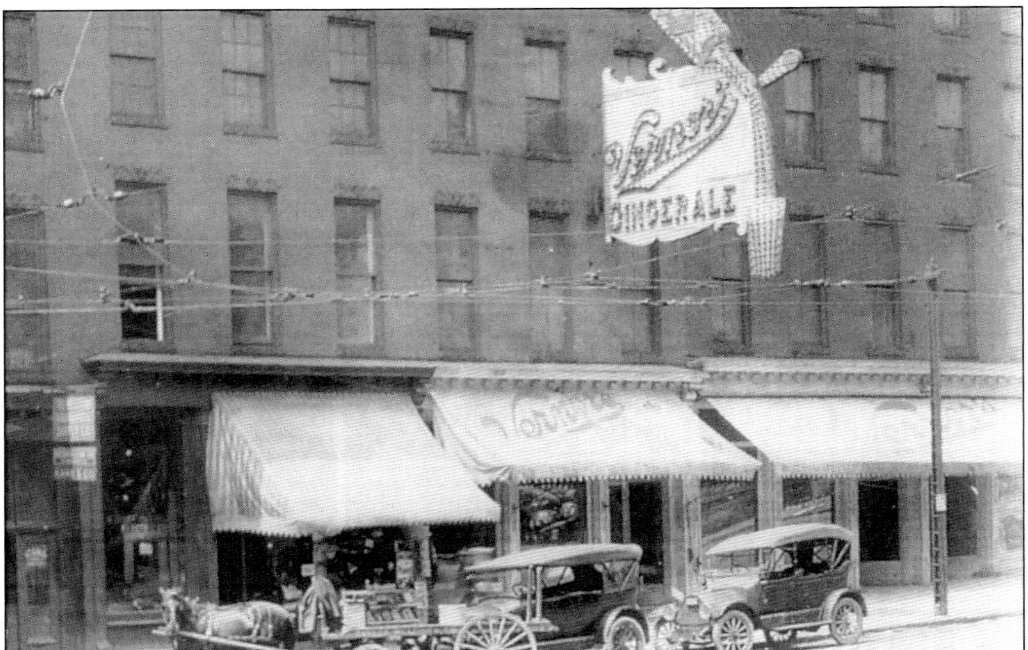

Dating Jewish couples often stopped at the Vernor's Ginger Ale Plant on the west side of lower Woodward. (Courtesy Burton Historical Collection of the Detroit Public Library.)

The *Detroit News* told of the groundbreaking ceremony of the new Shaarey Zedek in 1913.

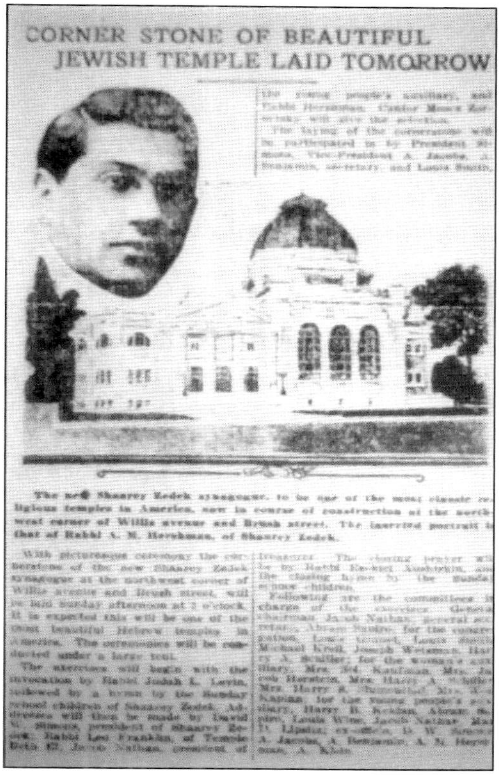

CORNER STONE OF BEAUTIFUL JEWISH TEMPLE LAID TOMORROW

The new Shaarey Zedek synagogue, to be one of the most classic religious temples in America, now in course of construction at the northwest corner of Willis avenue and Brush street. The inserted portrait is that of Rabbi A. M. Hershman, of Shaarey Zedek.

With picturesque ceremony the cornerstone of the new Shaarey Zedek synagogue at the northwest corner of Willis avenue and Brush street, will be laid Sunday afternoon at 2 o'clock. It is expected this will be one of the most beautiful Hebrew temples in America. The ceremonies will be conducted under a large tent.

The exercises will begin with the invocation by Rabbi Judah L. Levin, followed by a hymn by the Sunday school children of Shaarey Zedek. Addresses will then be made by David W. Simons, president of Shaarey Zedek; Rabbi Leo Franklin, of Temple Beth El; Jacob Nathan, president of

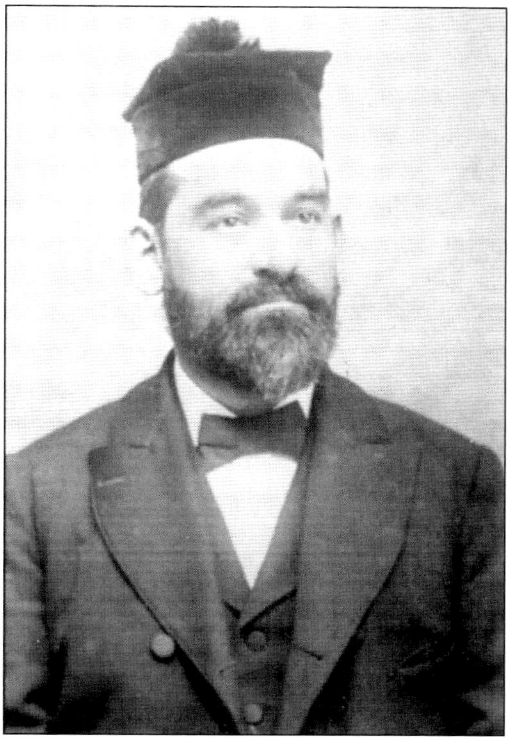

Meyer Smith had served as sexton of Shaarey Zedek for 23 years at the time of the groundbreaking of the new synagogue at Brush and Willis. (Courtesy archives of Congregation Shaarey Zedek.)

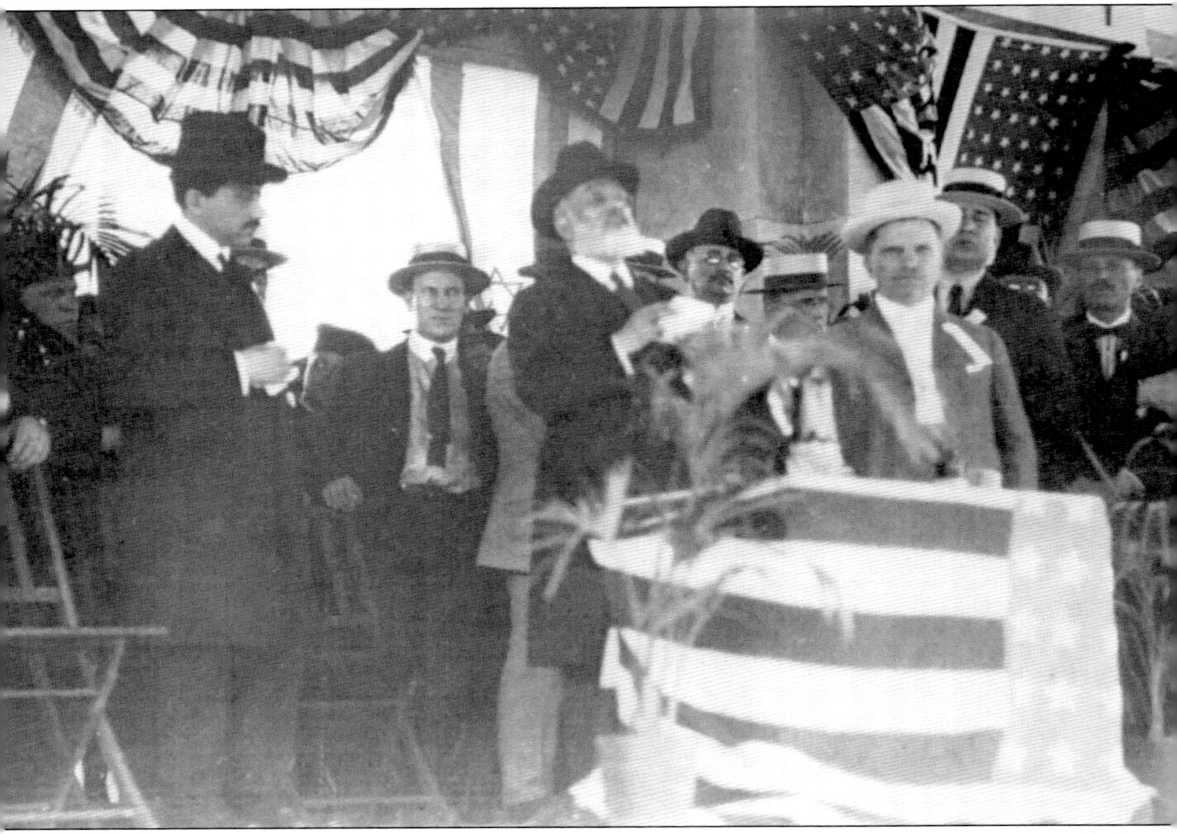

Rabbi Judah L. Levin, the head of Detroit's orthodox congregations, addressed those assembled for the ceremonies. Rabbi A.M. Hershman, spiritual leader of Shaarey Zedek, is on the left and D.W. Simons, president of the congregation, is on the other side of Rabbi Levin. (Courtesy Archives of Congregation Shaarey Zedek.)

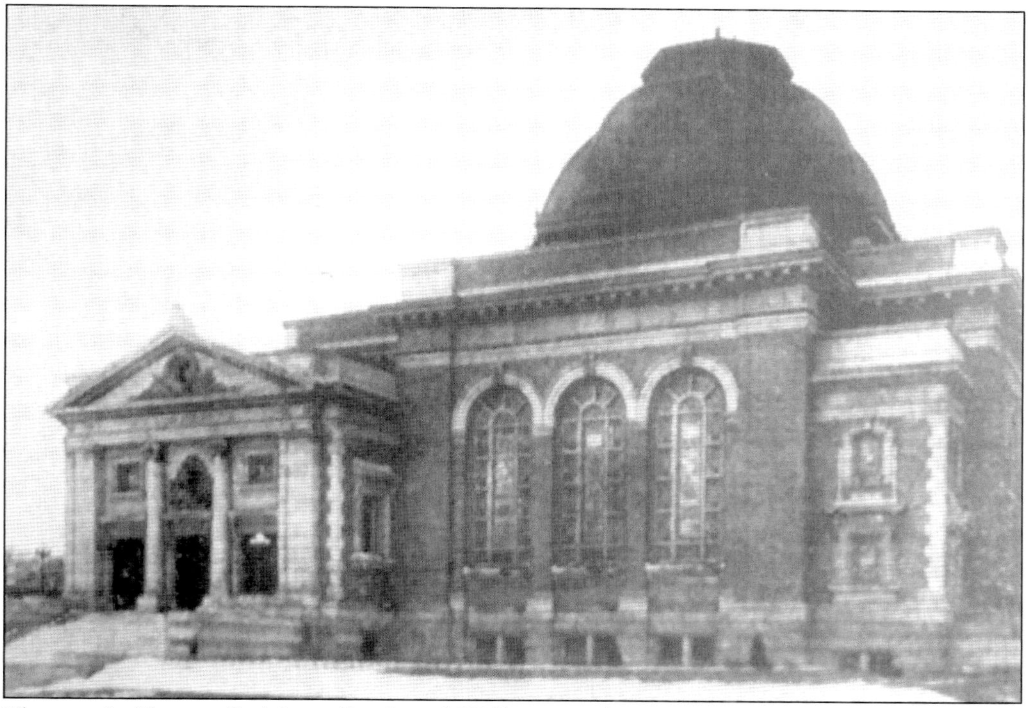

The stately Shaarey Zedek on Brush and Willis opened in 1915. Today the site is part of the Detroit Medical Center. (Courtesy archives of Congregation Shaarey Zedek.)

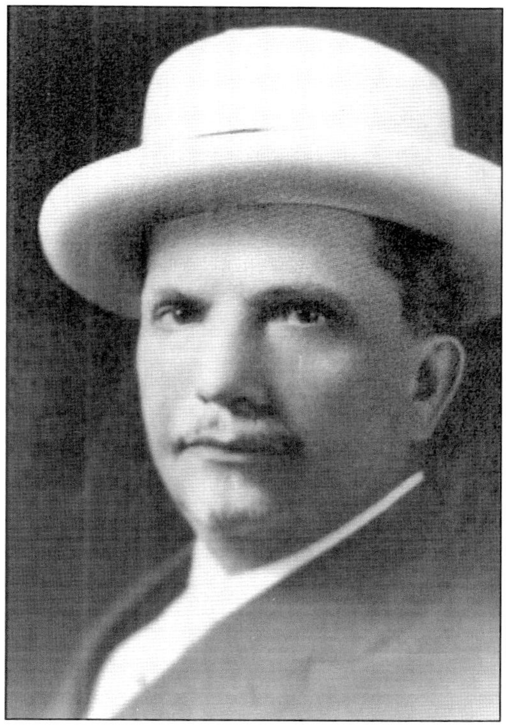

David W. Simons assumed the presidency of Shaarey Zedek in 1908 and held the post for twelve years. Simons was also well-known outside the Jewish community as he was active in city commerce and government. (Courtesy Archives of Congregation Shaarey Zedek.)

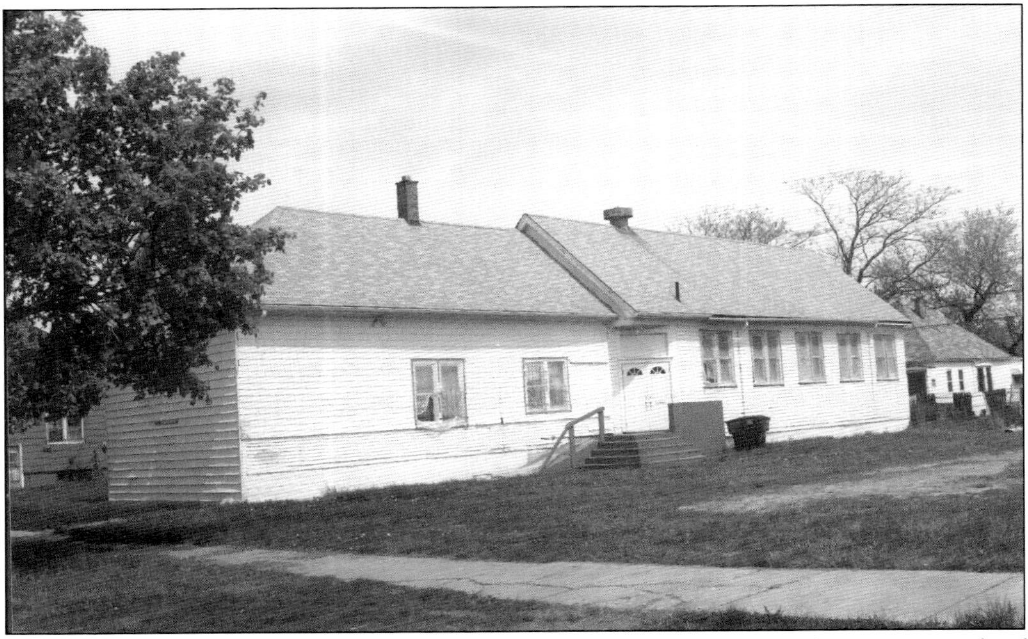

Congregation Beth Itzchok organized and built a small building on Fischer Street north of Mack in 1914. It housed.a small synagogue in front and a residence for the rabbi in back.

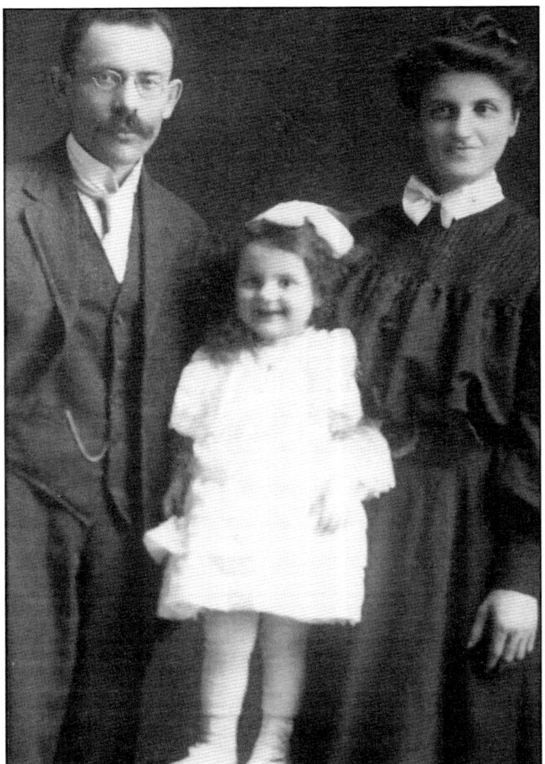

Scholarly Jacob Lazaroff became the first spiritual leader of Beth Itzchok. His daughter, Emma, would become world-famous in the coming decades, as a soprano and as a tireless worker on behalf of Jewish causes. (Courtesy Emma Lazaroff Schaver.)

After serving in the United States Navy, Louis Raskin became a Detroit fireman. A quarter of a century later, his son Danny would become a well-known columnist for the local *Jewish News*. (Courtesy Danny Raskin.)

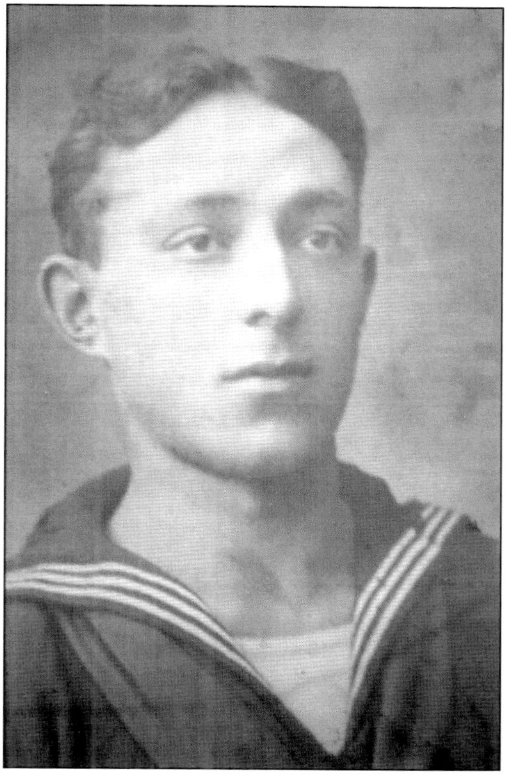

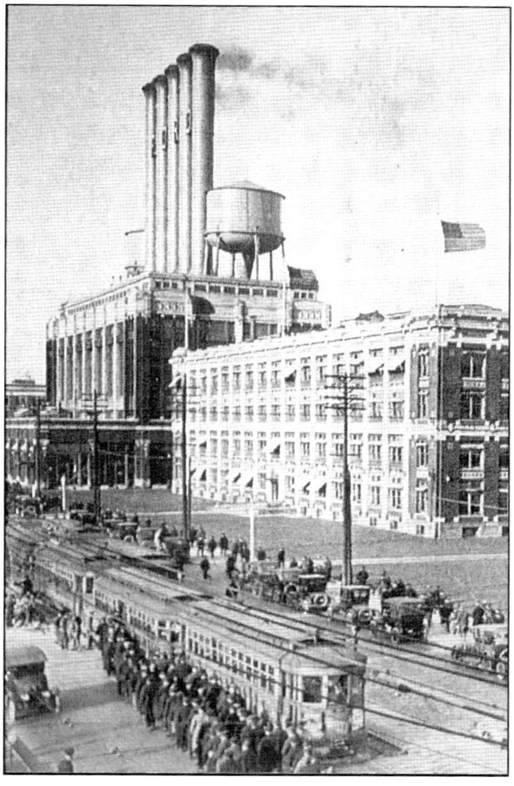

Detroit was home to 43 automobile companies when the Albert Kahn-designed Ford plant opened on Woodward in Highland Park, prior to World War I. The factory provided employment to many European immigrants. (Courtesy Burton Historical Collection of the Detroit Public Library.)

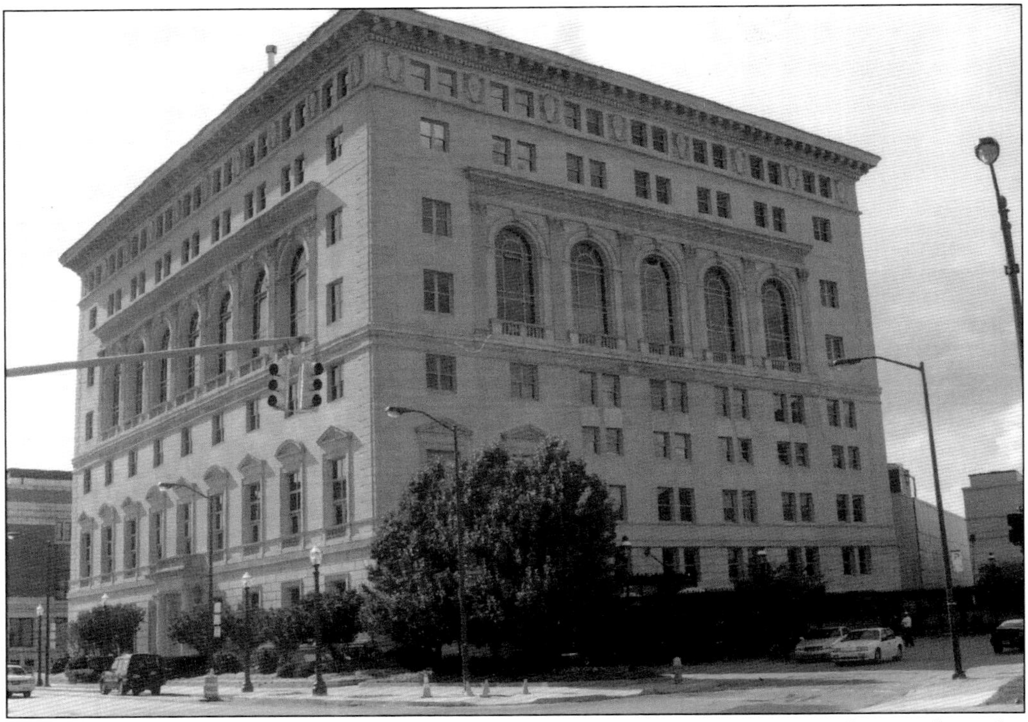

The elegant Detroit Athletic Club opened on Madison Avenue in 1915. Albert Kahn, who designed the building, refused an invitation to the first luncheon to protest the club's policy of barring Jews from membership.

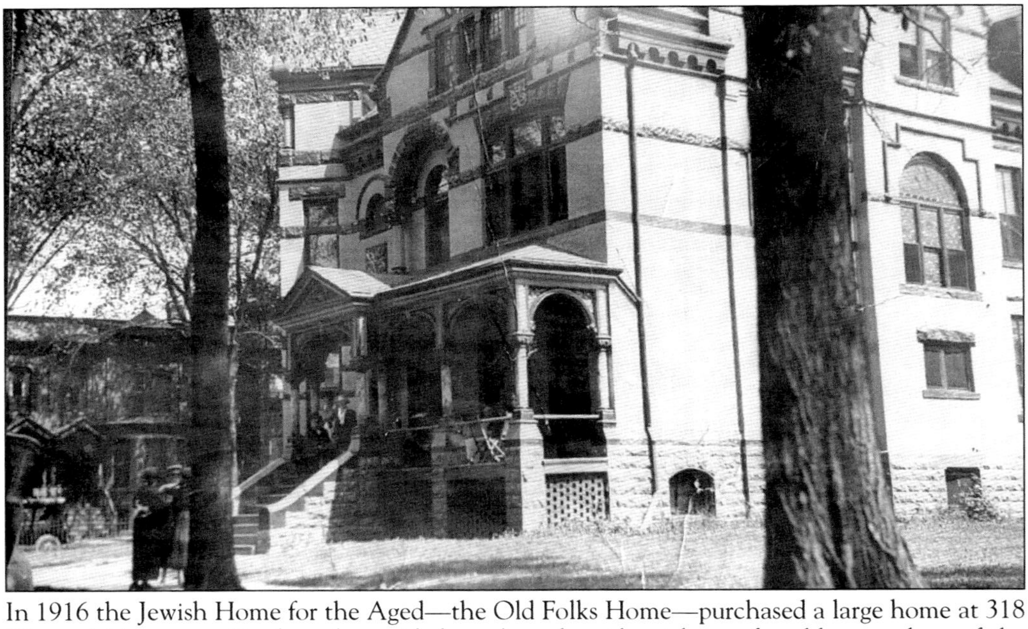

In 1916 the Jewish Home for the Aged—the Old Folks Home—purchased a large home at 318 Edmund Place near Brush and provided meals and residential care for older members of the community. (Courtesy Leonard N. Simons Jewish Community Archives.)

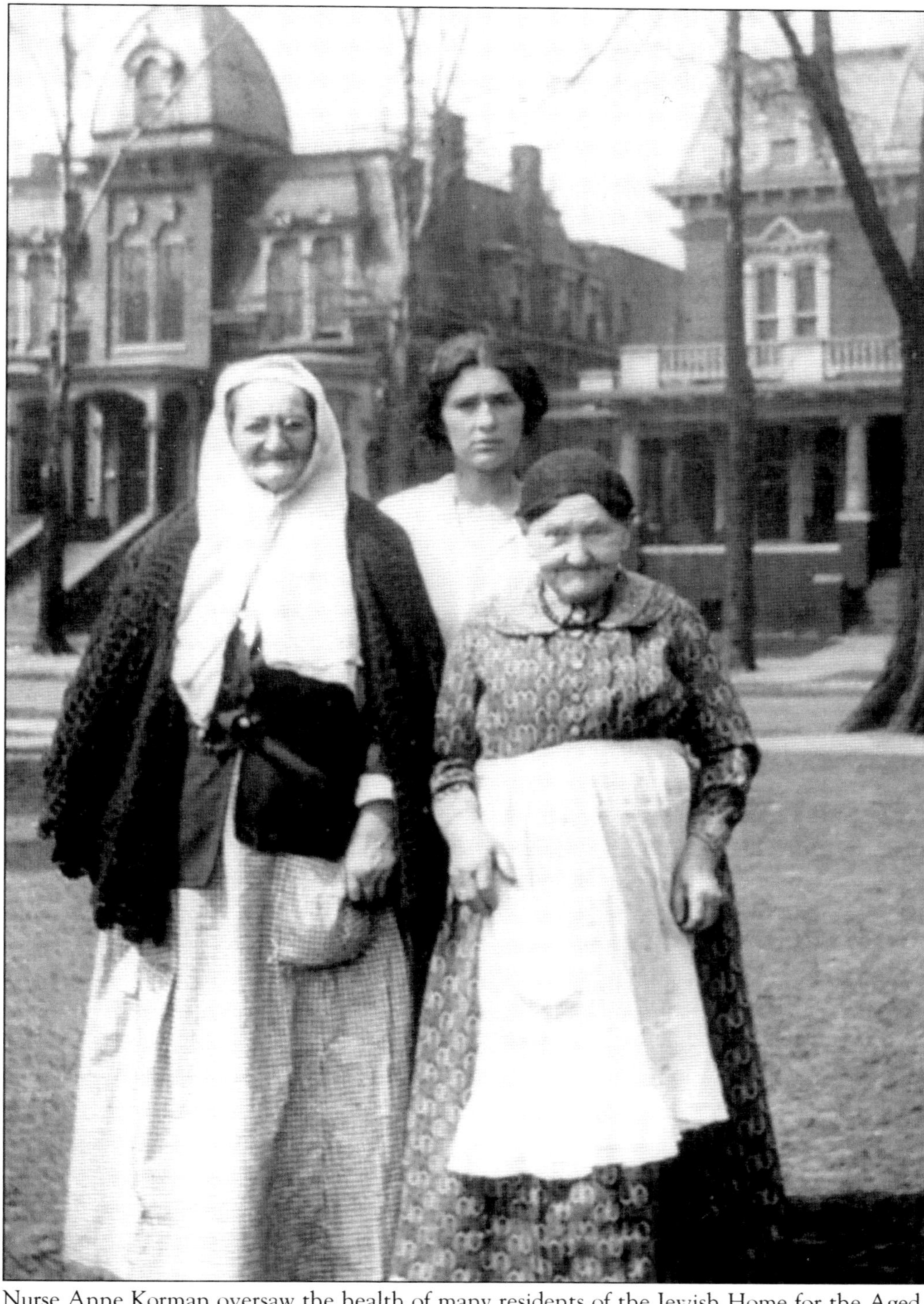

Nurse Anne Korman oversaw the health of many residents of the Jewish Home for the Aged, including Mrs. S.L. Goldman on the left, and Mrs. B. Freedlander. (Courtesy Leonard N. Simons Jewish Community Archives.)

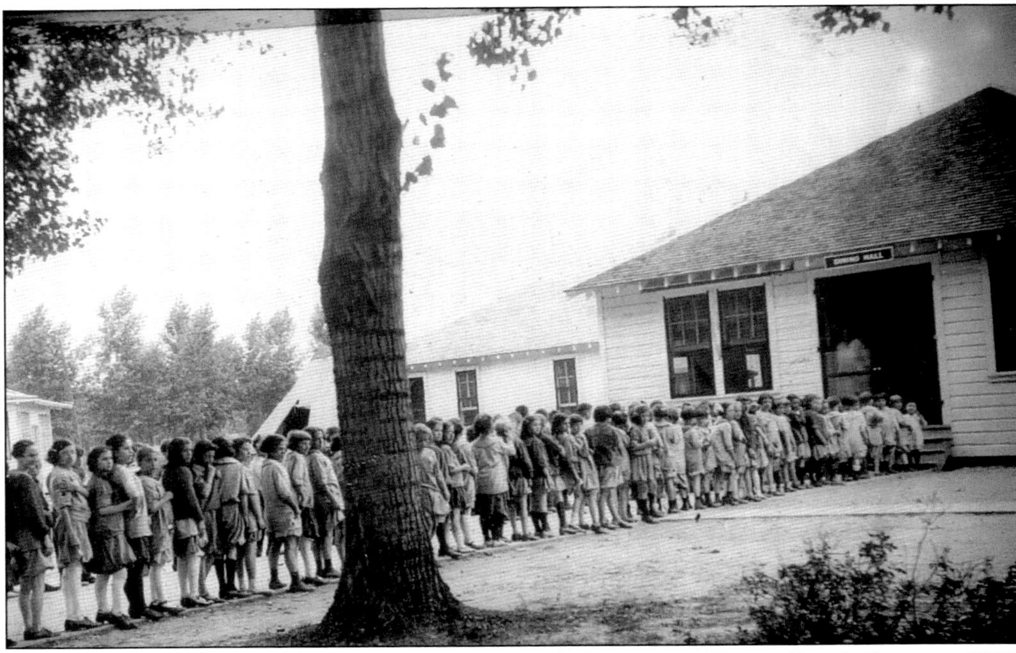

Campers line up outside the dining hall at the Fresh Air Society Venice Beach Camp in 1917. (Courtesy Leonard N. Simons Jewish Community Archives.)

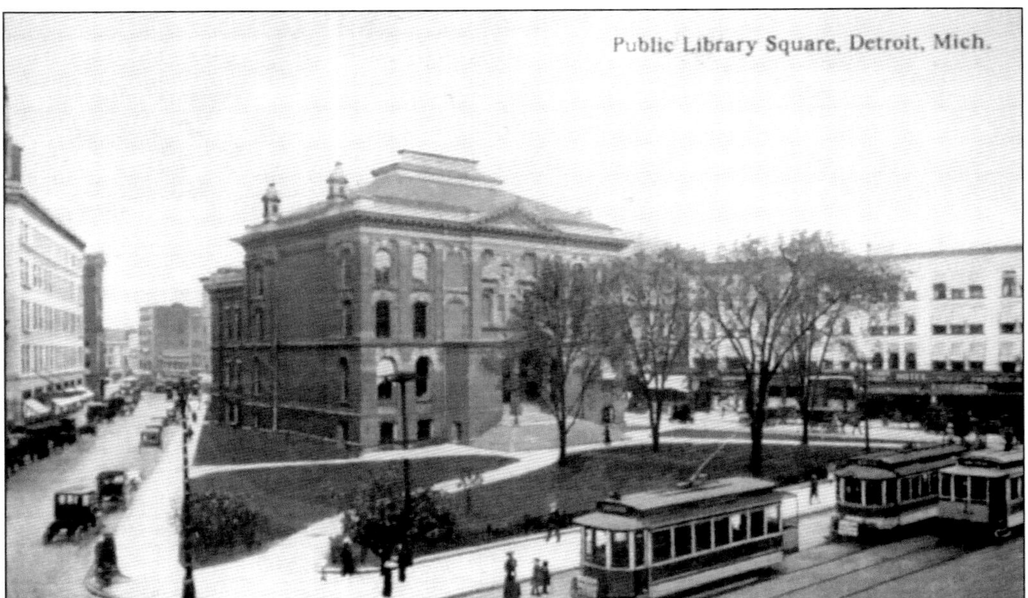

Jewish children also made frequent trips to the Downtown Library just east of Hudson's.

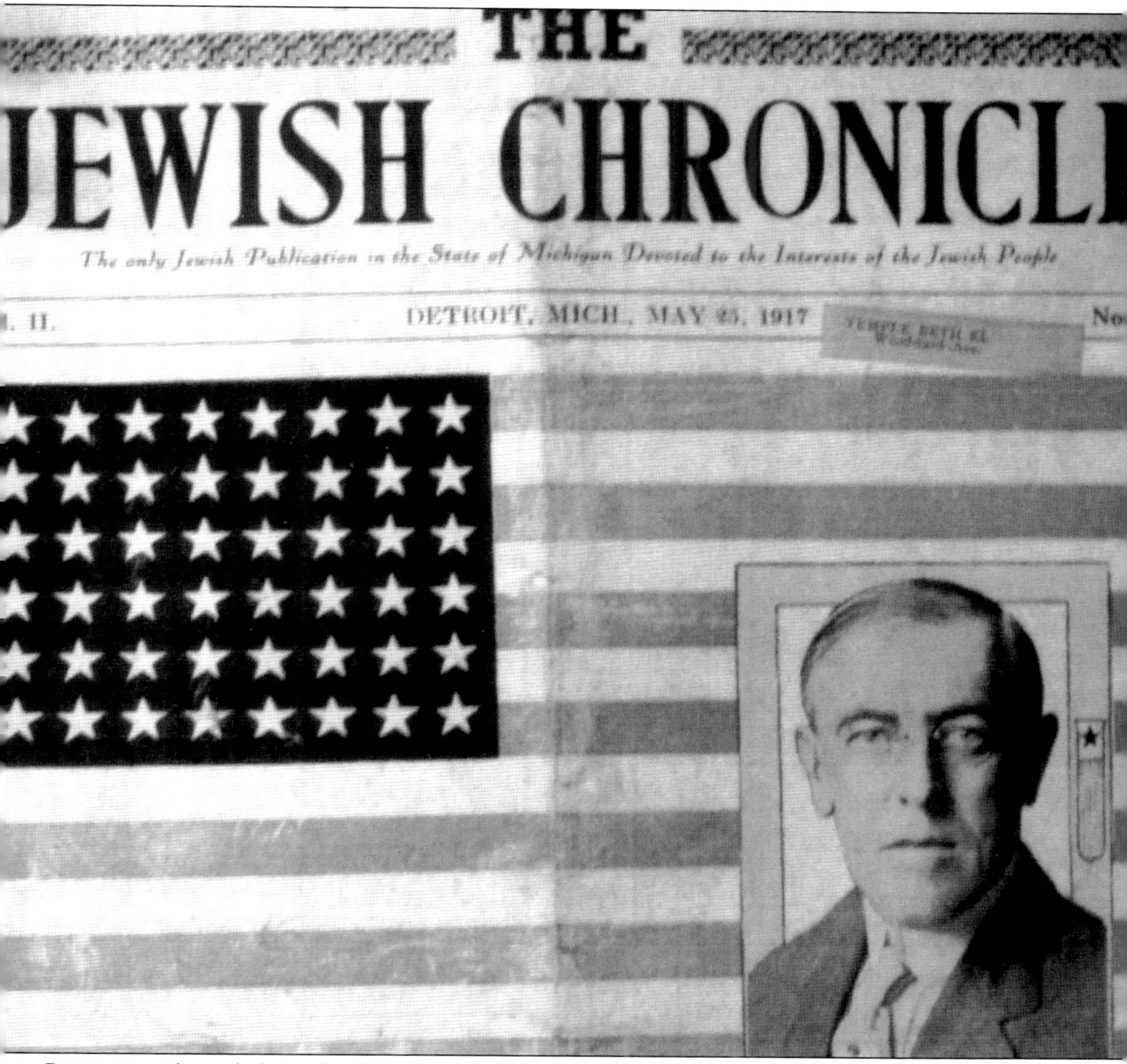

Patriotism abounded in the Jewish community during World War I. President Woodrow Wilson's picture often appeared in Detroit's weekly *Jewish Chronicle*. Wilson was considered a good friend of the Jews and appointed Louis D. Brandeis an associate justice with the Supreme Court—the first Jew to sit on the court. (Courtesy Rabbi Leo M. Franklin Archives of Temple Beth E1.)

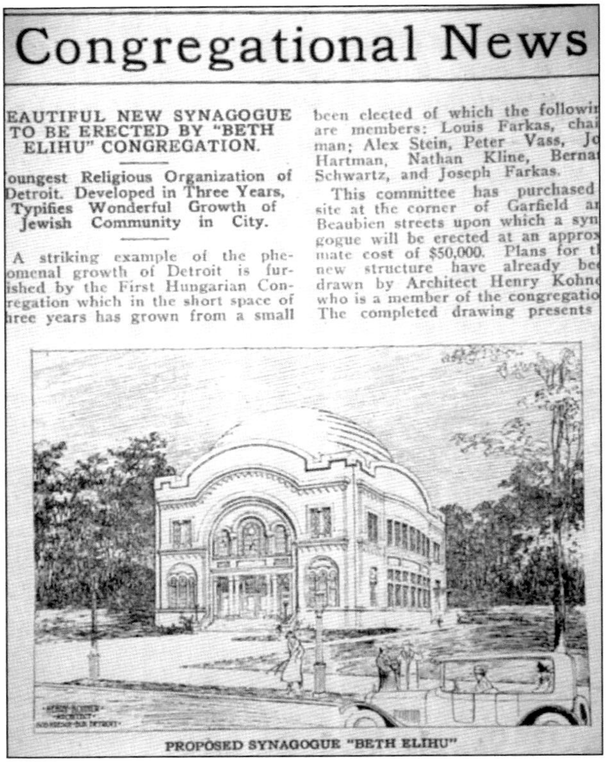

Congregational News

EAUTIFUL NEW SYNAGOGUE TO BE ERECTED BY "BETH ELIHU" CONGREGATION.

'oungest Religious Organization of Detroit. Developed in Three Years, Typifies Wonderful Growth of Jewish Community in City.

A striking example of the phe- omenal growth of Detroit is fur- ished by the First Hungarian Con- regation which in the short space of hree years has grown from a small been elected of which the followi are members: Louis Farkas, cha man; Alex Stein, Peter Vass, Jo Hartman, Nathan Kline, Berna Schwartz, and Joseph Farkas.

This committee has purchased site at the corner of Garfield a Beaubien streets upon which a syn gogue will be erected at an approx mate cost of $50,000. Plans for t new structure have already be drawn by Architect Henry Kohn who is a member of the congregatio The completed drawing presents

PROPOSED SYNAGOGUE "BETH ELIHU"

The weekly *Jewish Chronicle* told of Hungarian Jews planning Congregation Beth Elihu's synagogue on Garfield and Beaubien.

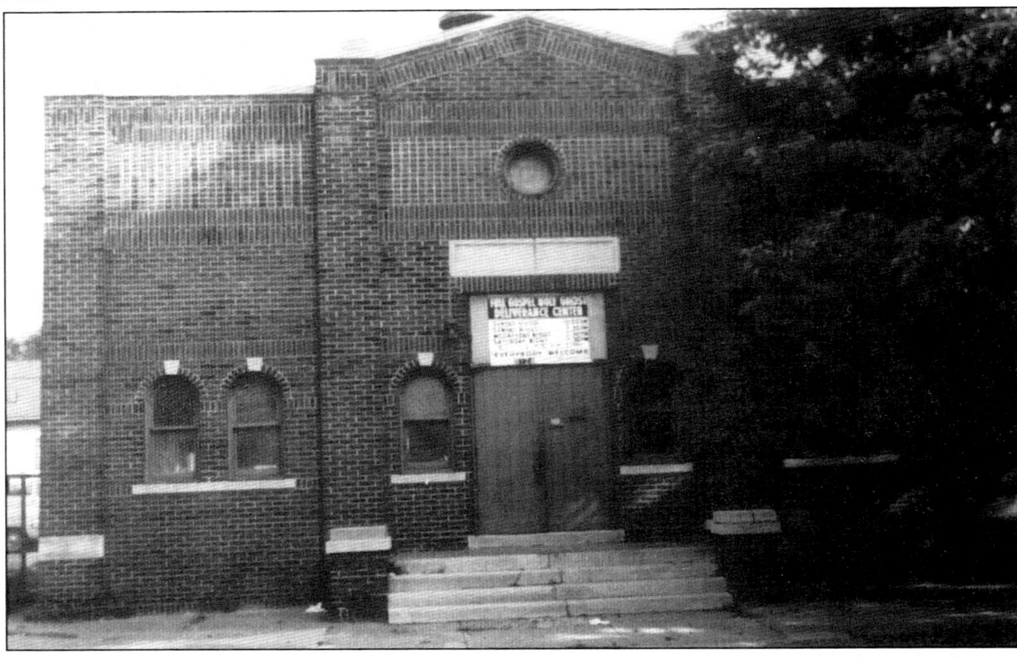

Another group of Hungarian Jews opened the First Hebrew Congregation of Delray, also known as Orthodox Hungarian Jewish Congregation. The building on Burdeno near Fort Wayne was Detroit's first orthodox congregation to locate west of Woodward.

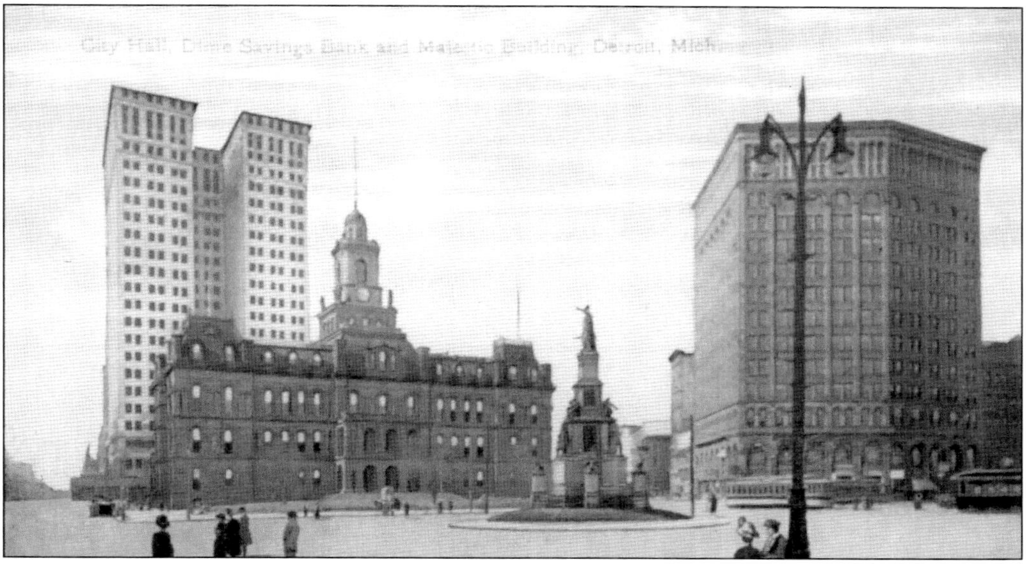

There were fewer men on Detroit's streets during World War I. Max Madison, who enlisted in the Marines in April 1917, became Detroit's first Jewish war casualty a year after his enlistment.

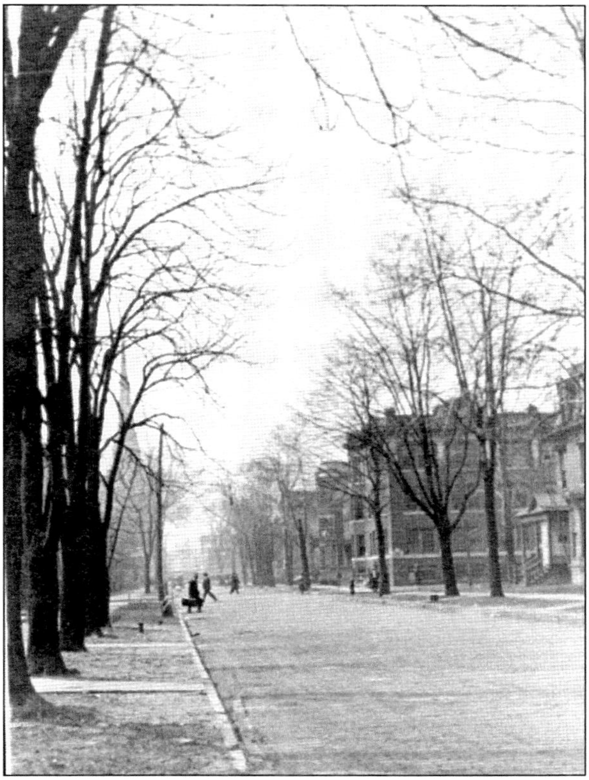

There also were fewer Jewish men on Winder Street going to work during rush hour. (Courtesy Burton Historical Collection of the Detroit Public Library.)

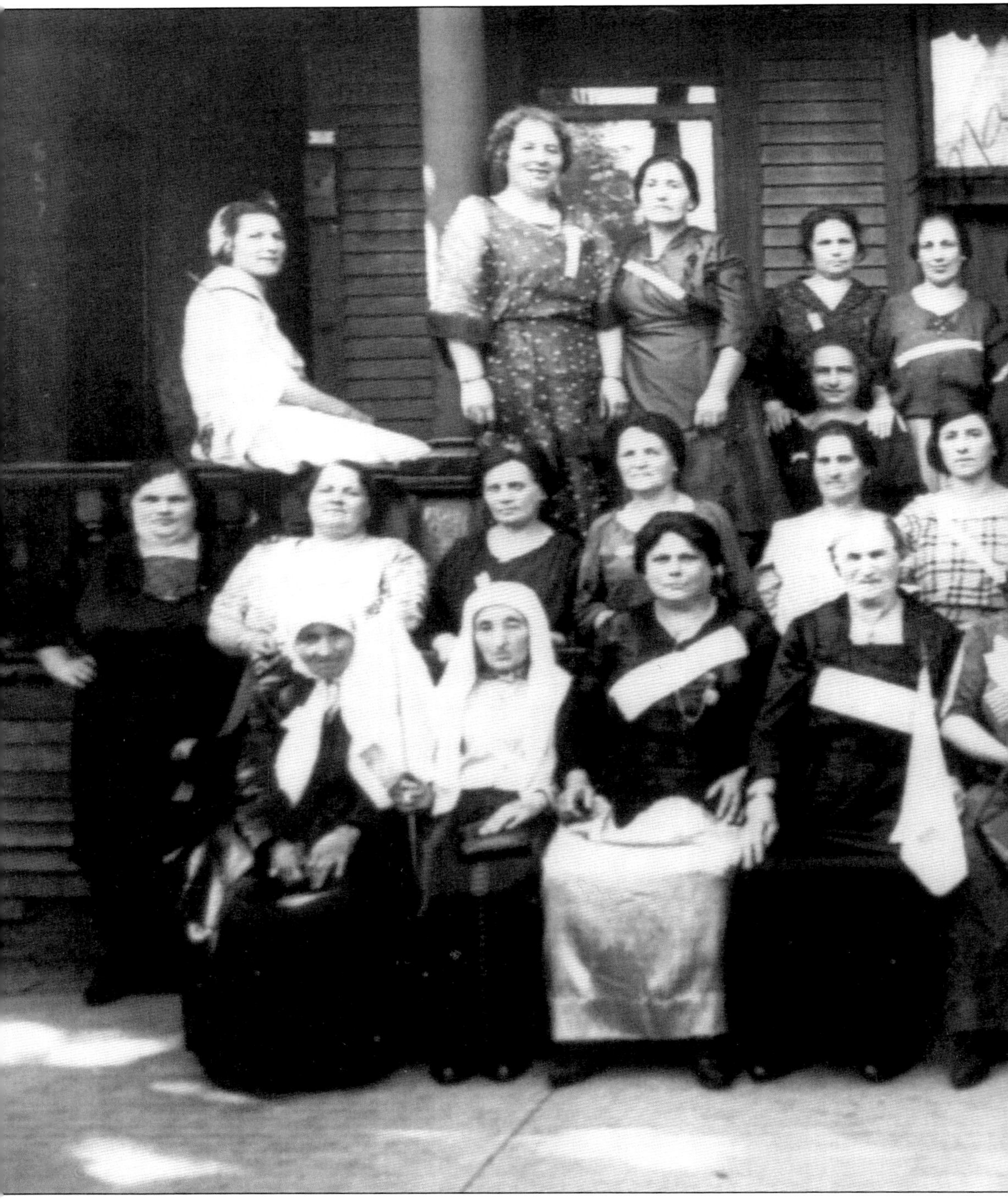

While many men were off to war, the women of the Jewish community did their part. The Ladies' Auxiliary of Beth Isaac—located on the lower floor of a frame dwelling on Belmont, a block north of Boston Boulevard—sold cakes and held fundraisers. At the Phoenix Club, the Jewish Women's Club Unit often met on behalf of the Red Cross, as did the Sisterhood of

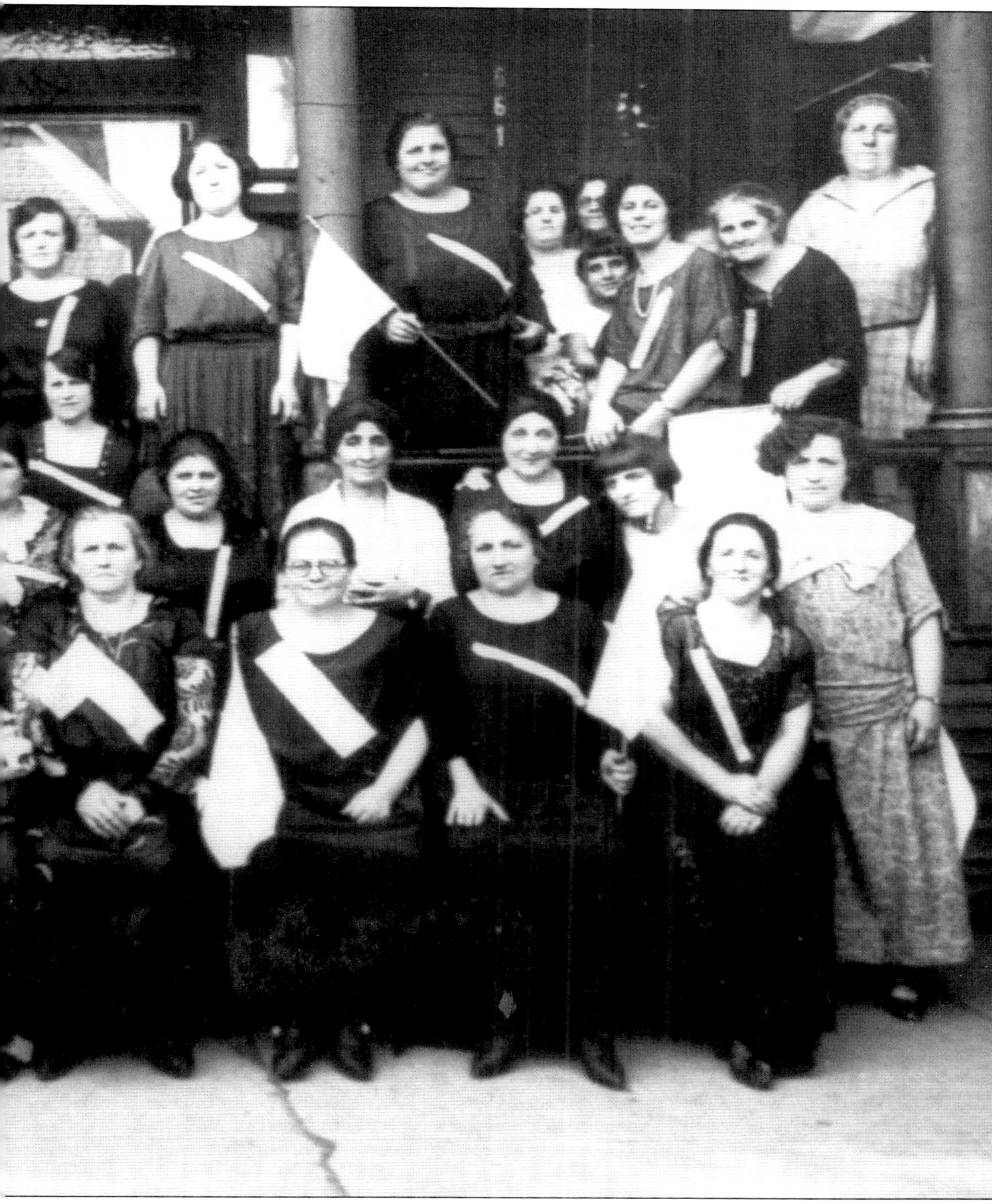

Shaarey Zedek. Rooms in the synagogue's basement were converted into hospital sewing rooms, where bandages or other items for Red Cross use were prepared. (Courtesy Leonard N. Simons Jewish Community Archives.)

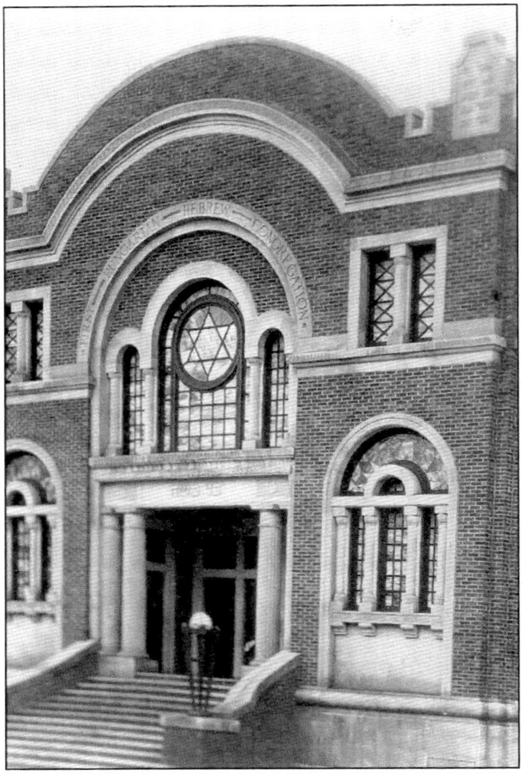

The Beth Elihu First Hungarian Hebrew Congregation evolved into Congregation B'nai Moshe, and the synagogue on Garfield and Beaubien was dedicated on March 3, 1918. (Courtesy Manning Brothers Historical Photographic Collection.)

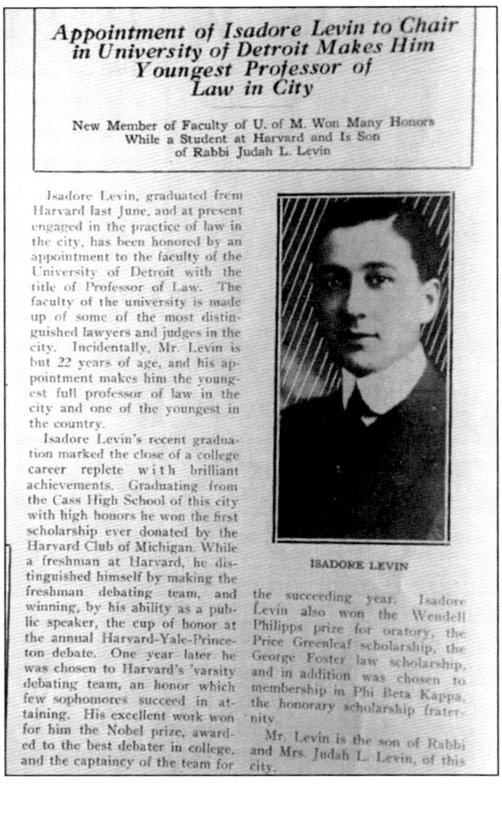

Appointment of Isadore Levin to Chair in University of Detroit Makes Him Youngest Professor of Law in City

New Member of Faculty of U. of M. Won Many Honors While a Student at Harvard and Is Son of Rabbi Judah L. Levin

Isadore Levin, graduated from Harvard last June, and at present engaged in the practice of law in the city, has been honored by an appointment to the faculty of the University of Detroit with the title of Professor of Law. The faculty of the university is made up of some of the most distinguished lawyers and judges in the city. Incidentally, Mr. Levin is but 22 years of age, and his appointment makes him the youngest full professor of law in the city and one of the youngest in the country.

Isadore Levin's recent graduation marked the close of a college career replete with brilliant achievements. Graduating from the Cass High School of this city with high honors he won the first scholarship ever donated by the Harvard Club of Michigan. While a freshman at Harvard, he distinguished himself by making the freshman debating team, and winning, by his ability as a public speaker, the cup of honor at the annual Harvard-Yale-Princeton debate. One year later he was chosen to Harvard's 'varsity debating team, an honor which few sophomores succeed in attaining. His excellent work won for him the Nobel prize, awarded to the best debater in college, and the captaincy of the team for the succeeding year. Isadore Levin also won the Wendell Philipps prize for oratory, the Price Greenleaf scholarship, the George Foster law scholarship, and in addition was chosen to membership in Phi Beta Kappa, the honorary scholarship fraternity.

Mr. Levin is the son of Rabbi and Mrs. Judah L. Levin, of this city.

ISADORE LEVIN

Isadore Levin, the son of Rabbi Judah L. Levin, graduated from Harvard and practiced law in Detroit after holding the rank of captain during World War I.

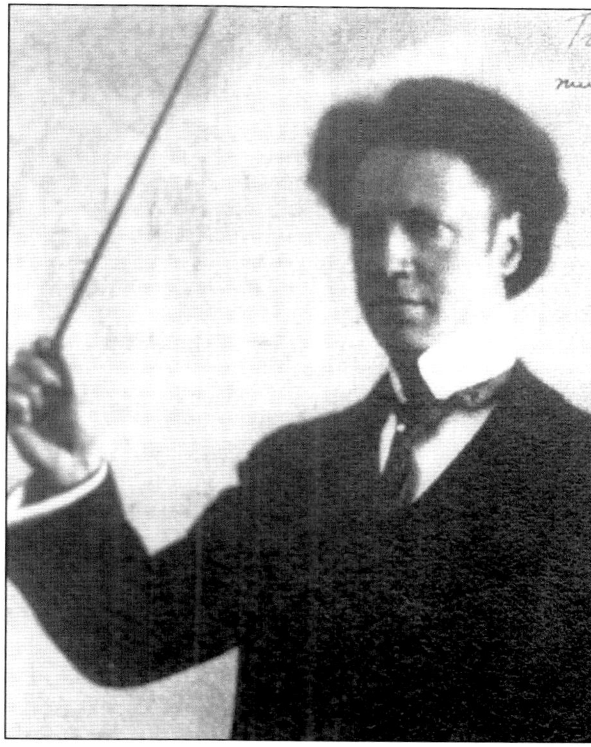

Ossip Gabrilowitsch, internationally known Russian pianist, moved to Detroit as conductor of the Detroit Symphony Orchestra. Gabrilowitsch was married to soprano Clara Clemens, the daughter of Mark Twain. Only the famous author and a few others were aware of Gabrilowitsch's Jewish background. (Courtesy Burton Historical Collection of the Detroit Public Library.)

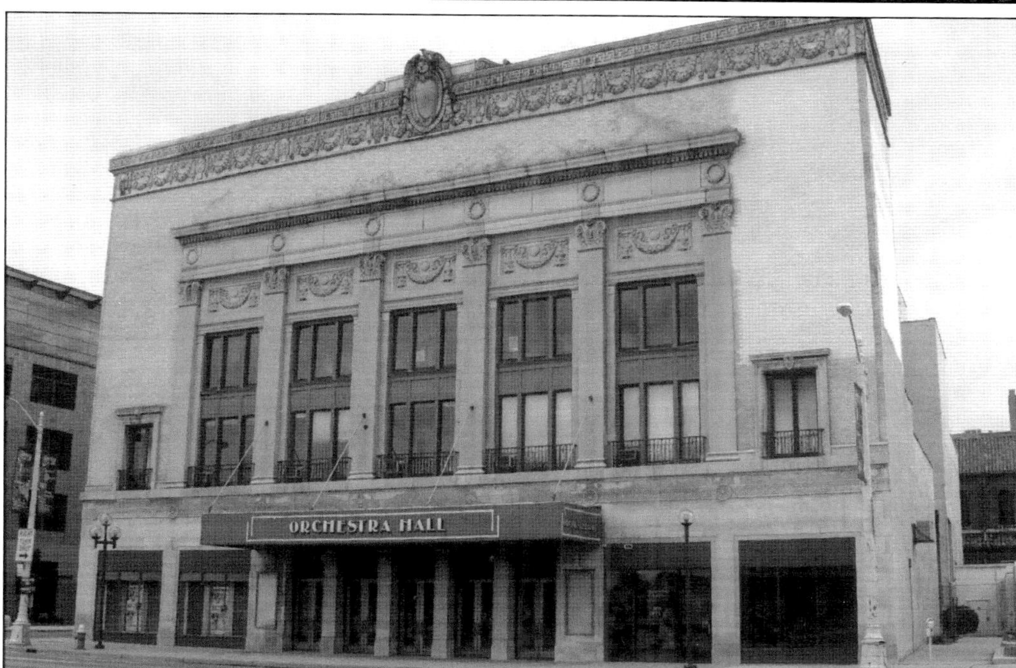

Gabrilowitsch urged the building of Orchestra Hall and led the DSO on opening night in front of over 2,000 people on October 23, 1919.

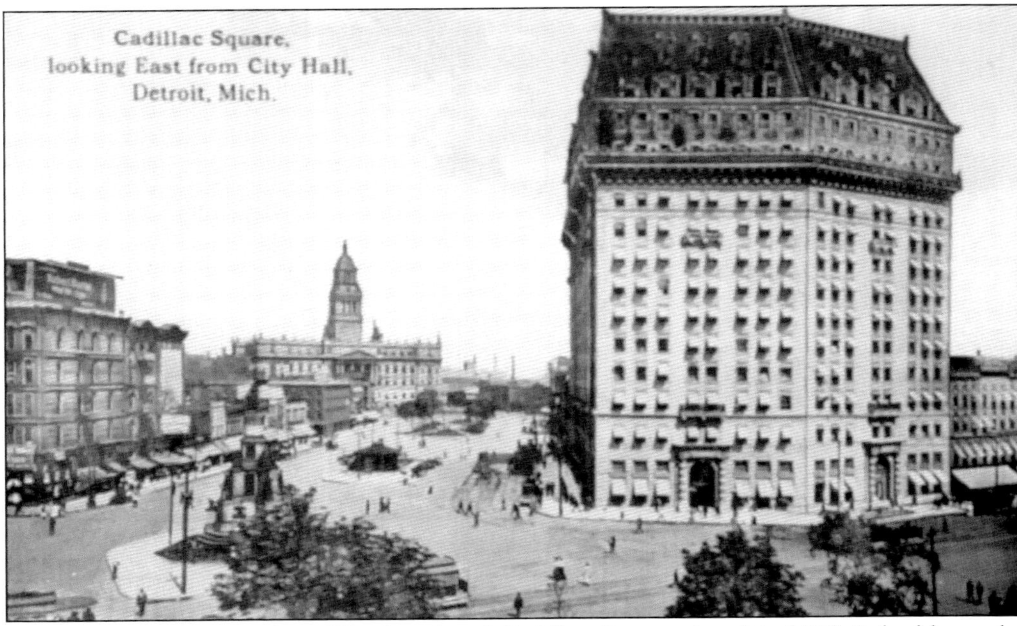

The Pontchartrain Hotel on Woodward and Cadillac Square closed in 1919. It had been the scene of many Jewish communal affairs in the past decades.

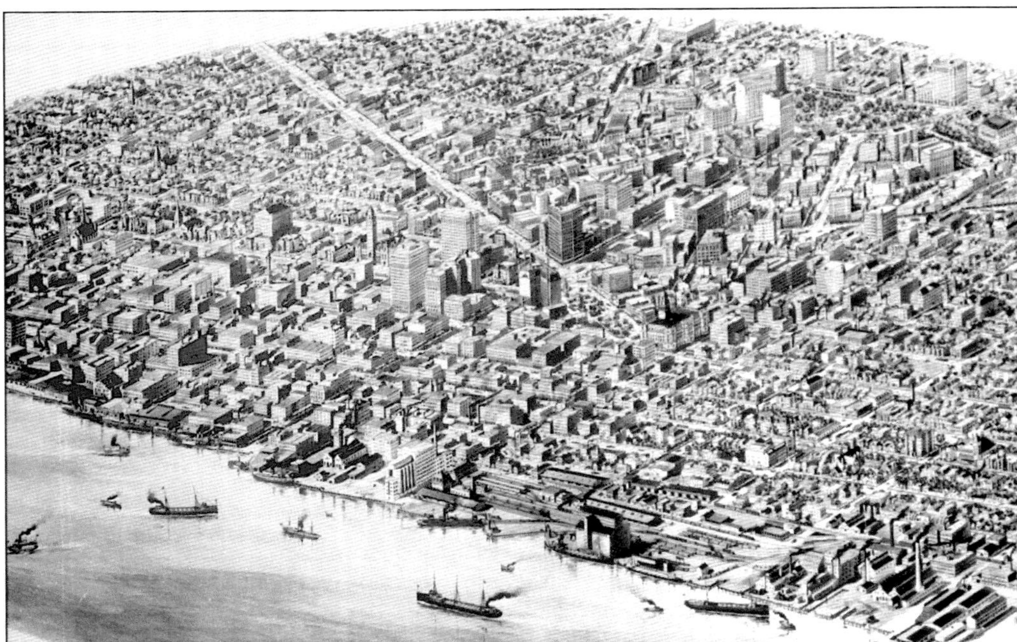

In 1919 the downtown hub of activity revolved around Michigan Avenue, Campus Martius, and the Cadillac Square area. The riverfront, which had many Jewish dry goods establishments, was getting shabbier. (Courtesy Burton Historical Collection of the Detroit Public Library.)

In 1919 newspapers reported that Rabbi Dr. Abraham Aaron Yudelovitch was elected Chief Rabbi of the United States at a meeting of more than 300 rabbis in New York.

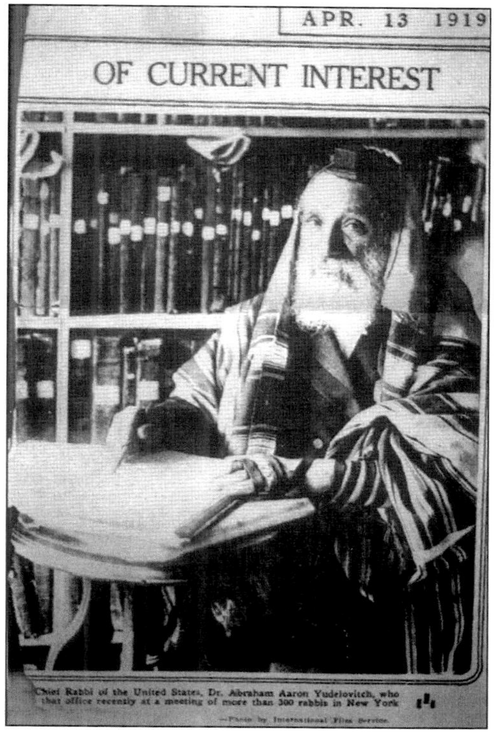

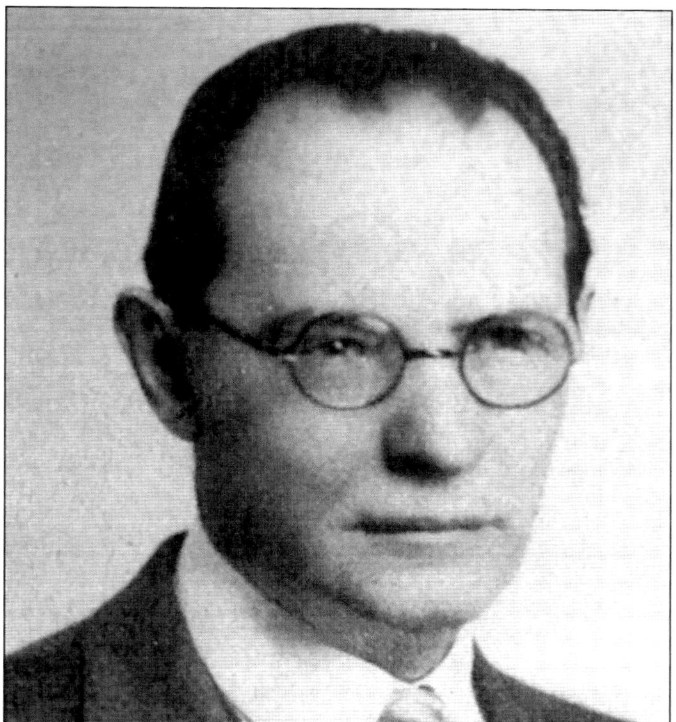

In 1919 the United Hebrew Schools organized as a religious educational institution. The aim of the organization was to create a system of institutions that would serve the needs of the community as a whole, not merely of one locality. The first branch was located at Wilkins and Hastings. Bernard Isaacs was the longtime Superintendent of the UHS. (Courtesy United Hebrew Schools.)

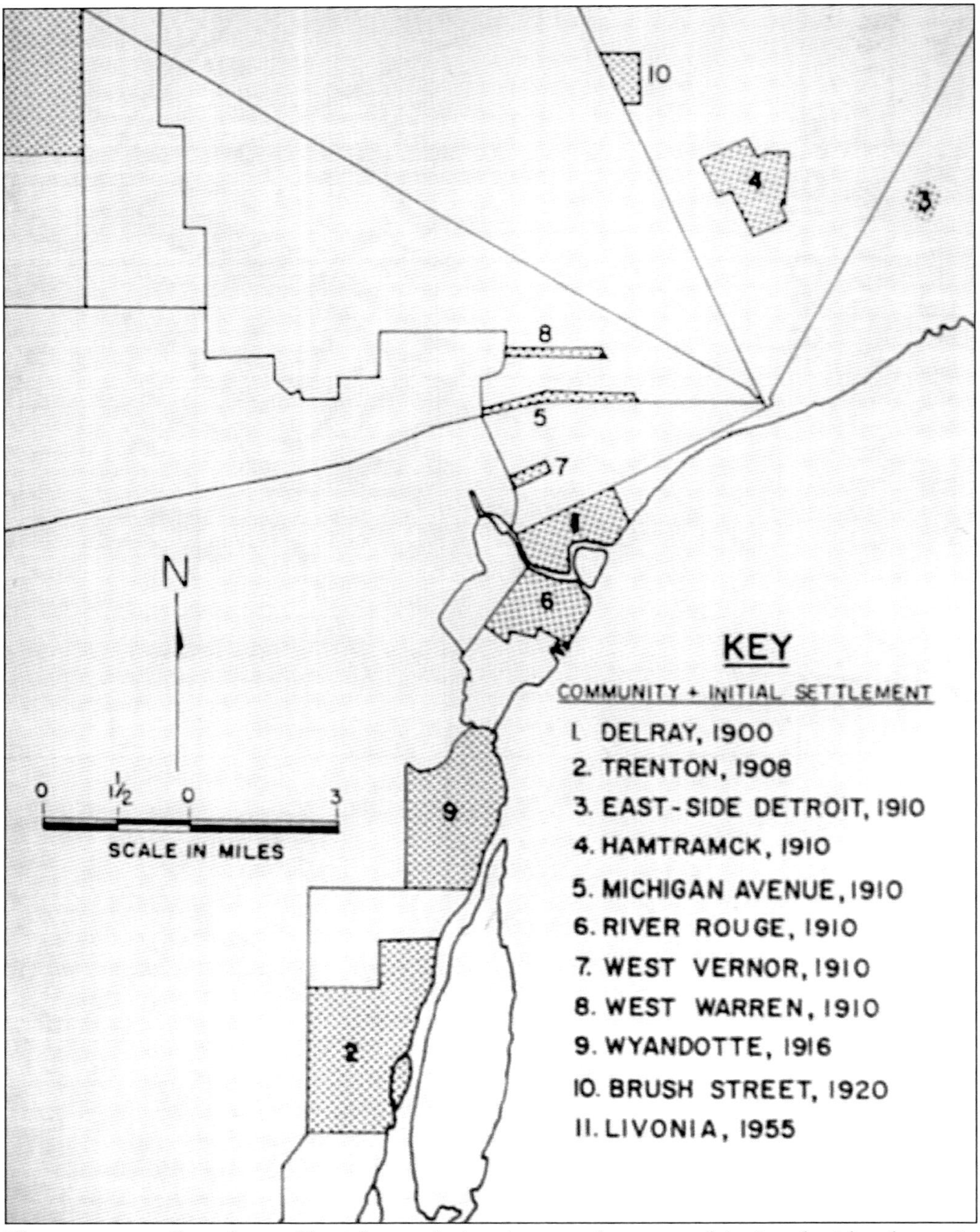

There were small pockets of Jewish population in several areas at this time besides the main Jewish neighborhoods south of Grand Boulevard surrounding the Hastings Street corridor. Each area had a small synagogue and usually hired visiting rabbis or rabbinical students on a part-time basis. By the end of World War I, some Jewish families lived as far north as Brush and McNichols (Six Mile Road). Thirty years later, many Detroiters were convinced that Livonia would eventually be the center of the metropolitan area's Jewish population. (Map courtesy of Phillip Applebaum.)

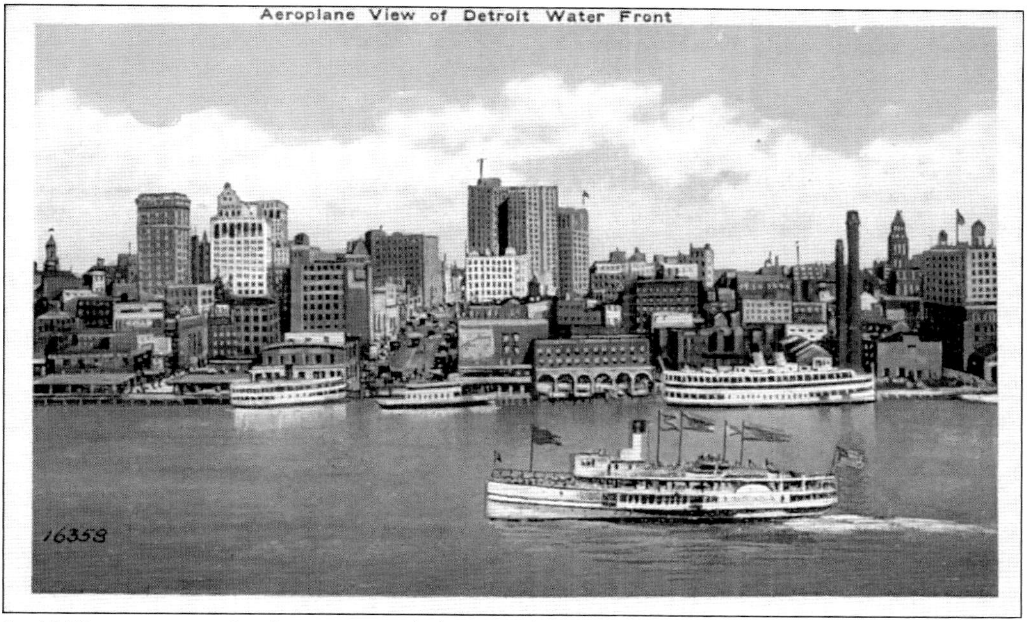

In 1920 community leaders estimated the Jewish population at 35,000. Detroit's population was 993,678, making it the fourth largest city in the nation. In only twenty years Detroit had gained over 700,000 residents.

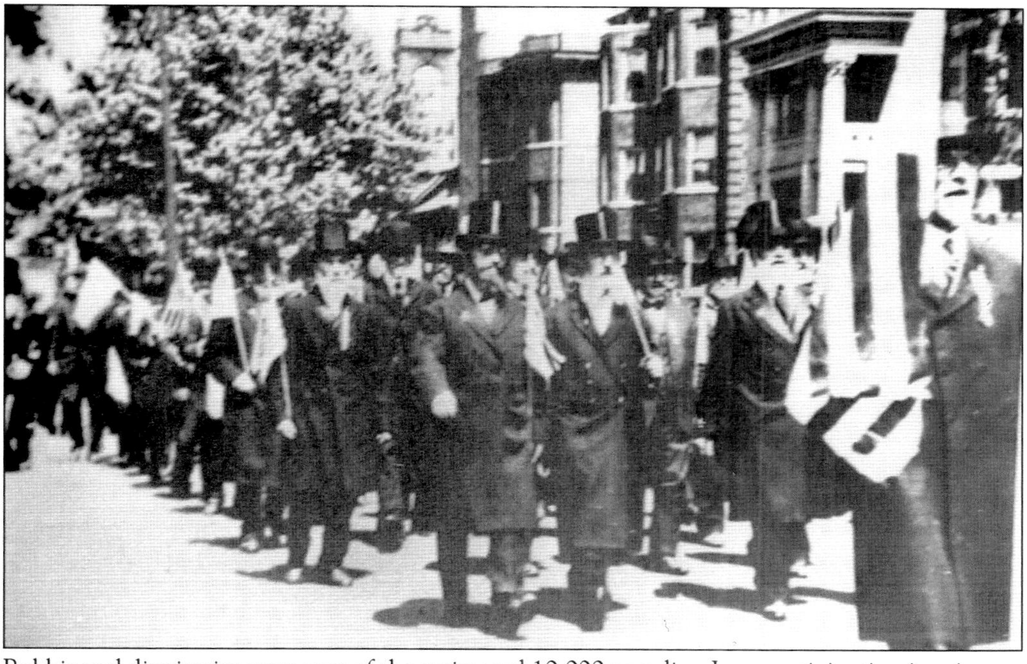

Rabbis and dignitaries were part of the estimated 10,000 parading Jews participating in a joyous demonstration celebrating the end of World War I and the Balfour Declaration calling for the establishment of a Jewish state in Palestine in the land of Abraham, Isaac, Jacob, King David, and King Solomon. (Courtesy Archives of Congregation Shaarey Zedek.)

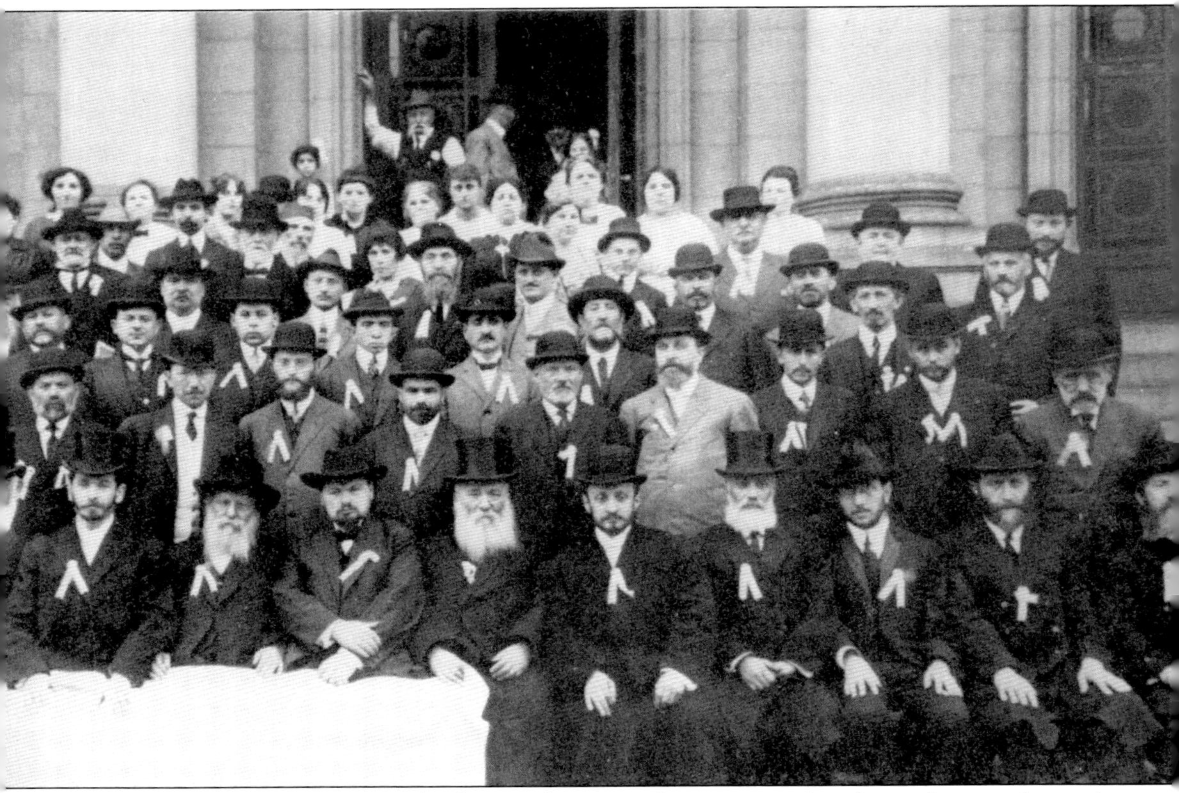

Detroit's rabbis, community leaders, and visiting dignitaries gather for a photograph on the steps at the Shaarey Zedek Synagogue at Brush and Willis. Detroit's four leading rabbis were in the front row on the right. White-bearded Rabbi Judah L. Levin, seventh from the left, Rabbi A. M. Hershman, spiritual leader of Shaarey Zedek (eighth from left), Rabbi Joseph Thumin of B'nai Moshe and Rabbi Ezekial Aishishkin of Beth David. (Courtesy Archives of Congregation Shaarey Zedek.)

Starting in 1920, automobile baron Henry Ford used his weekly Dearborn Independent newspaper to blame Jews for the world's social and economic problems. Besides being sold on the street, all Ford agencies carried the publication for customers. (Courtesy Burton Historical Collection of the Detroit Public Library.)

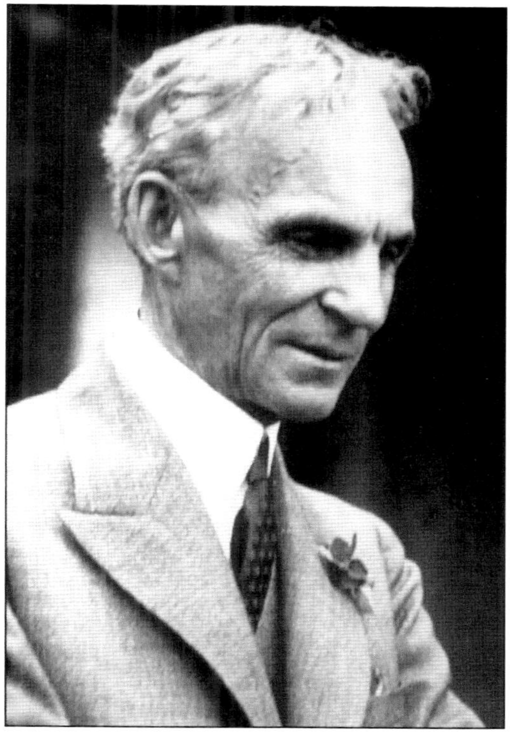

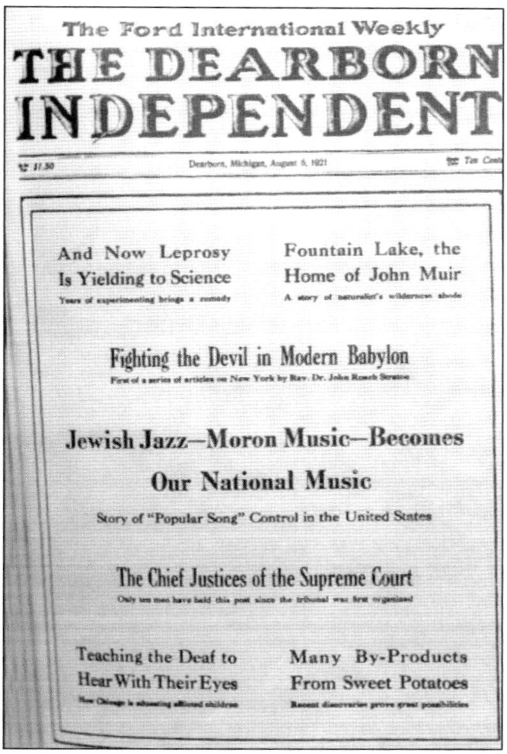

The Ford International Weekly

THE DEARBORN INDEPENDENT

Dearborn, Michigan, August 6, 1921

And Now Leprosy Is Yielding to Science
Years of experimenting brings a remedy

Fountain Lake, the Home of John Muir
A story of naturalist's wilderness abode

Fighting the Devil in Modern Babylon
First of a series of articles on New York by Rev. Dr. John Roach Straton

Jewish Jazz—Moron Music—Becomes Our National Music
Story of "Popular Song" Control in the United States

The Chief Justices of the Supreme Court
Only ten men have held this post since the tribunal was first organized

Teaching the Deaf to Hear With Their Eyes

Many By-Products From Sweet Potatoes
Recent discoveries prove great possibilities

Each issue of the Dearborn Independent for over a year carried anti-Jewish headlines under the banner of Henry Ford. (Courtesy Burton Historical Collection of the Detroit Public Library.)

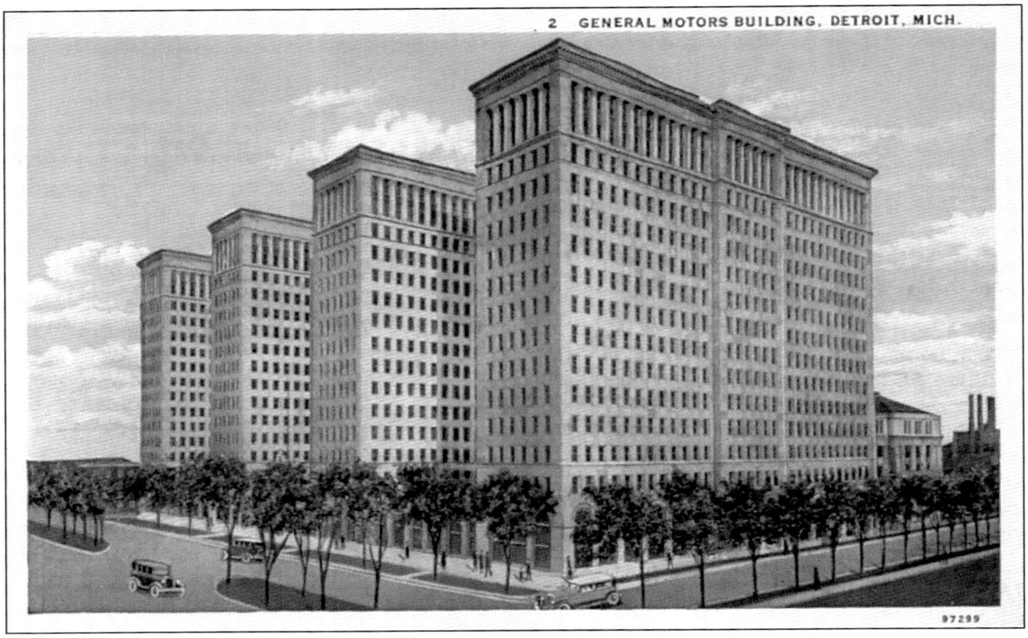

The Albert Kahn designed General Motors Building was completed in 1921.

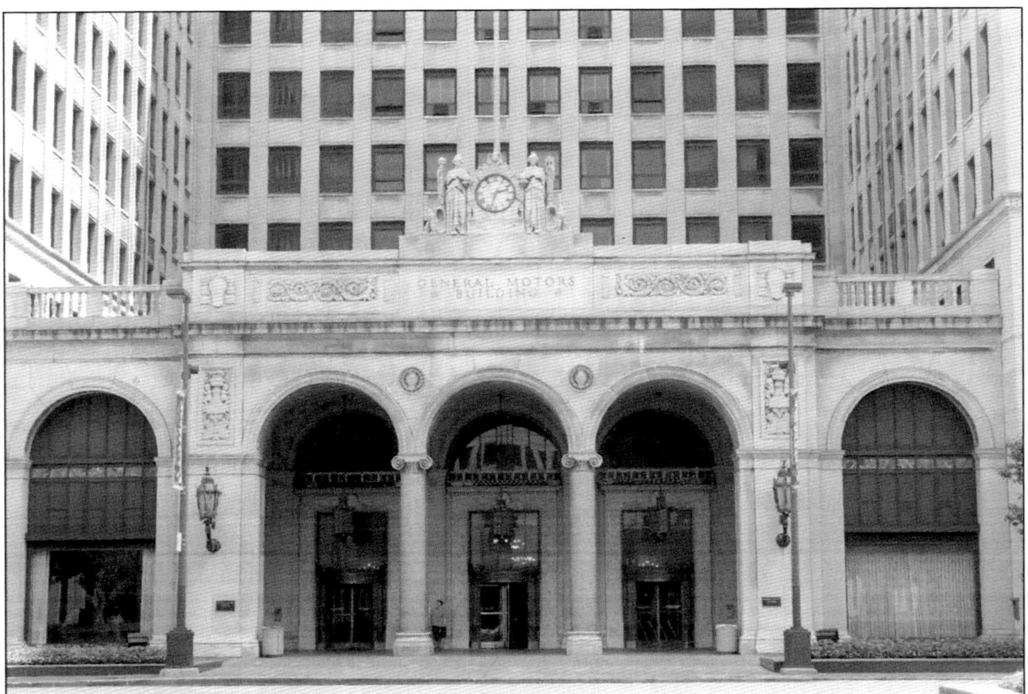

The impressive main entrance on Grand Boulevard was topped by a huge clock.

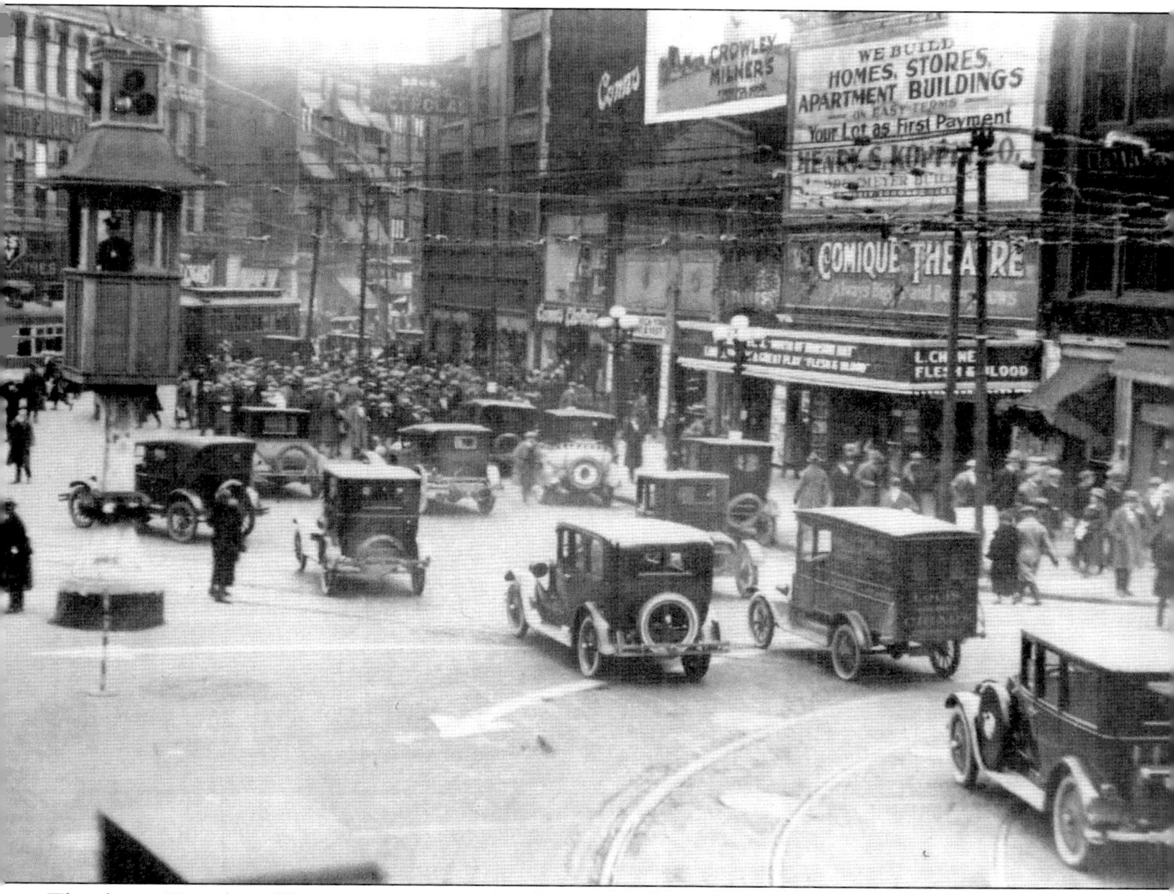

The busy Broadway/Gratiot area was the location of Engass Jewelry (left). Maurice and Clarence Engass conducted the jewelry company until its sale in 1958. Their father, Adolph, founded the company in 1865. Their grandfather was a Beth El president in 1859, and the Engass brothers were active members of the temple and belonged to numerous Jewish and civic groups. (Courtesy Burton Historical Collection of the Detroit Public Library.)

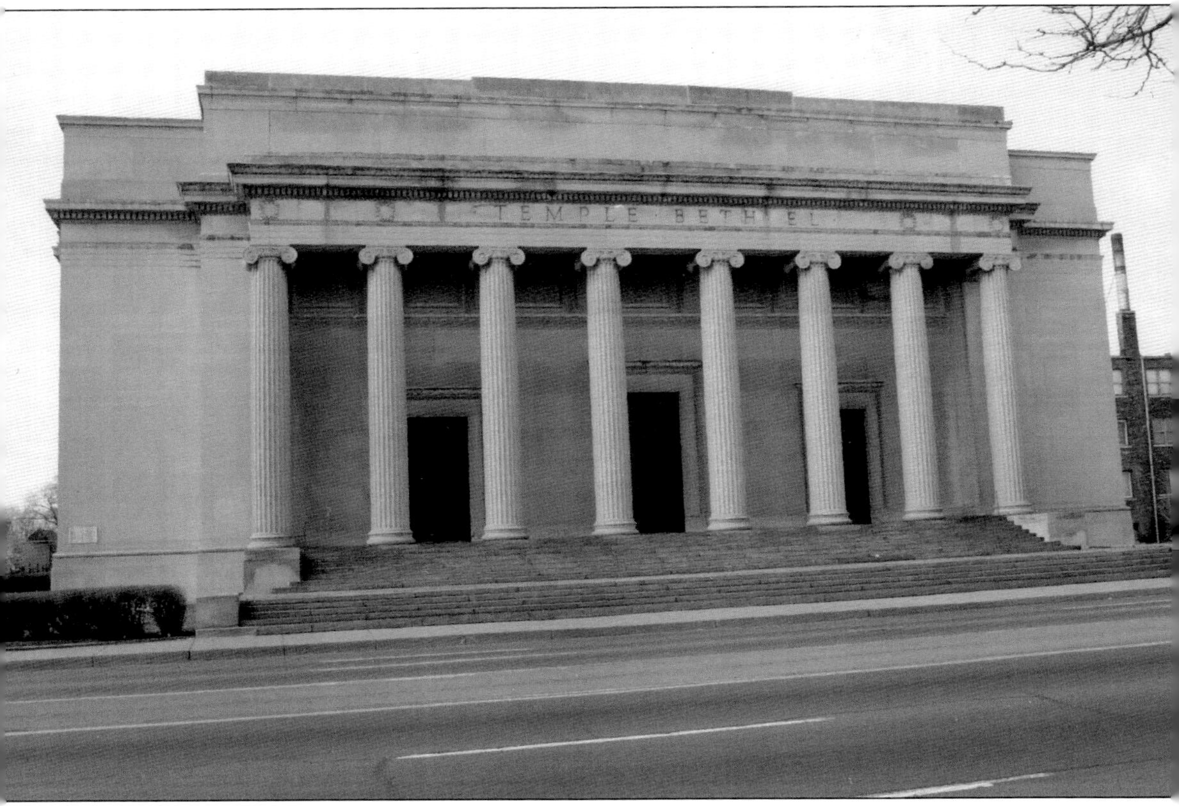

A thousand members, including the building's architect, Albert Kahn, belonged to Temple Beth El when the new structure on the west side of Woodward at Gladstone was dedicated in 1922. The congregation elected Rabbi Franklin for life tenure.

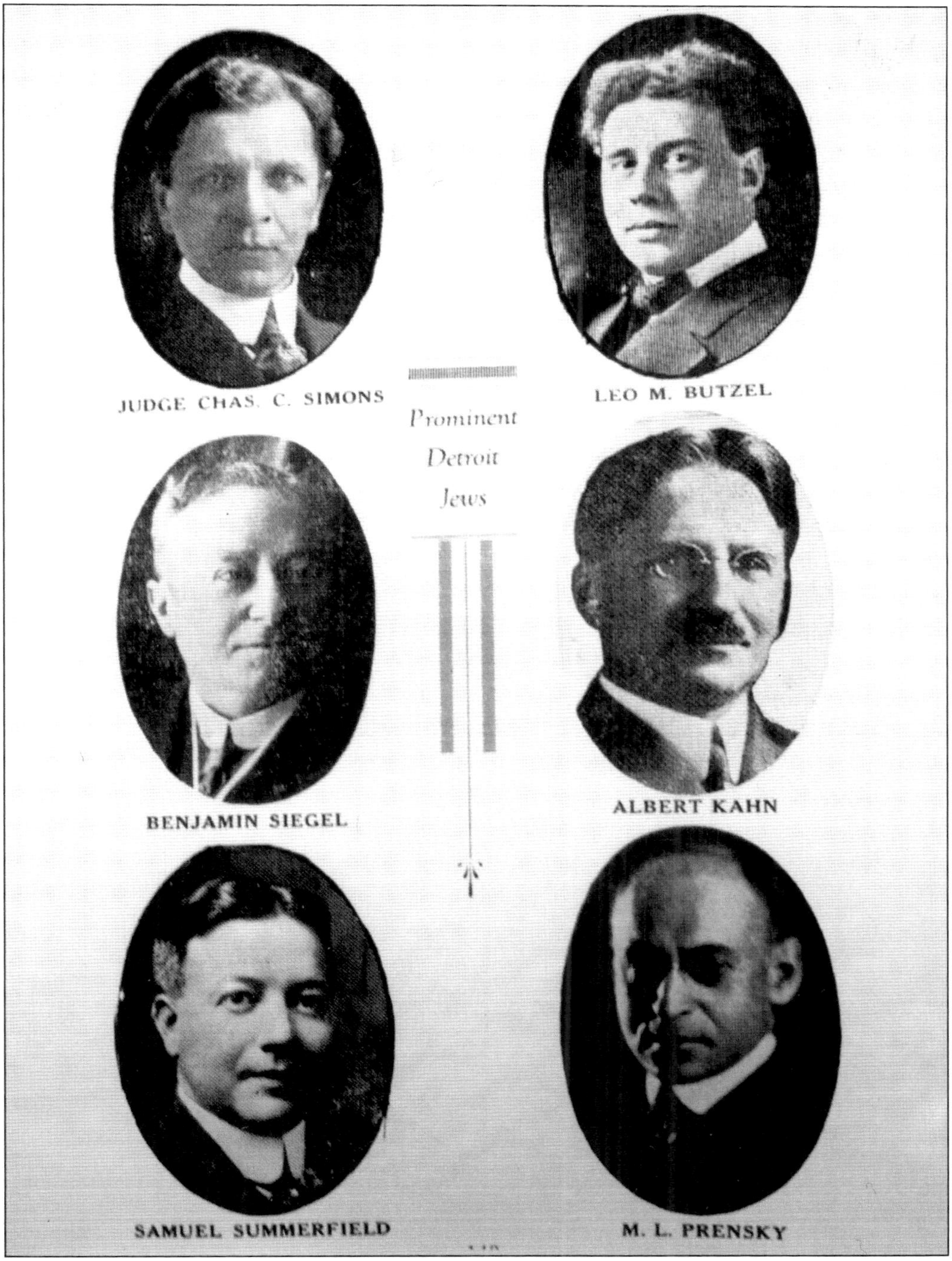

Prominent Jewish Detroiters in the 1923 *Jewish Community Blue Book*. Judge Simons was Michigan state senator in 1903 and 1904. Albert Kahn's name lives on as many of the buildings he designed generations ago in Detroit still stand. (Courtesy Rabbi Leo M. Franklin Archives of Temple Beth El.)

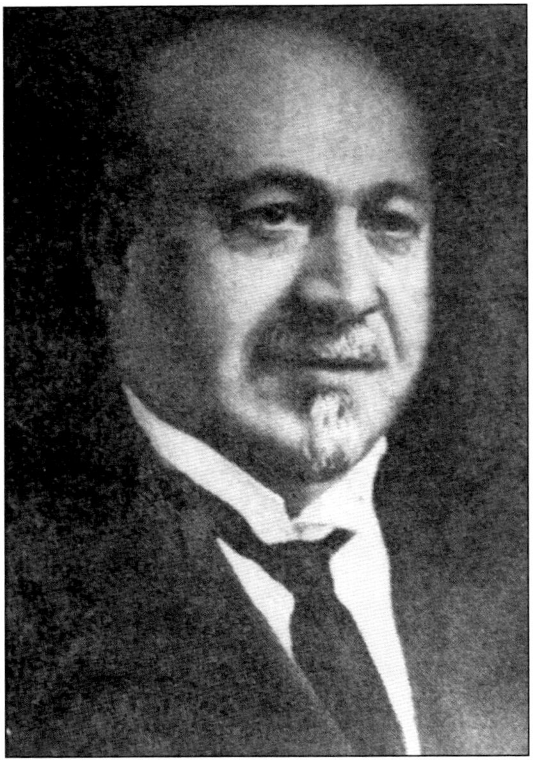

Esser Rabinowitz was the first president of the United Hebrew Schools and served in that capacity for ten years.

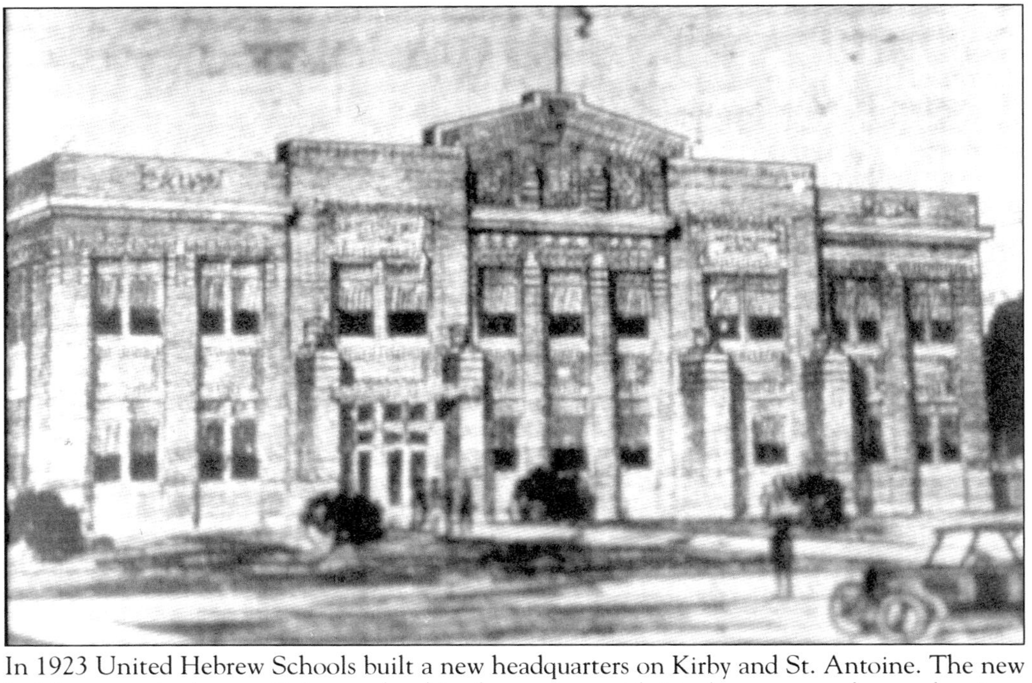

In 1923 United Hebrew Schools built a new headquarters on Kirby and St. Antoine. The new building was the largest Hebrew school in the country with 14 classrooms and an auditorium, which was used for weddings, concerts, lectures, and dances.

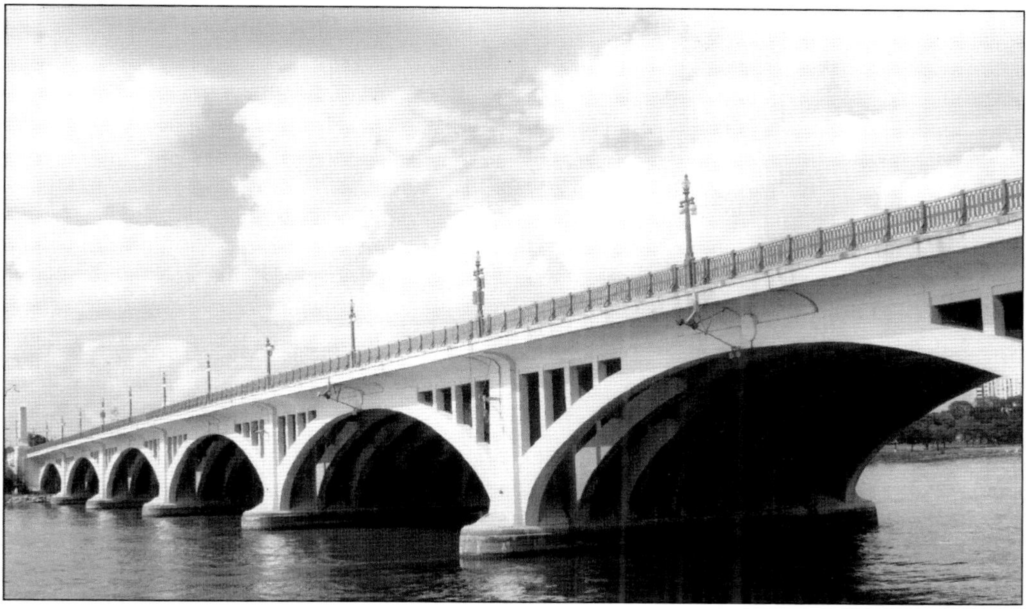

Jewish Detroiters were among the first to cross the new 2,356-foot long Belle Isle Bridge when it opened in 1923.

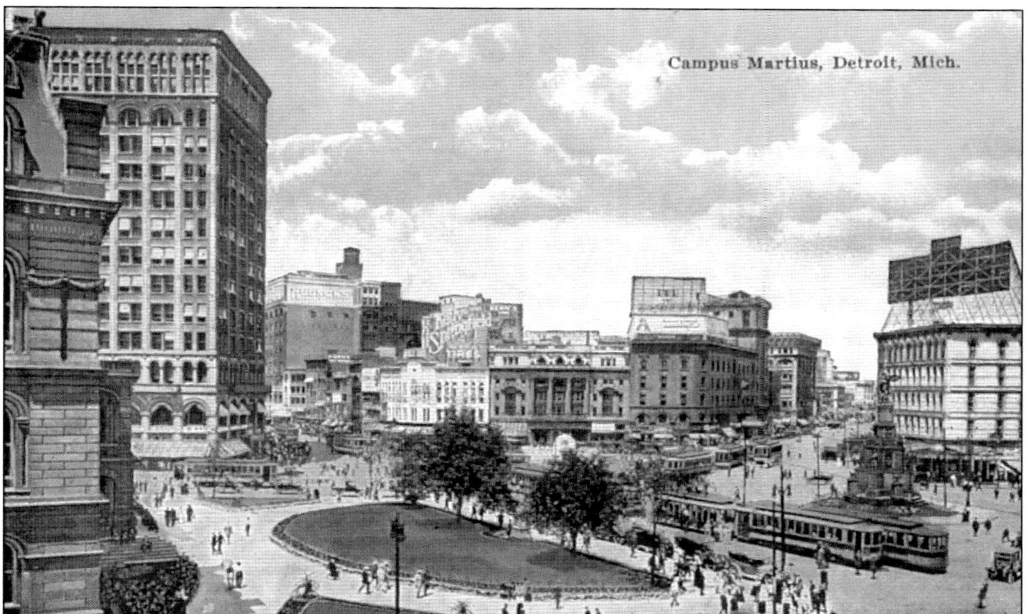

Streetcars along Hastings Street and Woodward went to Jefferson and passengers then boarded streetcars eastbound on Jefferson.

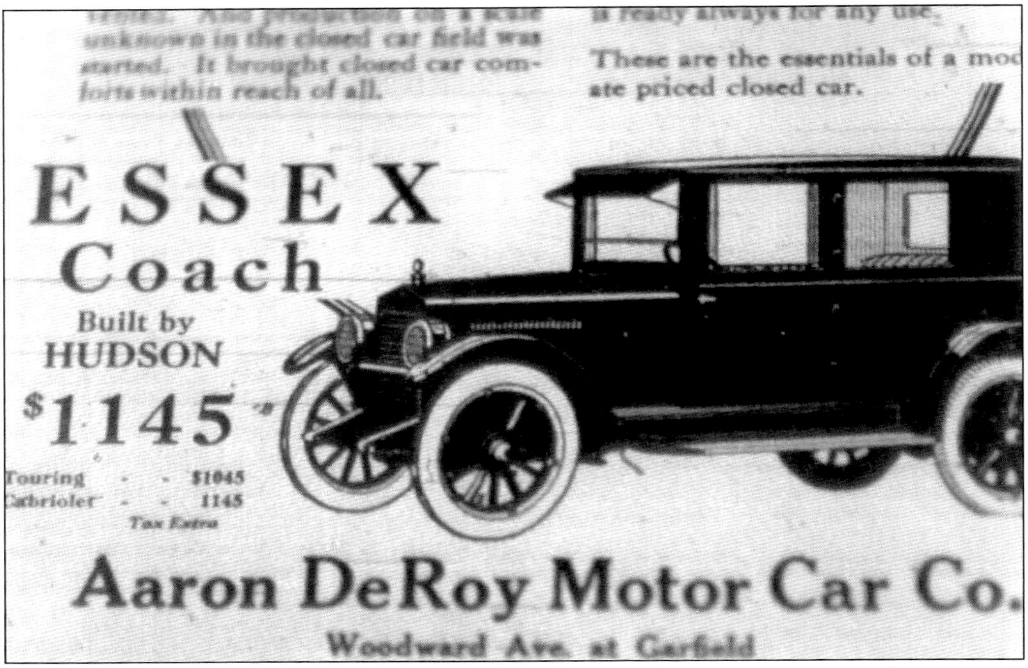

Aaron DeRoy's Motor Car Company on Woodward and Garfield was popular with all Detroiters, as was the 1923 Hudson Essex Coach. DeRoy was an active leader in Jewish charitable organizations.

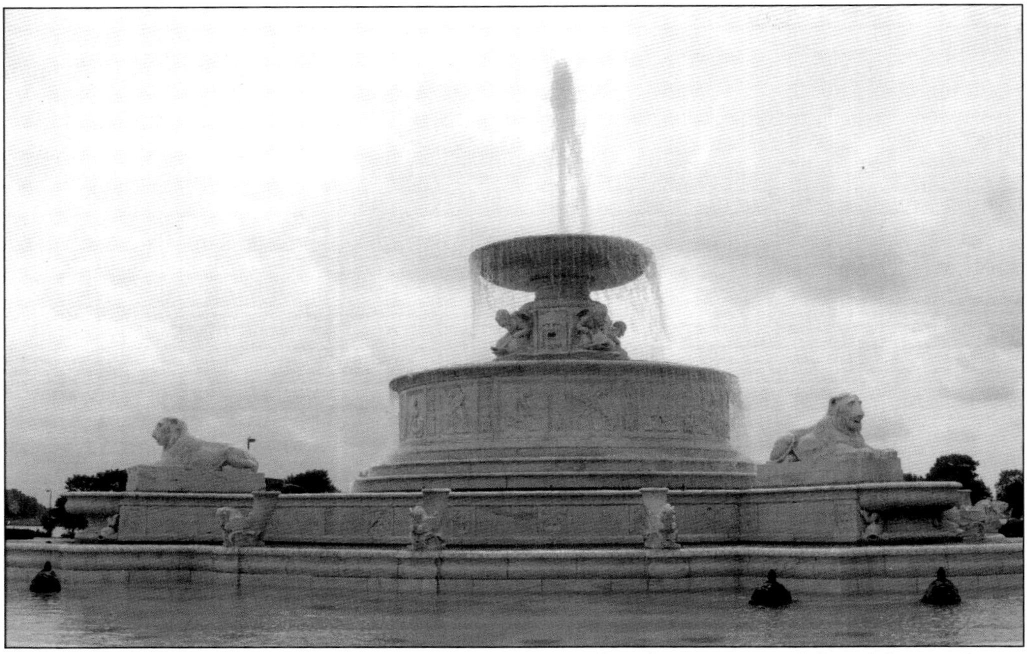

Belle Isle became an even more popular destination after the opening of the elaborate James Scott Memorial Fountain in 1925. Sightseers trekked to the western end of the island as it was extended a thousand yards to accommodate the reflecting lagoon and fountain.

Four

1925–1950

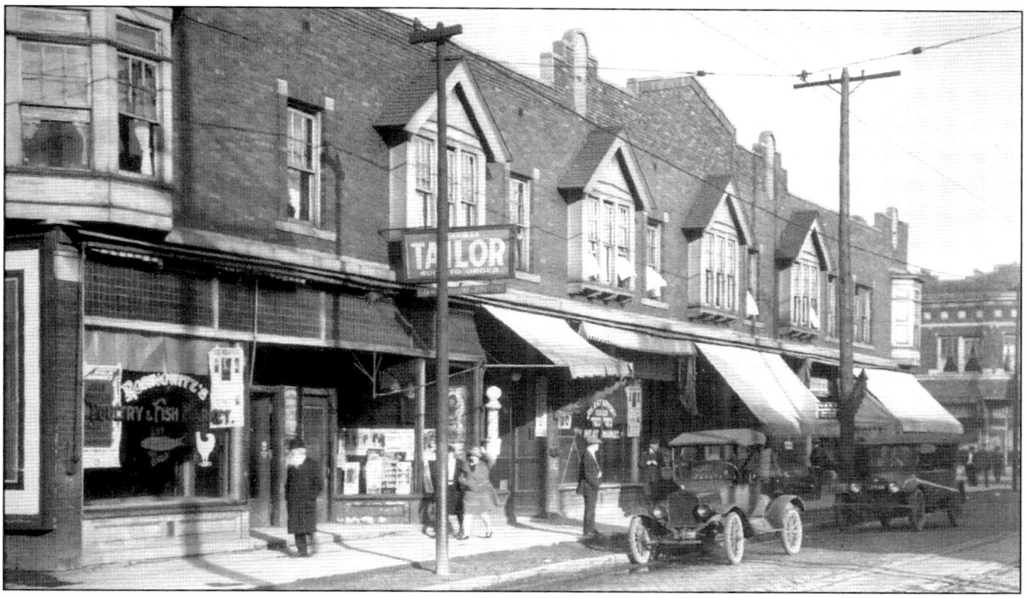

Hastings Street between Kirby and Frederick was a main shopping destination for the Jewish community, as it contained a kosher poultry and fish shop, a tailor shop, a barber shop, and a kosher meat market. Several orthodox synagogues were a short walk west. Shaarey Zedek was a half mile southwest, and Temple Beth E1 was over a mile northwest. Temple Beth El had 1,246 members in 1925, and Rabbi Leon Fram came from Chicago as assistant rabbi. Fram founded the Beth El College of Jewish Studies, one of the first evening schools in the country for adults. Weekly broadcasts of Beth El services began on WWJ radio. The United Hebrew Schools of Detroit had 2,000 children enrolled in its five branches. (Courtesy Manning Brothers Historic Photographic Collection.)

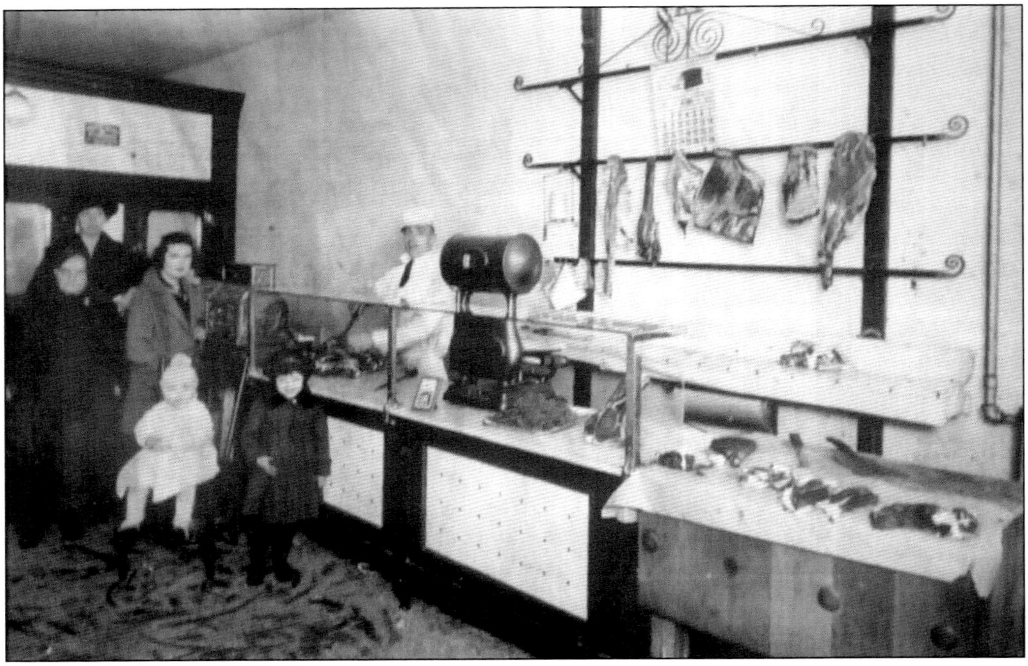

Jewish families were moving from the lower Hastings area south of Grand Boulevard to the Oakland district north of Grand Boulevard, centering around Holbrook. Oscar "Izzy" Goodgall operated a butcher shop at 8810 Oakland Avenue. (Courtesy Marcia Abel.)

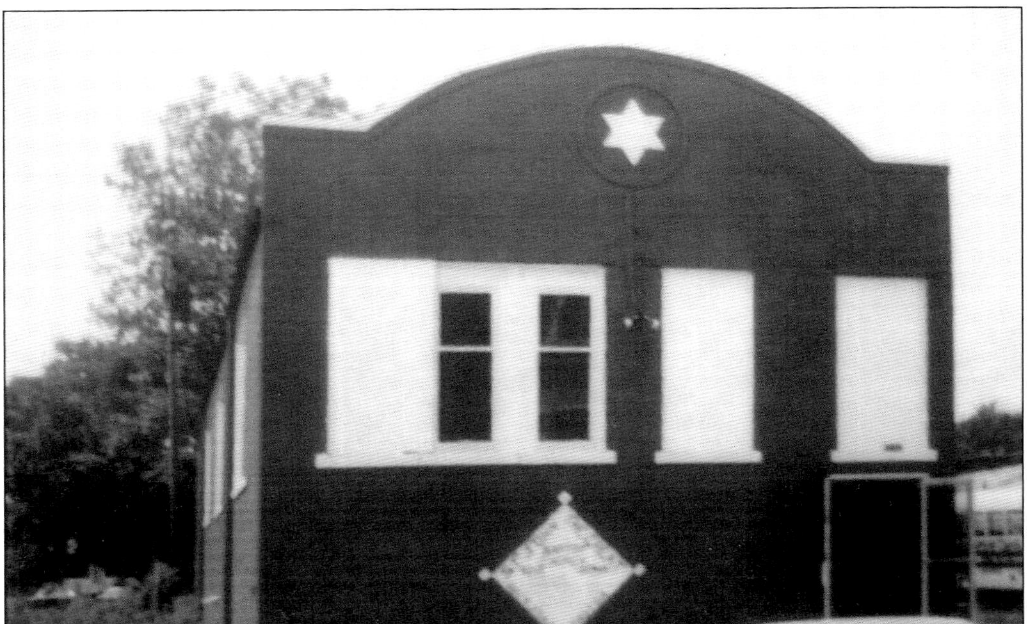

Nearby on Delmar, the United Hebrew Schools operated a small branch across the street from the Ahavas Achim Synagogue.

Ahavas Achim—the largest synagogue in the Oakland area—was organized in 1916 at this location on Delmar near Holbrook. It would move to several more locations before merging with Adat Shalom on Middlebelt Road south of 14 Mile Road.

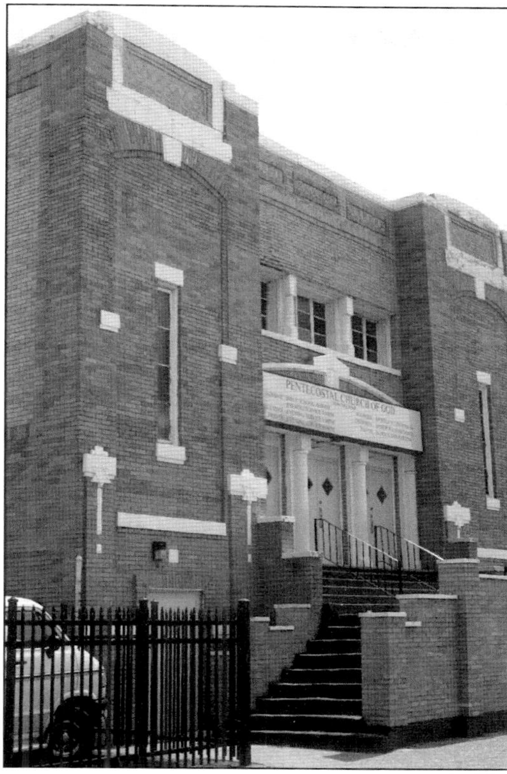

The Beth Moses—also known as the Jewish Orthodox Roumanian Congregation—was organized in 1903 in the lower Hastings corridor, and became the center of activities for Roumanian Jews when it was built on Owen near Oakland.

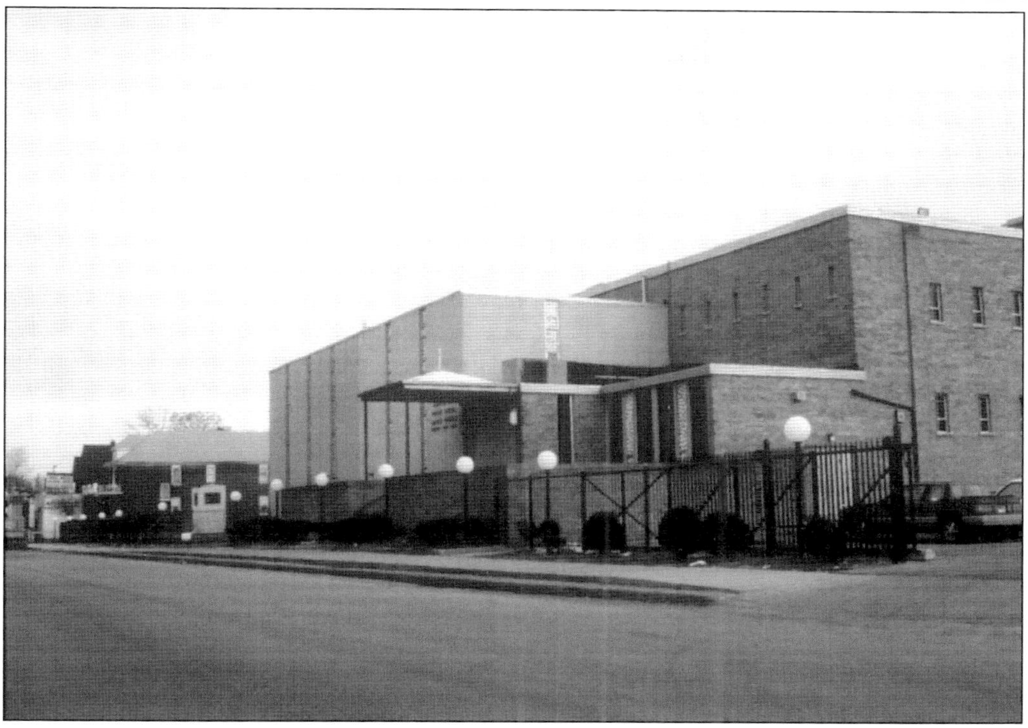

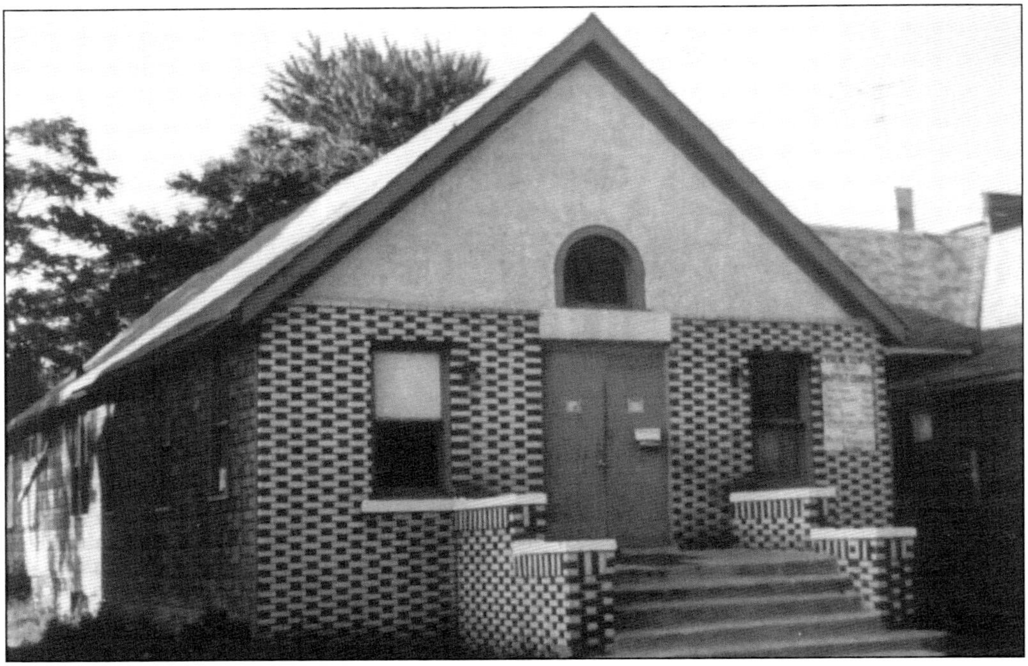

The Atereth Zvi was organized in 1921, and services were held in a private home on Cameron near Mt. Vernon before this small structure was built.

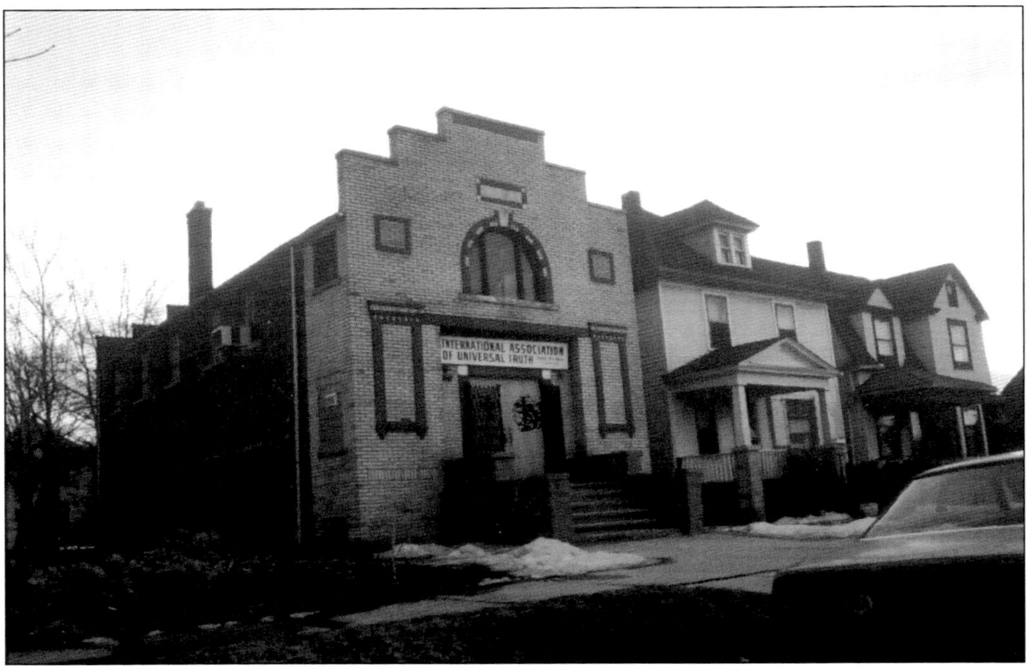

The B'nai Jacob—called the King Street Shul because of its location in the residential block of King Street east of Oakland—built this small synagogue in 1925.

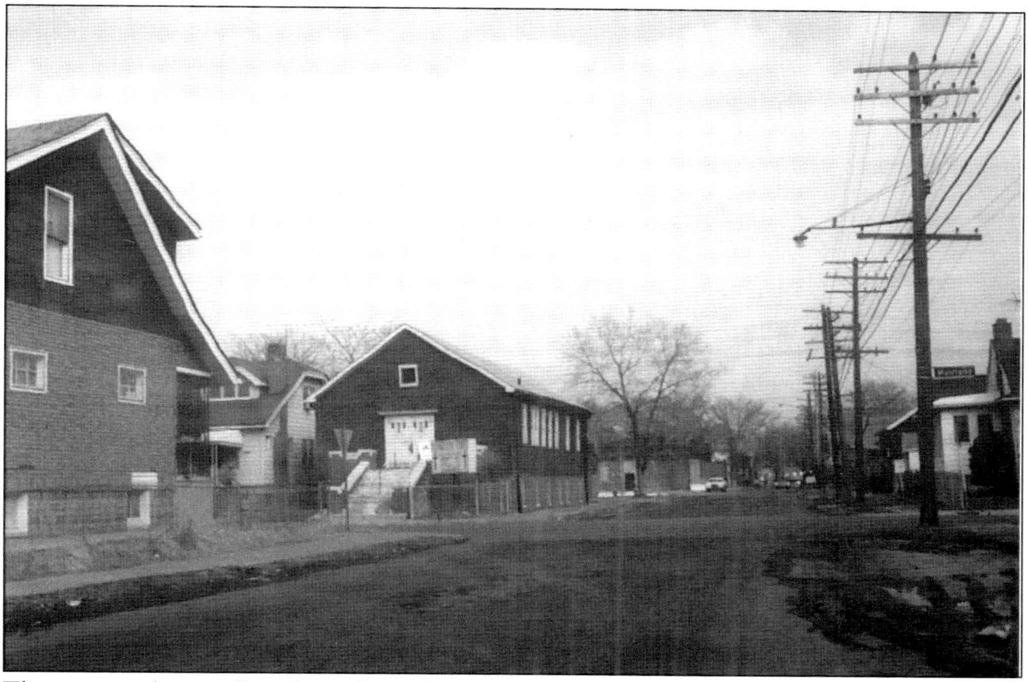

There were other small pockets of Jewish population. The Shaar Hashomayim was built in 1925 as Beth Israel on Muirland, located three-quarters of a mile south of the more affluent section north of McNichols, and a half mile east of Livernois. Today it sits between Puritan and the Lodge Freeway.

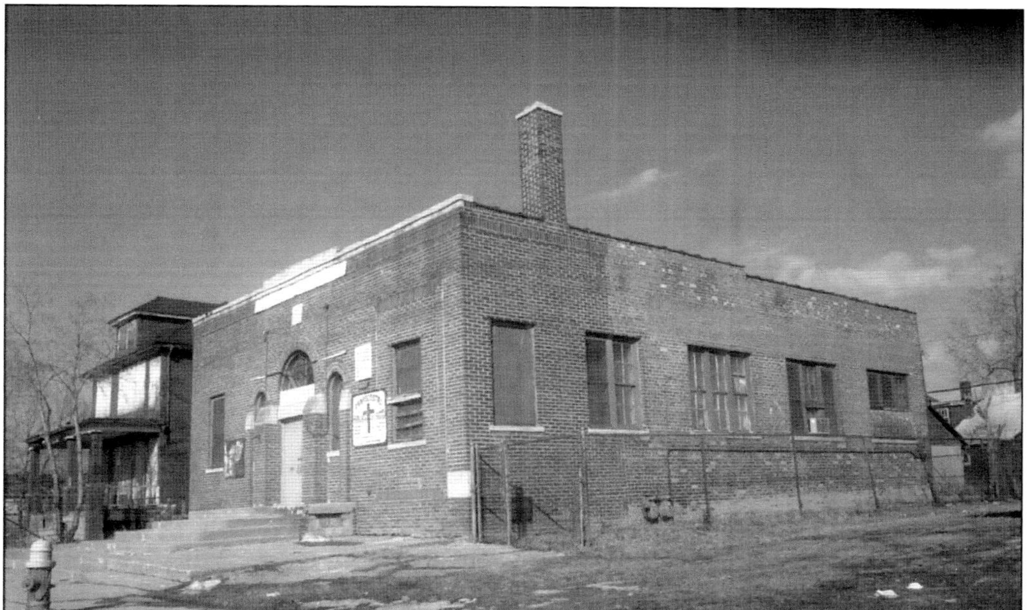

Shaarey Torah organized in 1926 at 17750 Brush, a half mile north of McNichols. It had used visiting rabbis at times and was the only congregation in the area.

The Yiddish Playhouse

2814 Hastings Street Phone Cherry 2523

A. LITTMAN and M. FISHSON, Managers.

Celia Adler is still with us. You will miss a treat if you do not see her.

Friday Night, April 2; Saturday, April 3, Matinee and Evening.

"STOLEN LOVE"

Sunday, April 4, Matinee and Evening; Monday Night, April 5; Tuesday Night, April 6.

"FORGOTTEN CHILDREN"

As Jews branched out to several areas, Hastings Street south of Grand Boulevard was still the cultural area for plays and lectures. New York-based Celia Adler was one of the leading actresses of the Yiddish Theater in the United States.

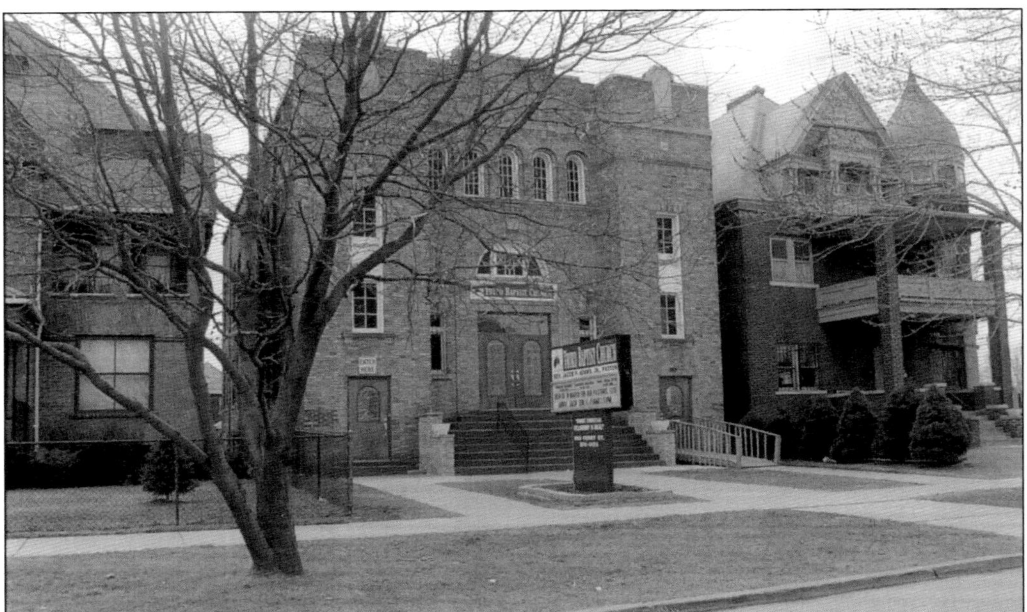

In 1923 the B'nai Israel, which used the home next door as its synagogue for several years, built its synagogue, which was used until 1933.

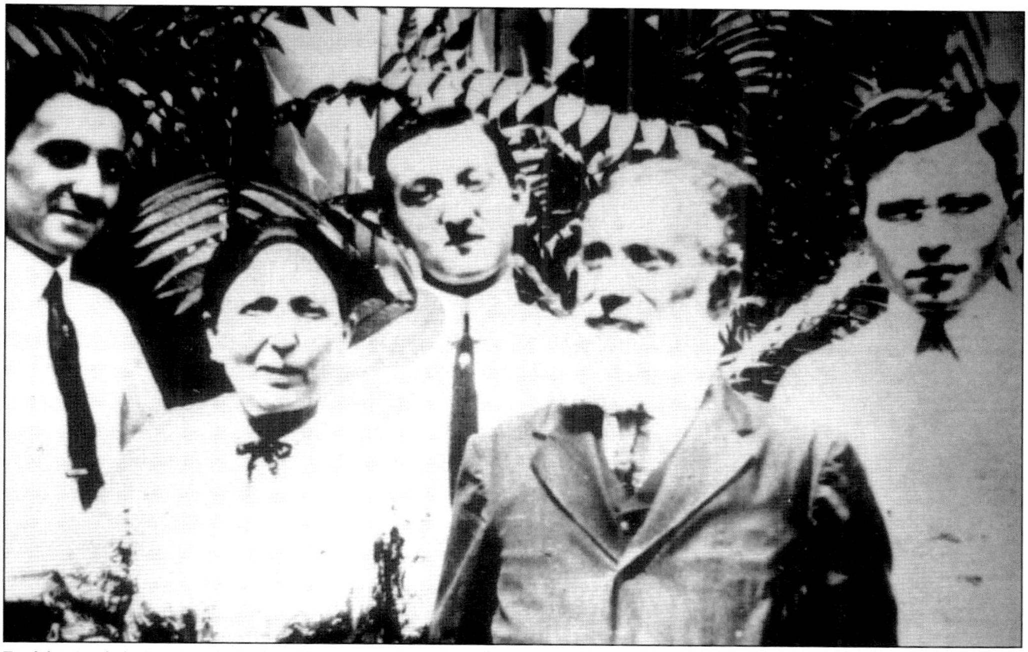

Rabbi Judah L. Levin's family were familiar faces on Ferry Street. Rabbi Levin passed away in 1926. (Courtesy Judith Levin Cantor)

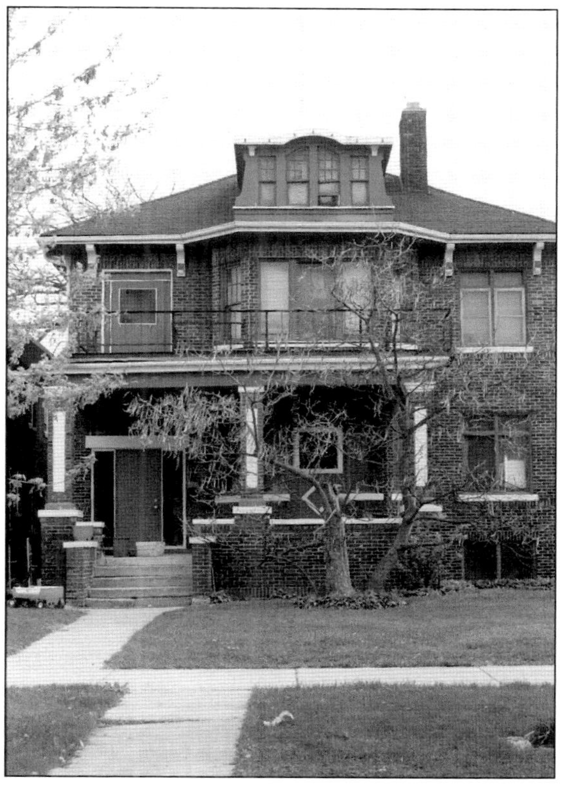

The Levin home on the southeast corner of Ferry and Brush. Eight thousand mourners gathered in the streets for Rabbi Levin's funeral on the Sunday morning before Passover. Police on motorbikes led the procession from the Levin home.

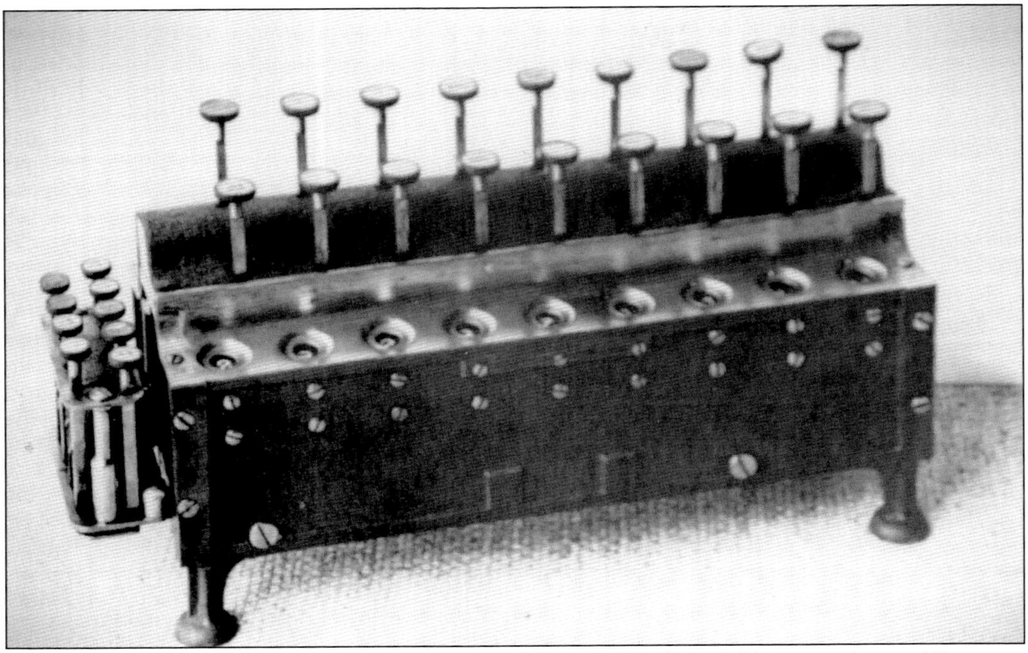

Rabbi Levin loved science and mathematics and patented an adding machine. (Courtesy Archives of Congregation Shaarey Zedek.)

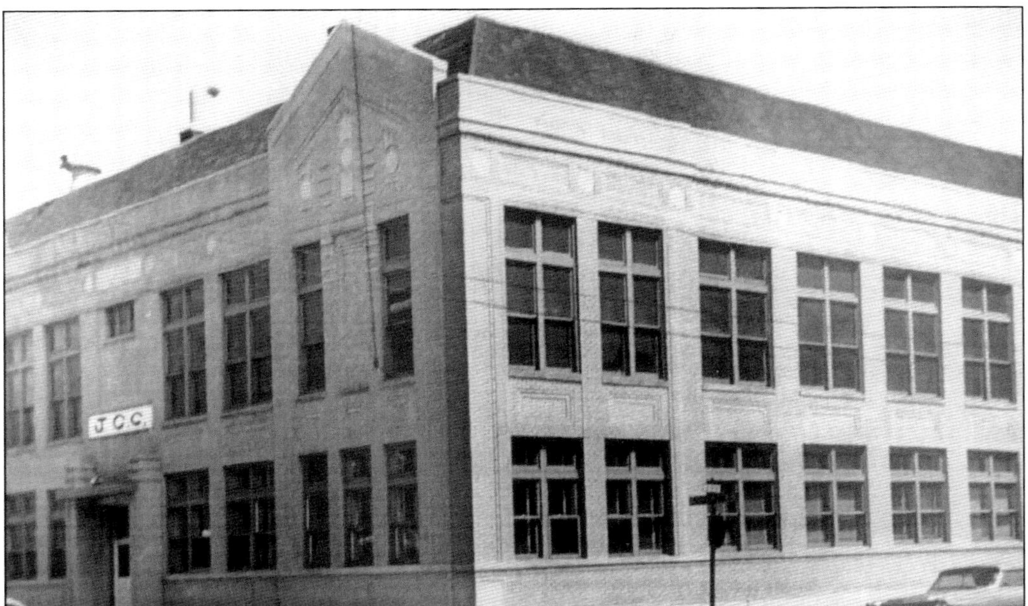

The Philadelphia/Byron branch of United Hebrew Schools in the Twelfth Street section was gaining enrollment as it was the fastest growing center of Jewish population.

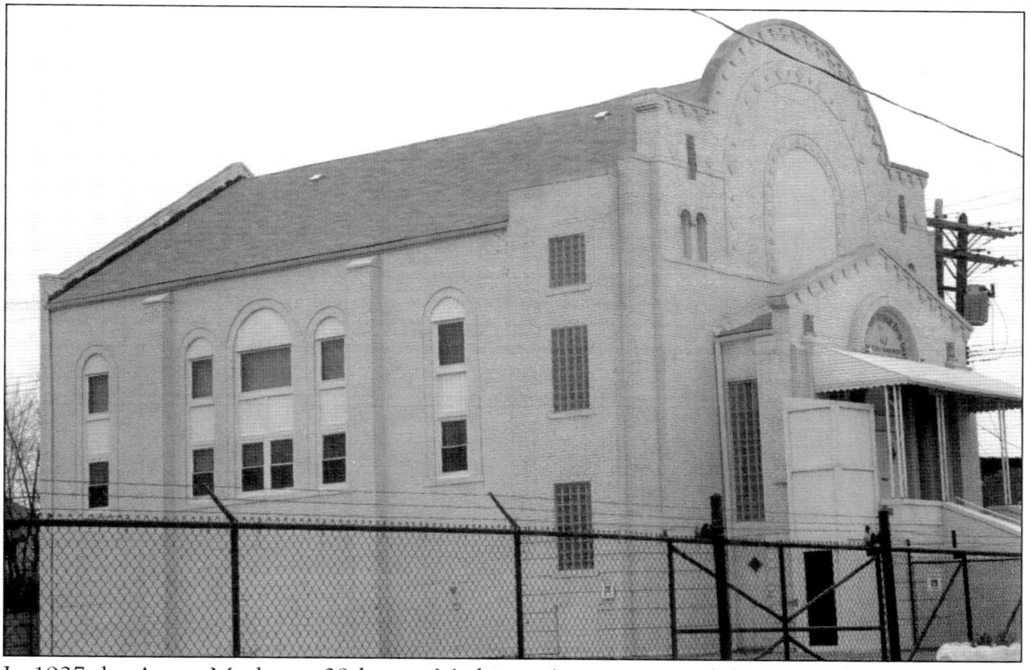

In 1927 the Aaron Moshe on 29th near Michigan Avenue, around the corner from a GM plant and less than two miles from the Tigers' ballpark, remodeled their nine-year-old synagogue. Most of the 35-member families had businesses in the area.

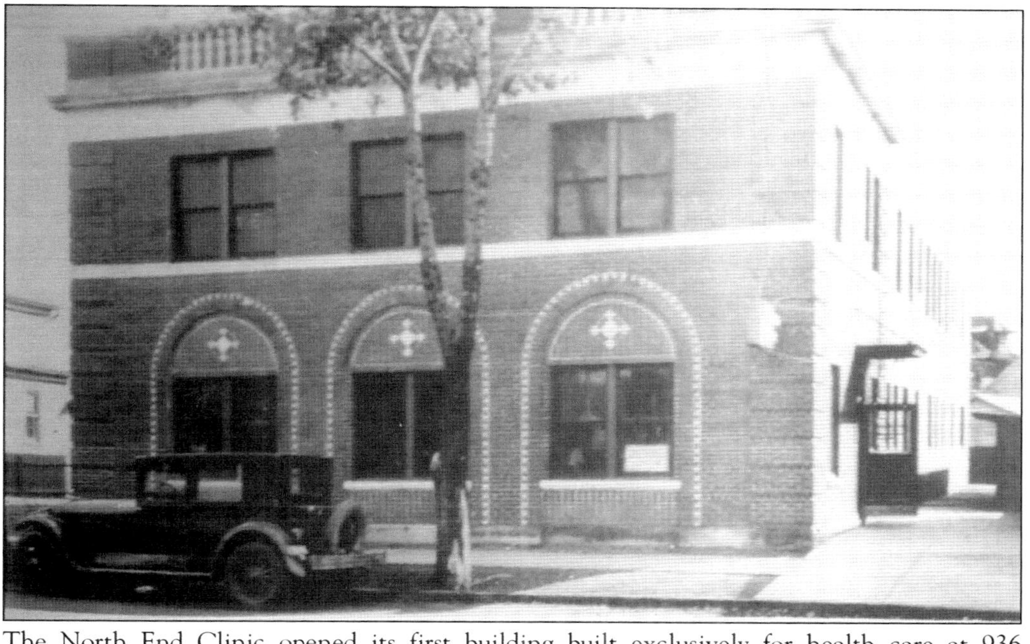

The North End Clinic opened its first building built exclusively for health care at 936 Holbrook near Oakland. It would serve as a Jewish health center for the indigent, and more than 40 doctors and six dentists donated their services. (Courtesy Leonard N. Simons Jewish Community Archives.)

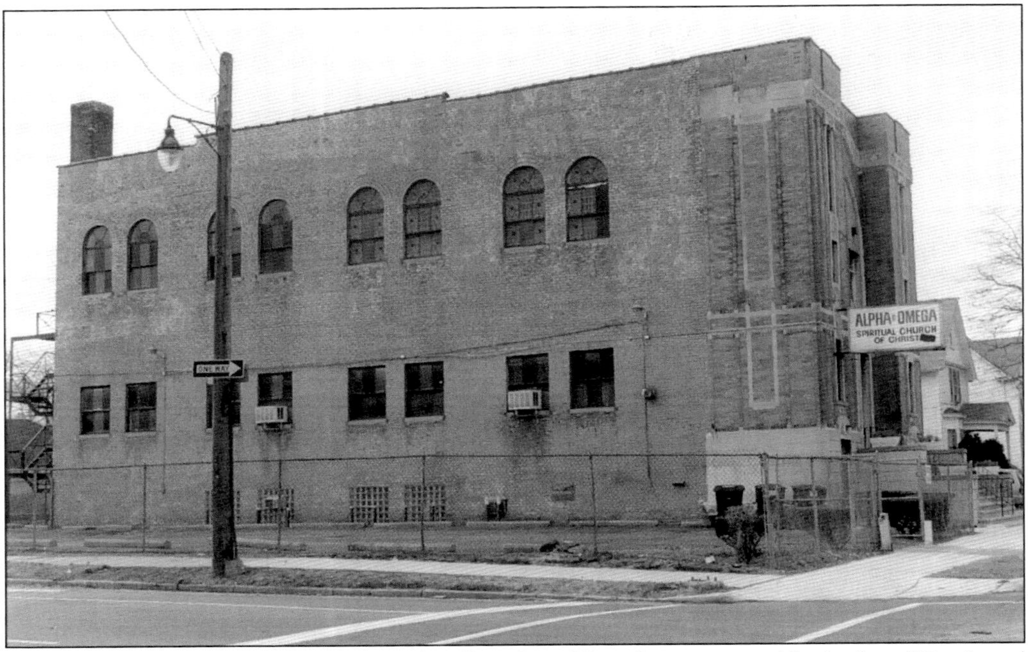

Ahavas Zion at the southwest corner of Holbrook and Beaubien was two blocks from Woodward near Temple Beth El. From the Beaubien side, it looks like the AlphaOmega Spiritual Church, as the sign states.

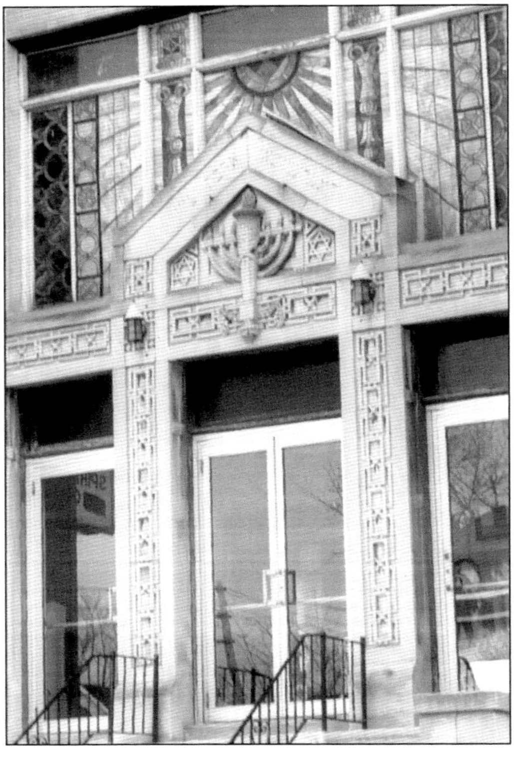

From the Holbrook side, it looks as it did in the 1920s and 1930s when Rabbi Samuel Fine was the spiritual leader.

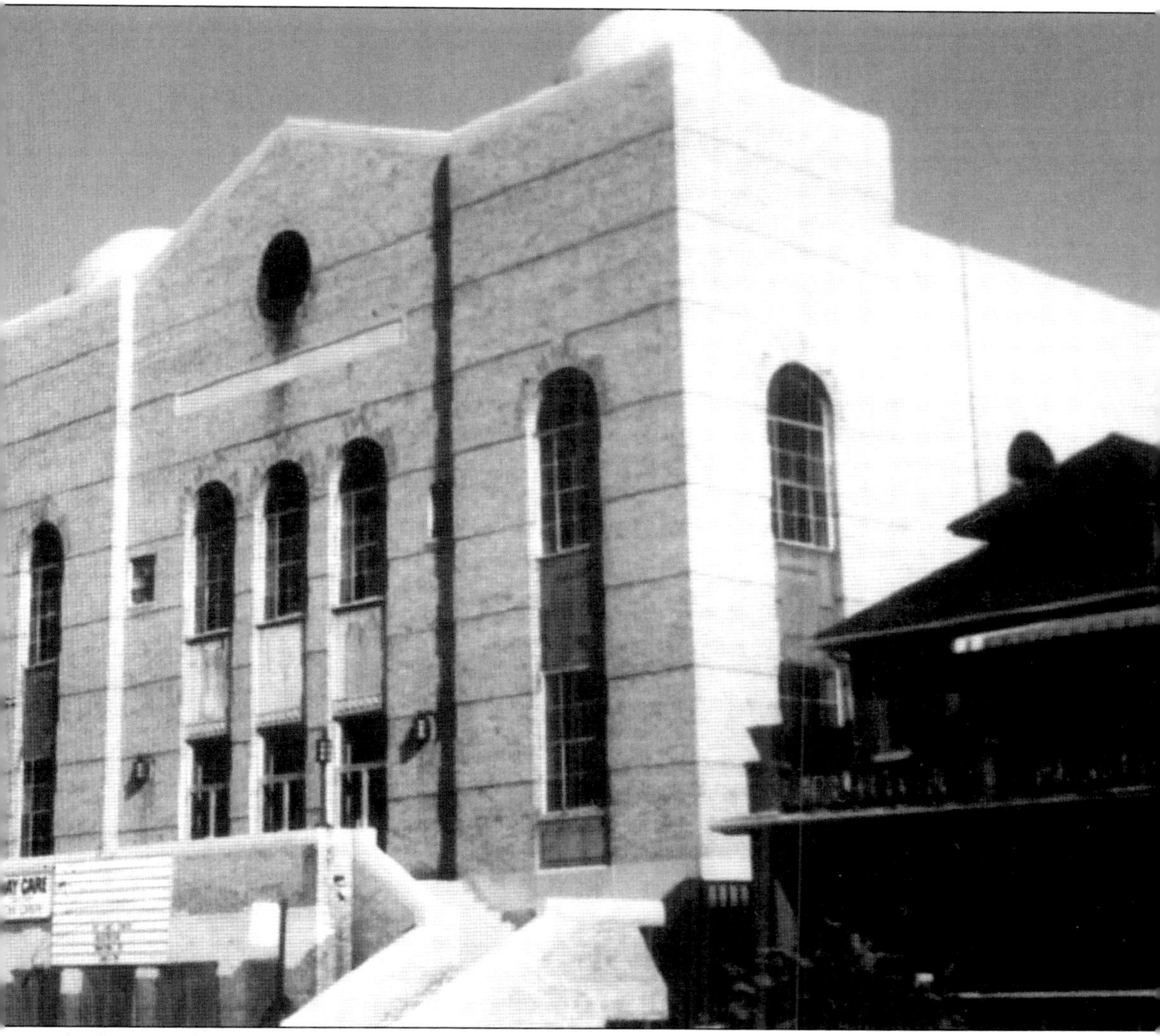

The huge Beth Tefilo Emanuel on Taylor and Woodrow Wilson completely dwarfs the four-flat next door. It was the largest synagogue in the Twelfth Street section and housed an afternoon Hebrew school. A half century after it ceased to exist as a synagogue, it's still known as the Taylor shul (synagogue). (Courtesy Joe Kramer.)

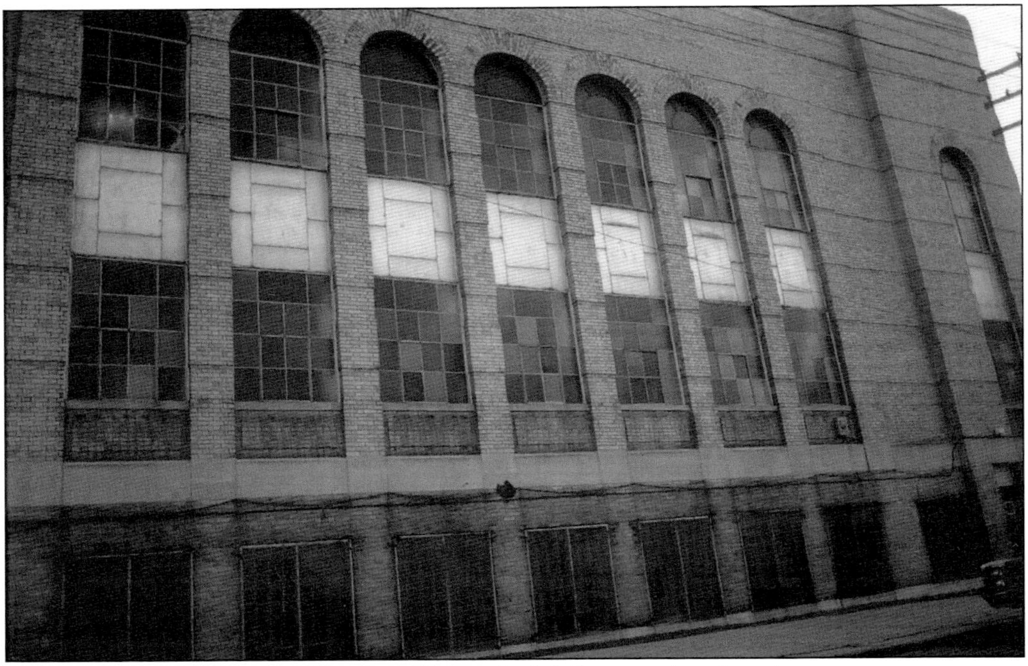

The huge side windows on Woodrow Wilson had different colored sections.

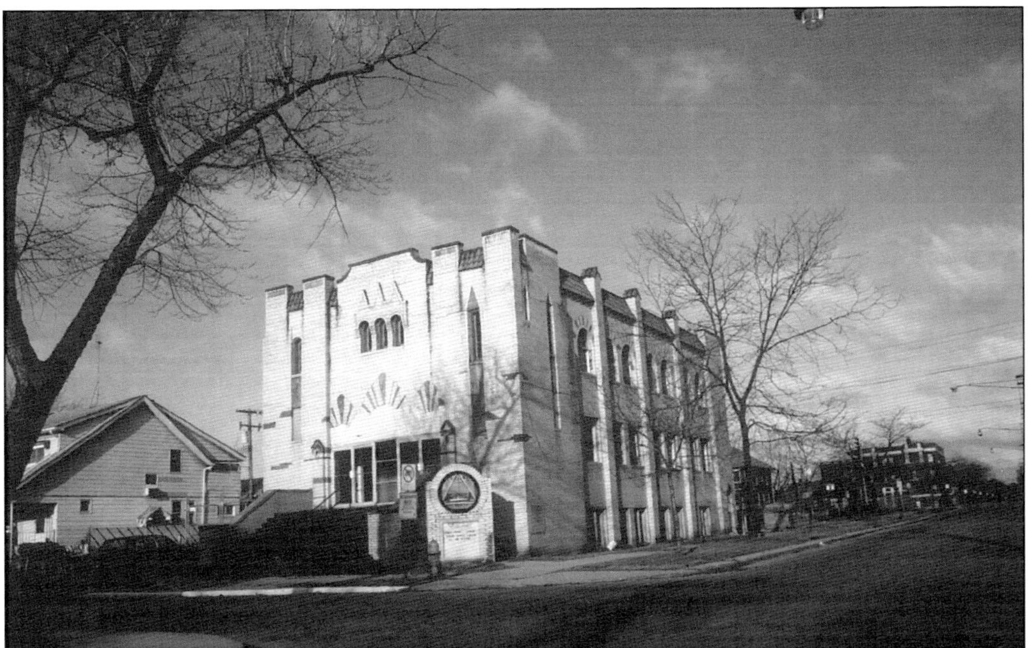

A few blocks south of Taylor on Pingree at Woodrow Wilson was the Beth Yehudah. It was dedicated in 1928 and soon became known as the Pingree Shul.

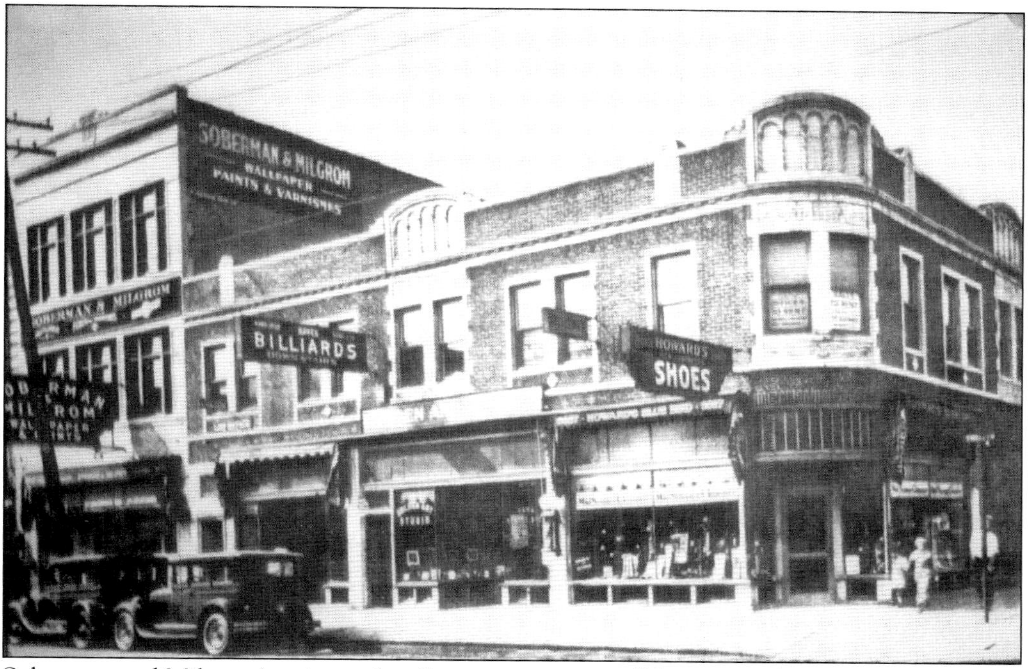

Soberman and Milgrom's paint and wallpaper store was well known in the Twelfth Street area. The business near Blaine Street would eventually become known as Mercury Paints. (Courtesy Manning Brothers Historic Photographic Collection.)

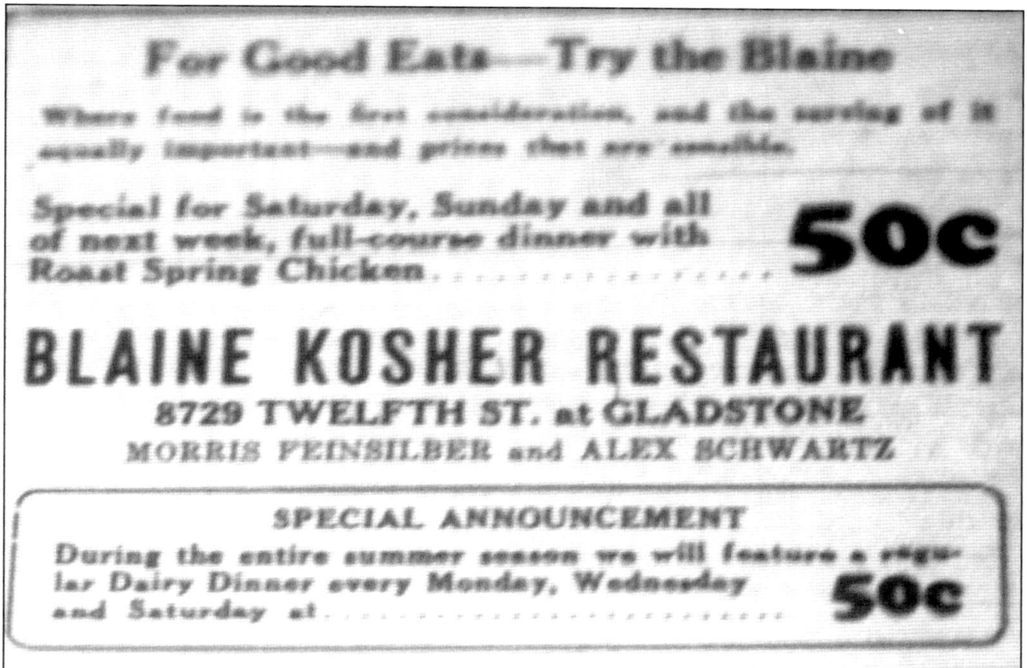

The Blaine Kosher Restaurant on Twelfth Street at Gladstone was an advertiser in the *Detroit Jewish Chronicle* in 1928.

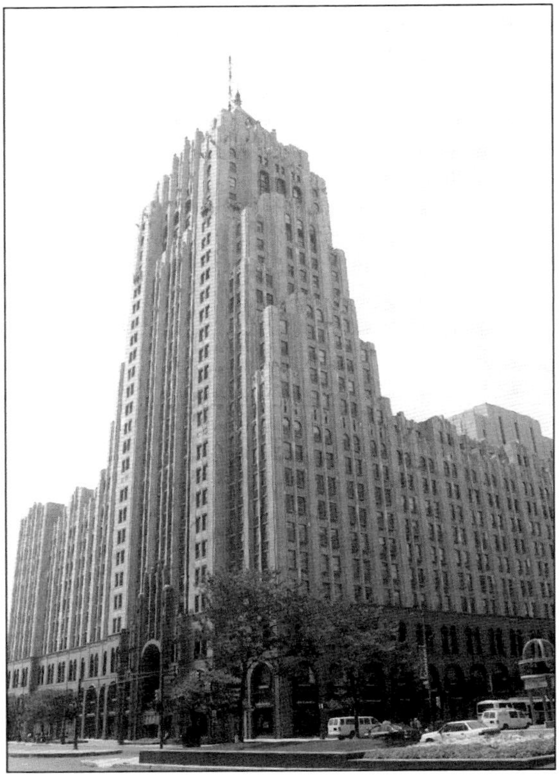

Jewish Detroiters beamed with pride when the Albert Kahn designed Fisher Building opened on Grand Boulevard at Second in 1928. The building featured a magnificent three-story marble-walled interior facade. Round arches framed shop windows facing the streets.

Kahn's grand Grand Boulevard buildings were only a short ride away from most Jewish Detroiters. Numerous Detroit landmarks went up in the latter part of the 1920s, including the two-story Book Cadillac Hotel, and taller buildings such as the David Stott Building, the Cadillac Square Tower, the Guardian Building, and the Penobscot Building.

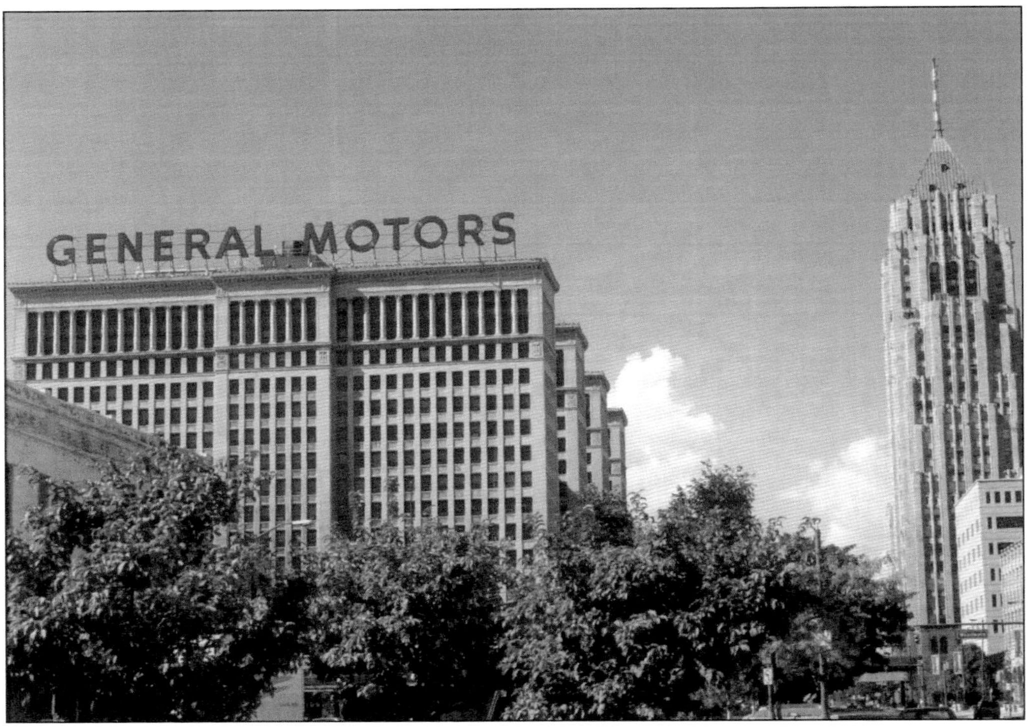

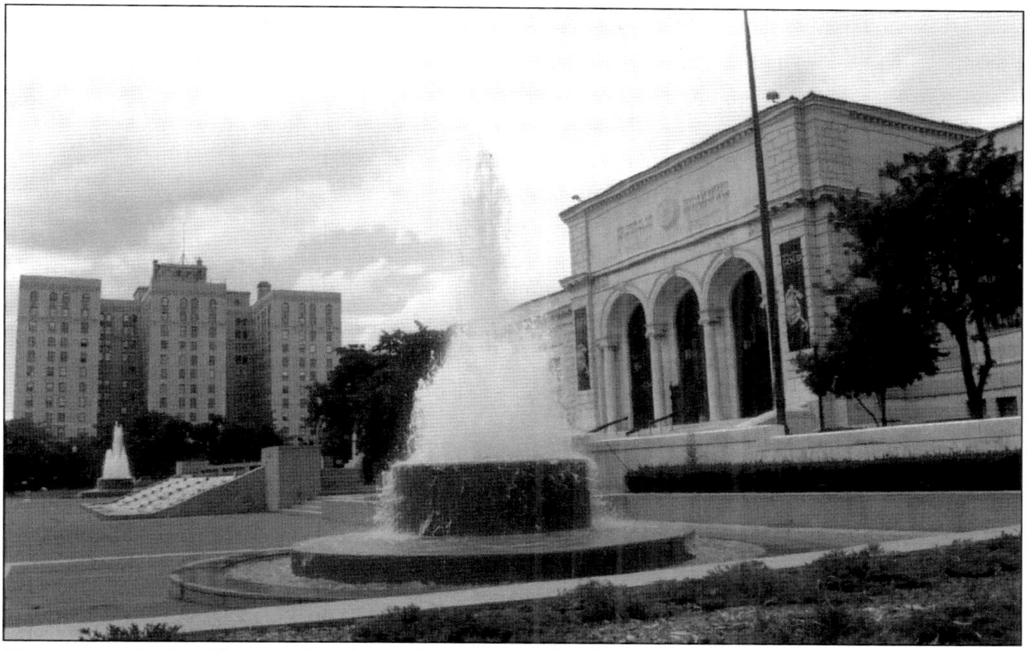

Detroiters also had beautiful cultural buildings. The Detroit Institute of Arts featured white Vermont marble, as did the Detroit Public Library across the street.

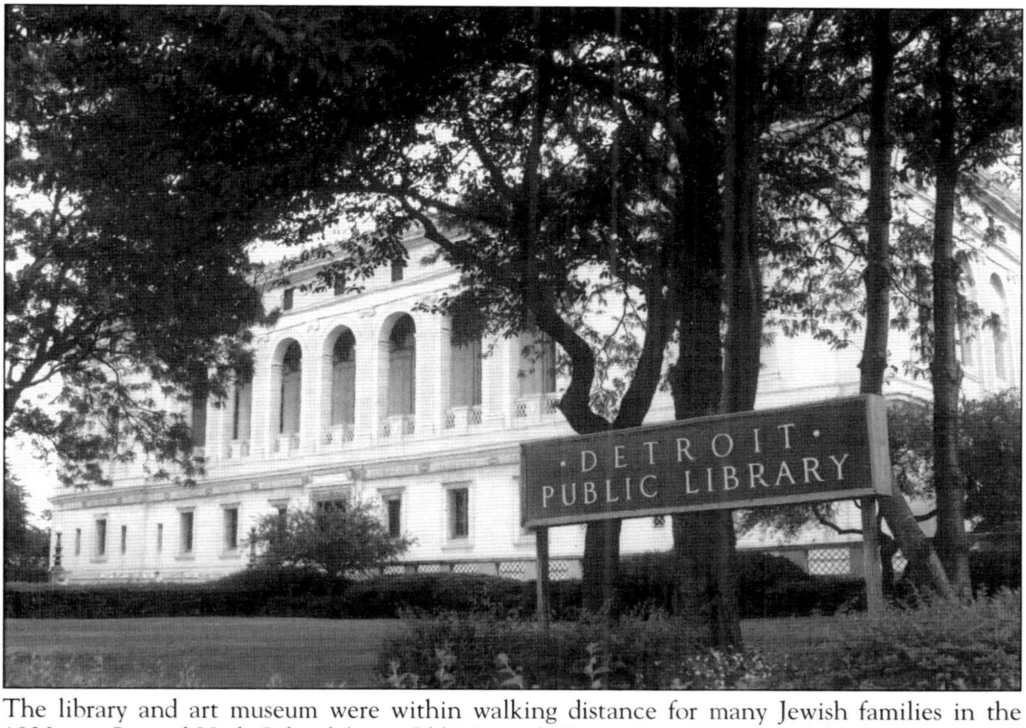

The library and art museum were within walking distance for many Jewish families in the 1920s, as Central High School (now Old Main of Wayne State University) had a large Jewish student population.

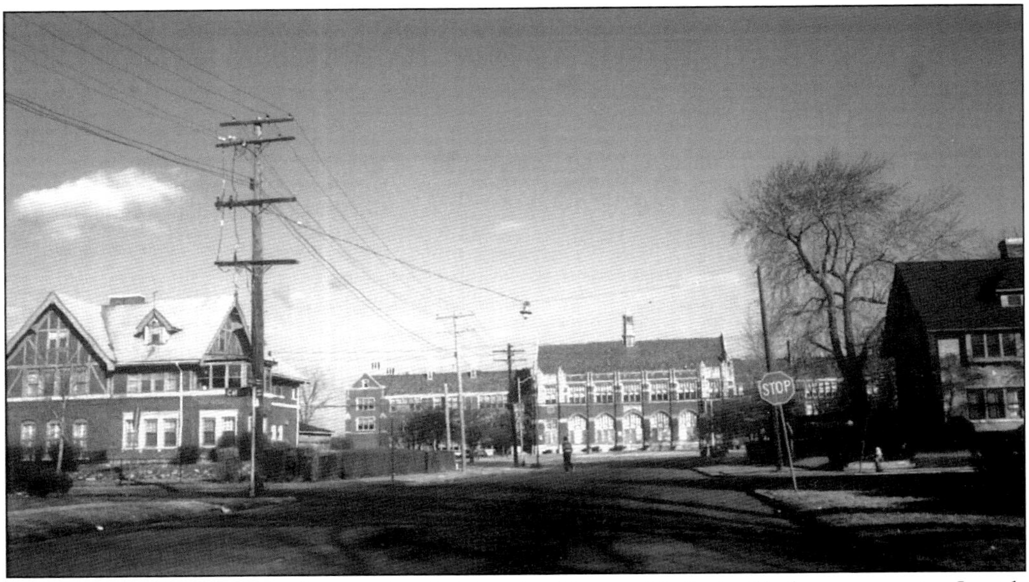

A new Central High School opened in 1928 in the Linwood-LaSalle-Elmhurst emerging Jewish neighborhood.

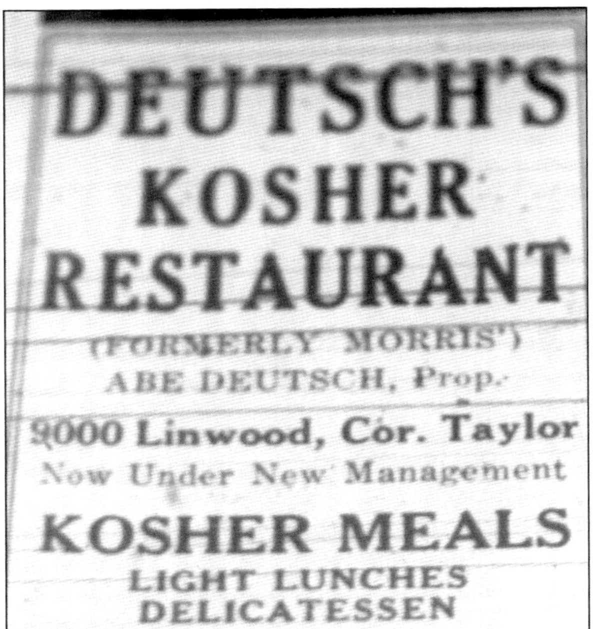

New Jewish restaurants and delicatessens opened on Linwood around the same time.

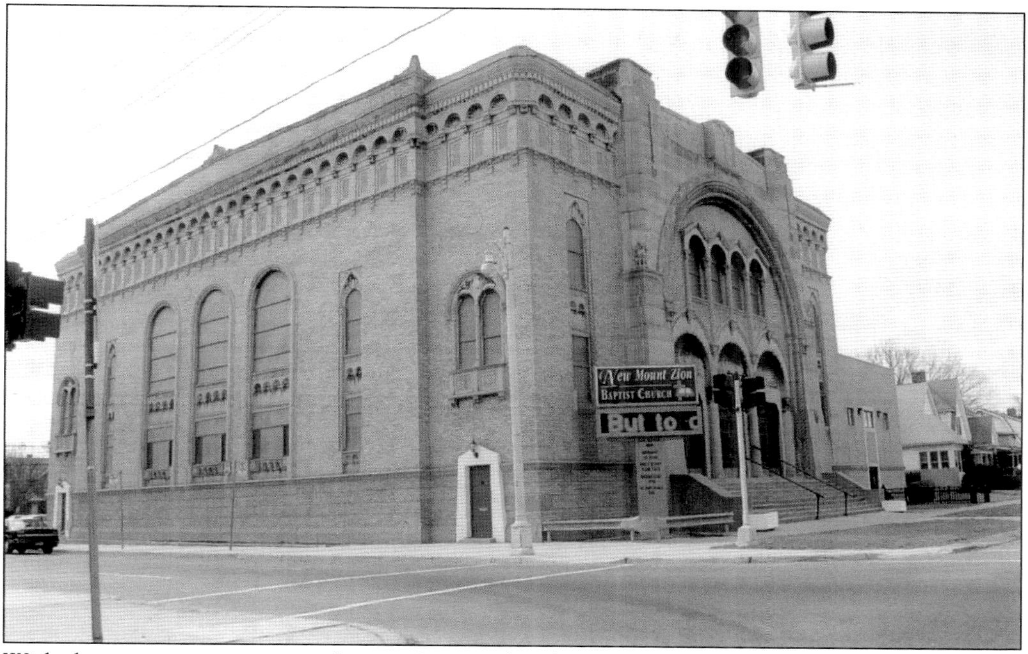

With the community moving closer to Linwood—about three-quarters of a mile west of Twelfth Street—the Beth David opened its huge, Moorish style synagogue in 1928 on Elmhurst and 14th, a block west of Linwood.

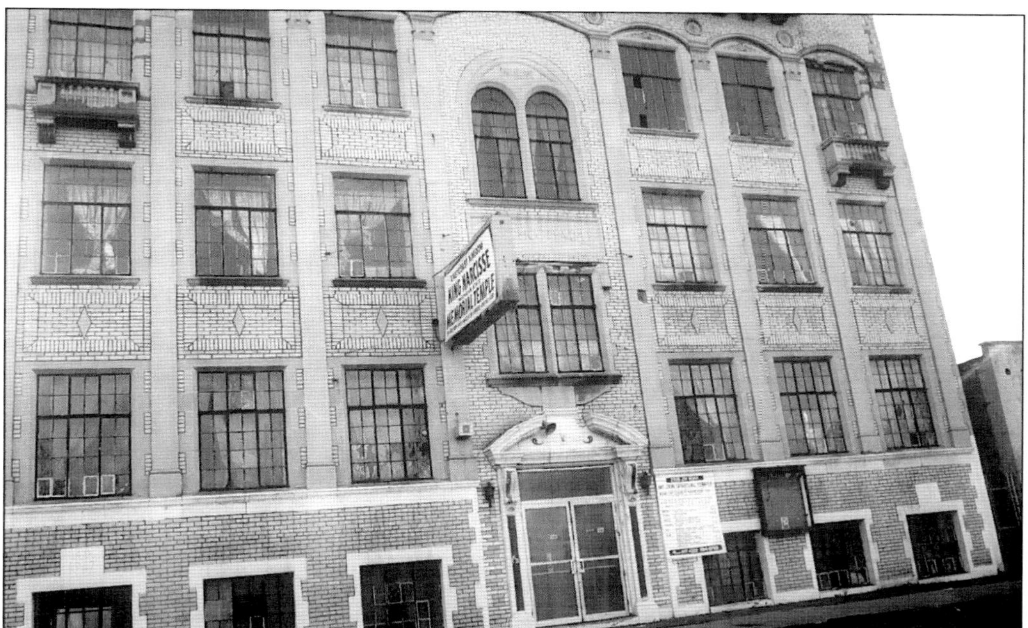

Congregations that couldn't afford to build synagogues rented floor space in the Jericho Temple on Joy Road near Linwood. Usually, two or more congregations conducted services on different floors of the building at the same time.

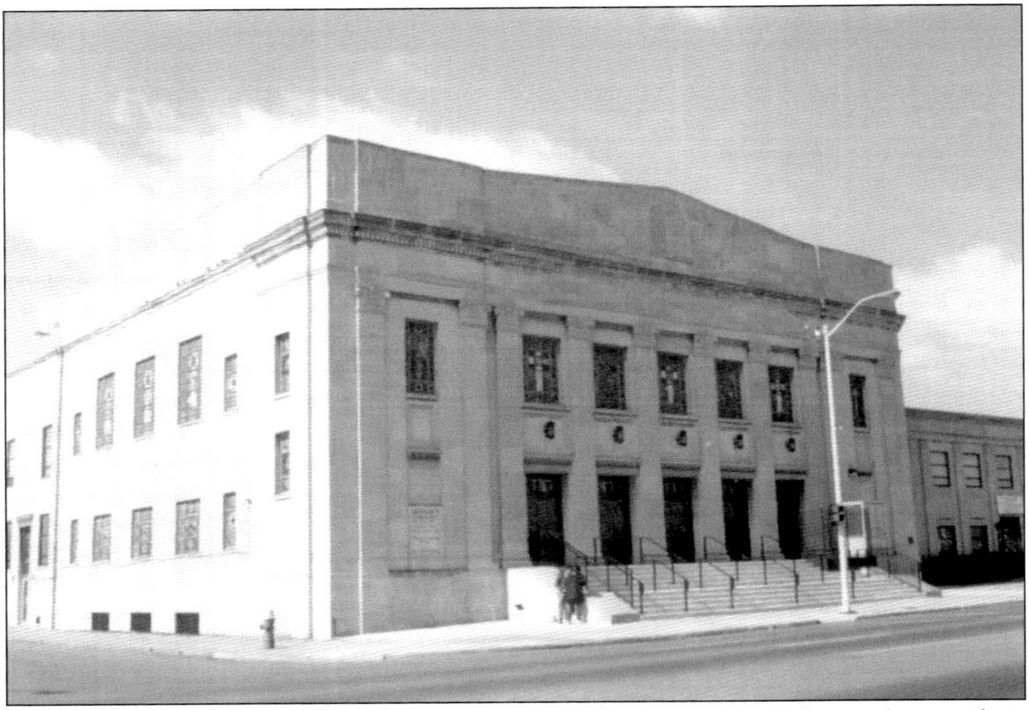

At this time, the B'nai Moshe relocated four and a half miles north and three miles west from Garfield and Beaubien to Dexter and Lawrence. It was the first synagogue built on Dexter.

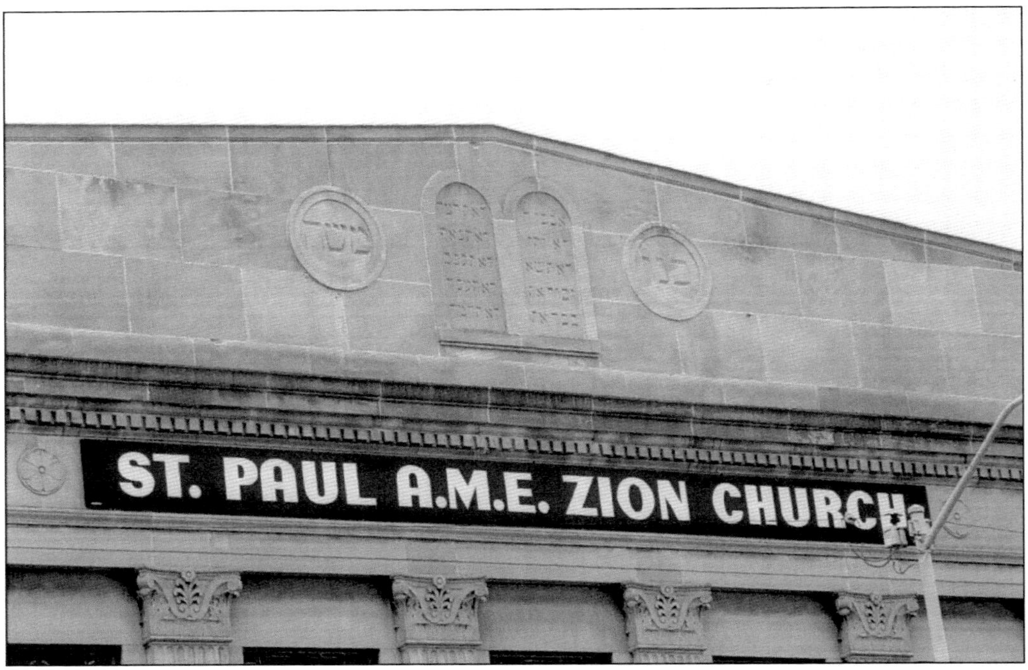

Even though it's the St. Paul A.M.E. Zion Church today, a close look at the top of the structure shows B'nai Moshe in Hebrew in the building's design.

Rabbi Moses Fischer, who became the synagogue's spiritual leader in 1923, would serve B'nai Moshe for the next two decades.

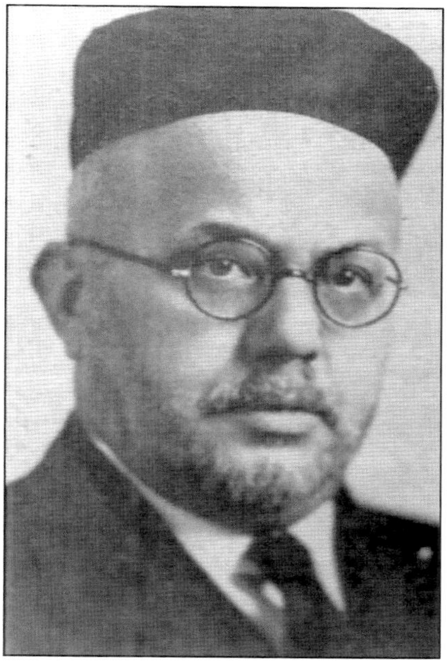

In 1929, on the eve of the stock market crash, Detroit's industry had 330,000 workers. More than thirty percent of Detroiters were employed in factories. Detroit was one of the fastest growing cities in the country. Jews and others were moving to Detroit from Europe and from other American cities. (Courtesy Burton Historical Collection of the Detroit Public Library.)

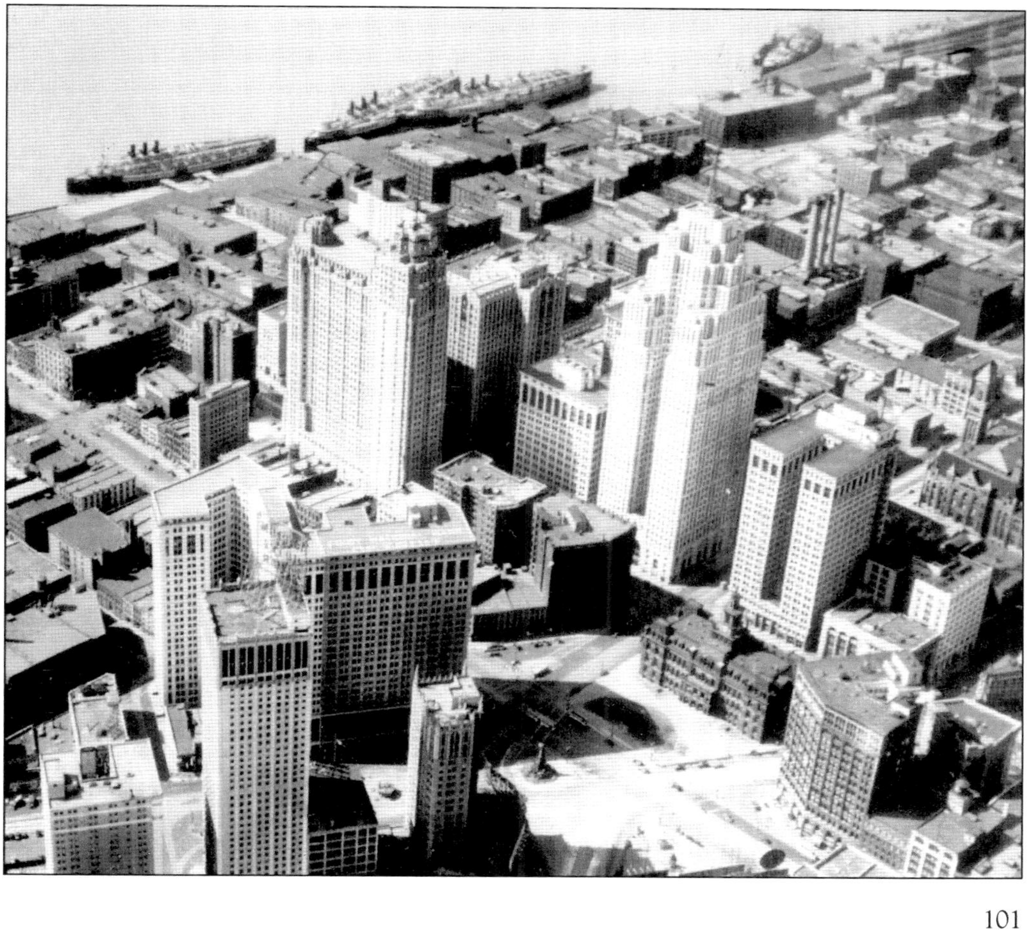

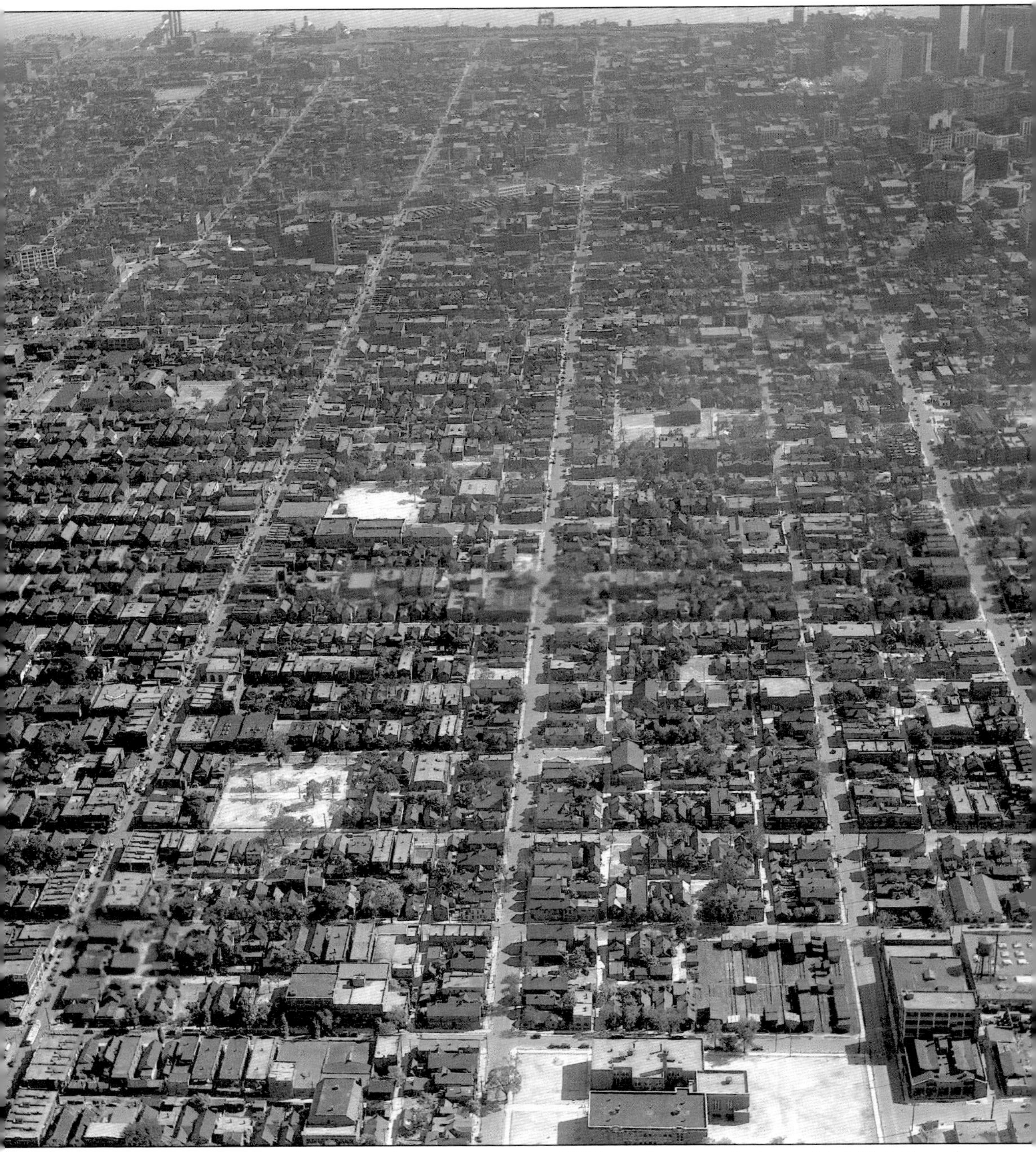

Detroit was the fourth largest American city in 1930, with a population of 1,568,662 and an incredible increase of 1,362,958 in only 30 years. Detroit's black population of 120,066 was 7.7 percent of the city's total. Blacks were settling in the older Jewish Hastings Street corridor south of Grand Boulevard. Hastings Street—razed in 1959 for the construction of the Chrysler Freeway—is shown in the photo extending from the Detroit River in the lower left hand corner. St. Antoine, Beaubien, and Brush ran west off Hastings. (Courtesy Walter Reuther Library of Wayne State University.)

It was estimated that in 1931, twenty percent of Detroit's work force was idle because of the Depression. Thousands of Detroiters—including many in the Jewish community—were out of work, out of money, and out of credit. Gertrude Wineman was a tireless worker in the 1931 drive to help those in need.

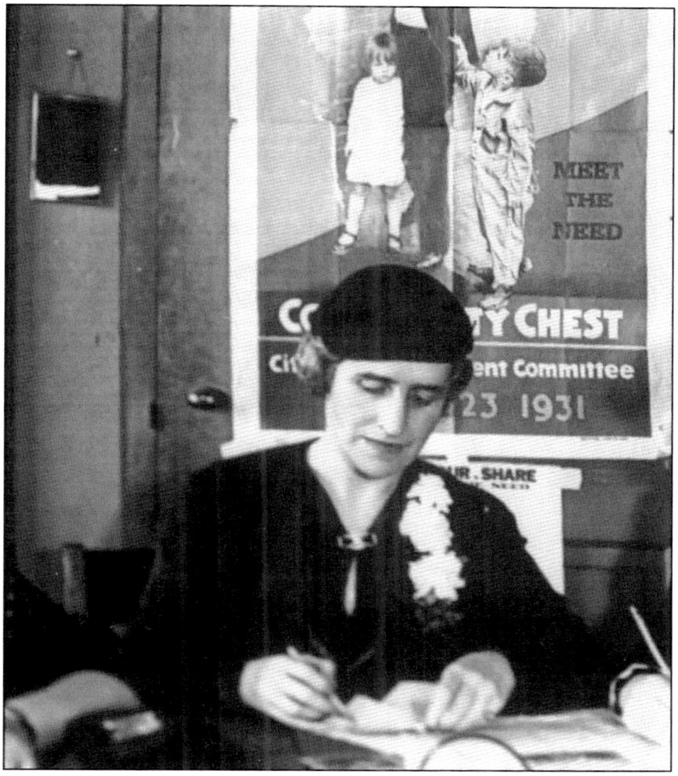

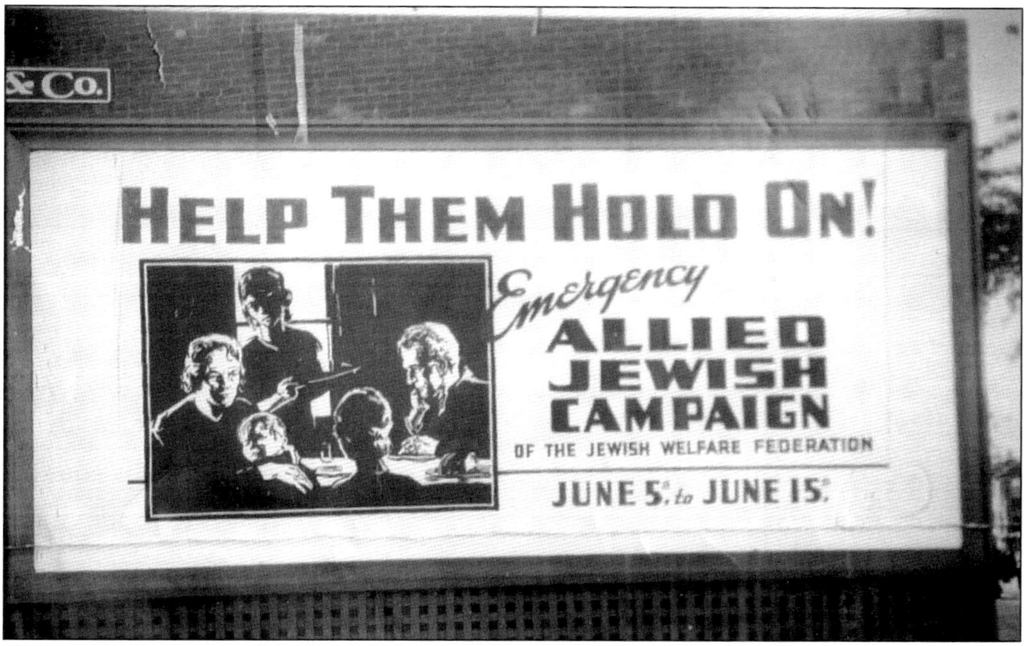

Signs on billboards in the Jewish community were a reminder of the plight of many families. (Photos courtesy Leonard N. Simons Jewish Community Archives.)

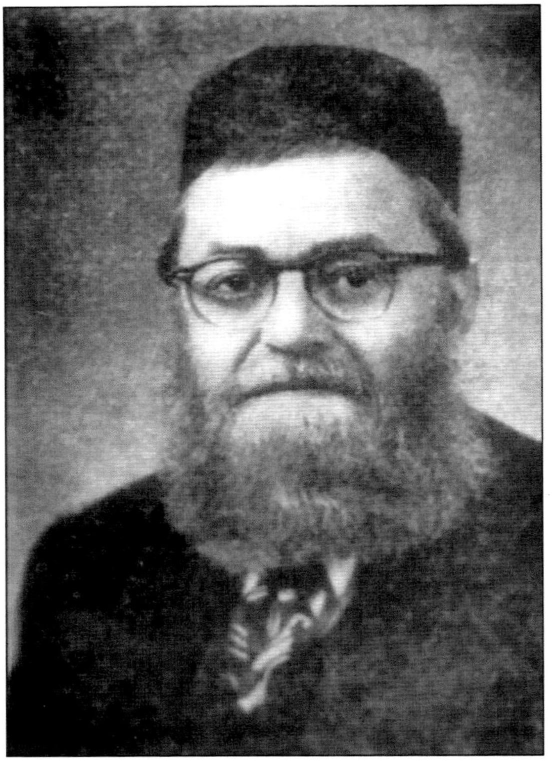

In 1931, Rabbi Joseph BenZion Rabinowitz moved to Detroit at the urging of men from the same European village. A home on Blaine off Twelfth Street was purchased; the Rabinowitz family lived upstairs and the first floor was converted into a synagogue.

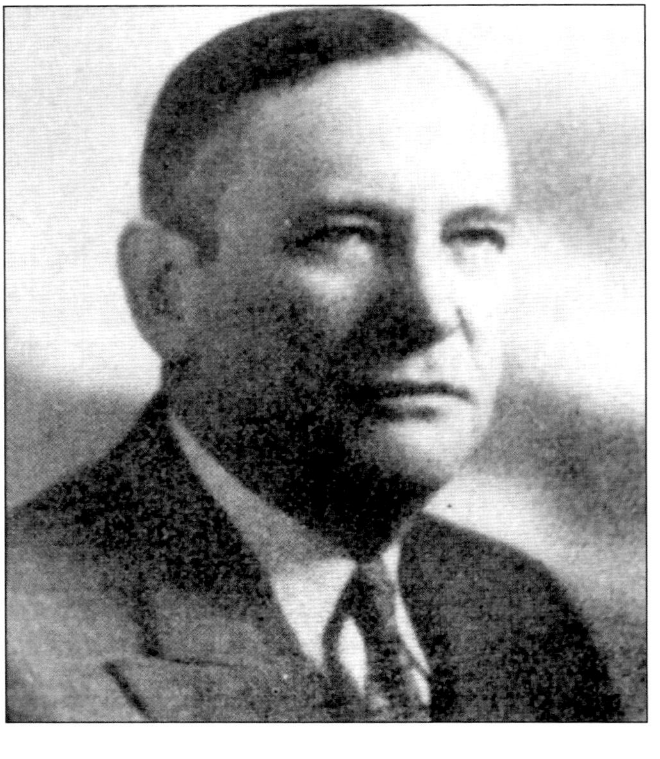

Well-known in the community, Robert Marwil was president of Congregation Shaarey Zedek and held office in several other Jewish organizations.

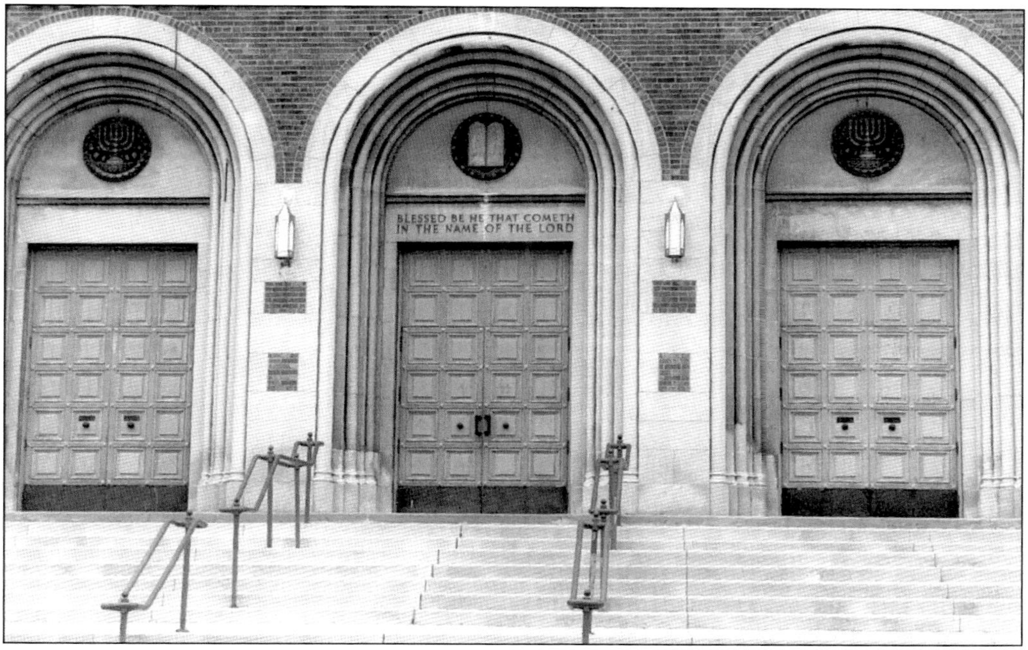

The famous doors of the new Shaarey Zedek Synagogue on Chicago Boulevard and Lawton opened in 1932.

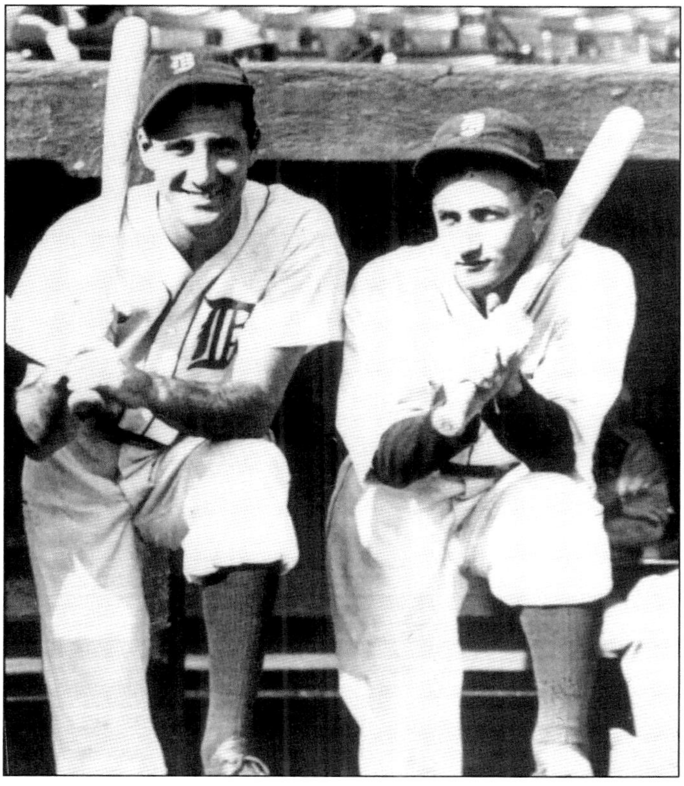

Hank Greenberg's bat and smile lit up the Jewish community as economic times were improving. Greenberg's good friend on the Tigers was Charlie Gehringer. The pair was often referred to as the G-Men. Greenberg's visit to Shaarey Zedek for part of Yom Kippur services during the heat of the 1934 pennant race made national news. (Courtesy Jim Campbell.)

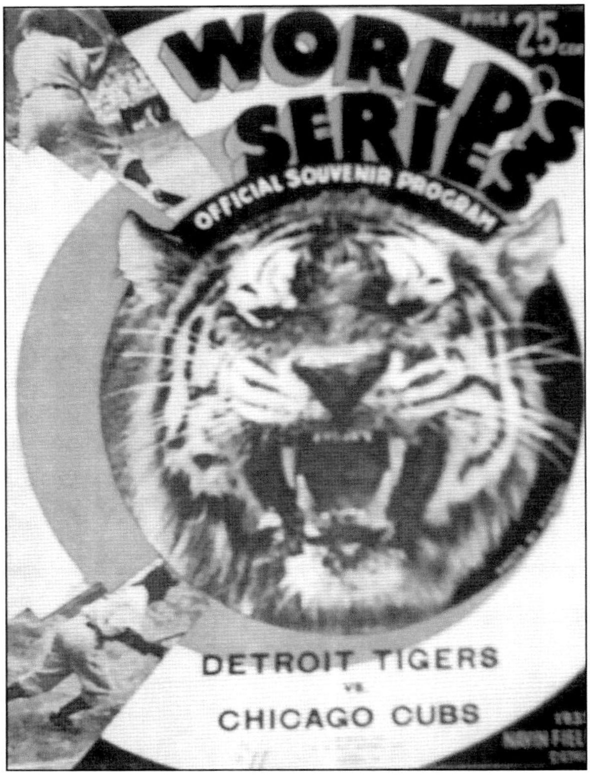

Detroit was known as the City of Champions in 1935 as the Tigers, Lions, and Red Wings all had championship seasons.

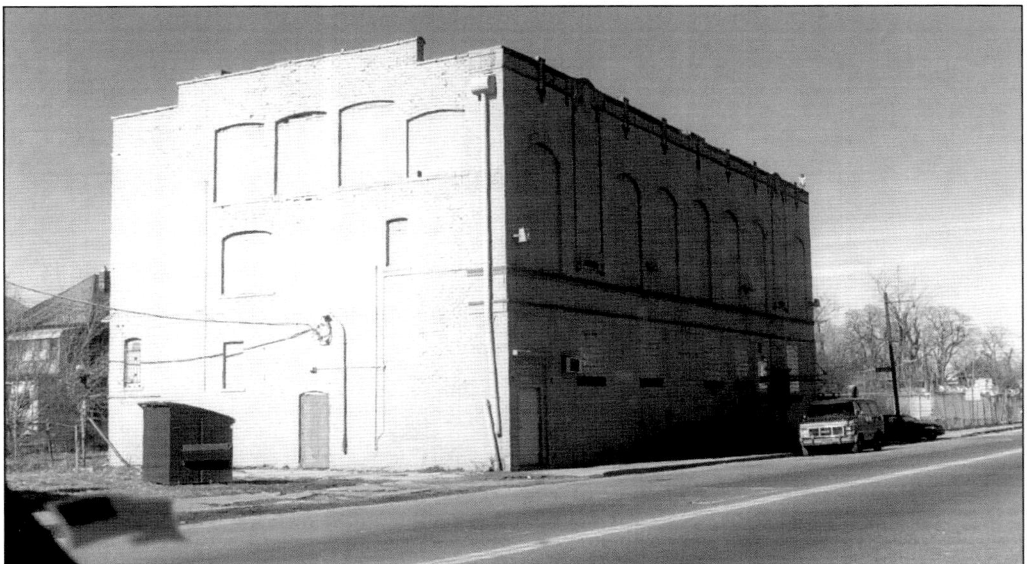

The famous "Schvitz" (Bathhouse) at 8295 Oakland was the place for animated talk on sports, politics, and other issues of the day. It attracted all types of men, from judges to gangsters.

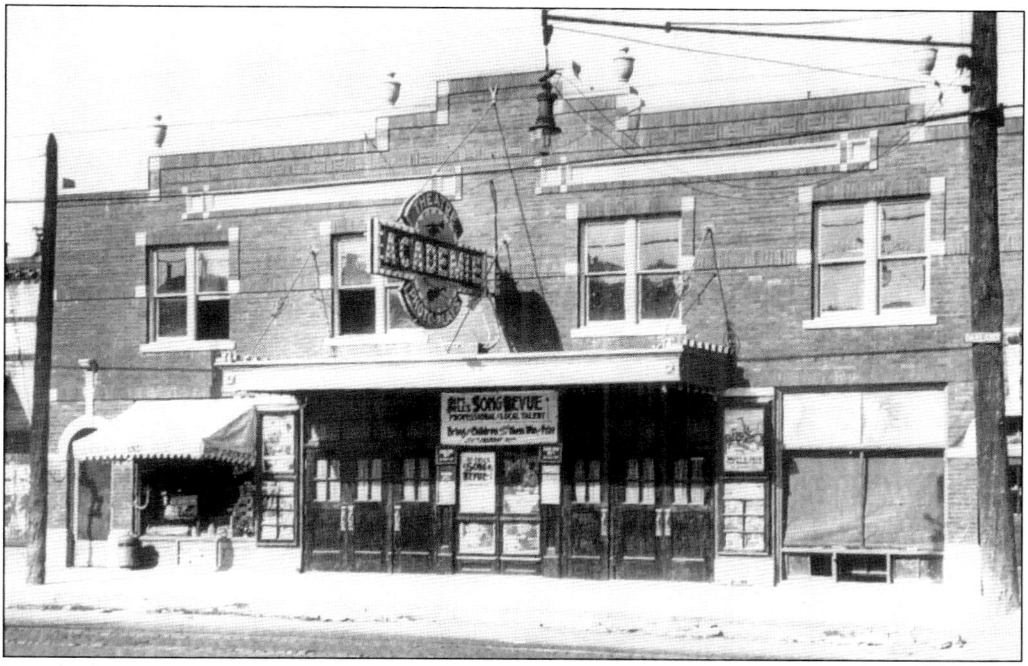

Not far from the "Schvitz" on Oakland was the Academie Theater, well known for hosting local talent shows. (Courtesy Manning Brothers Historic Photographic Collection.)

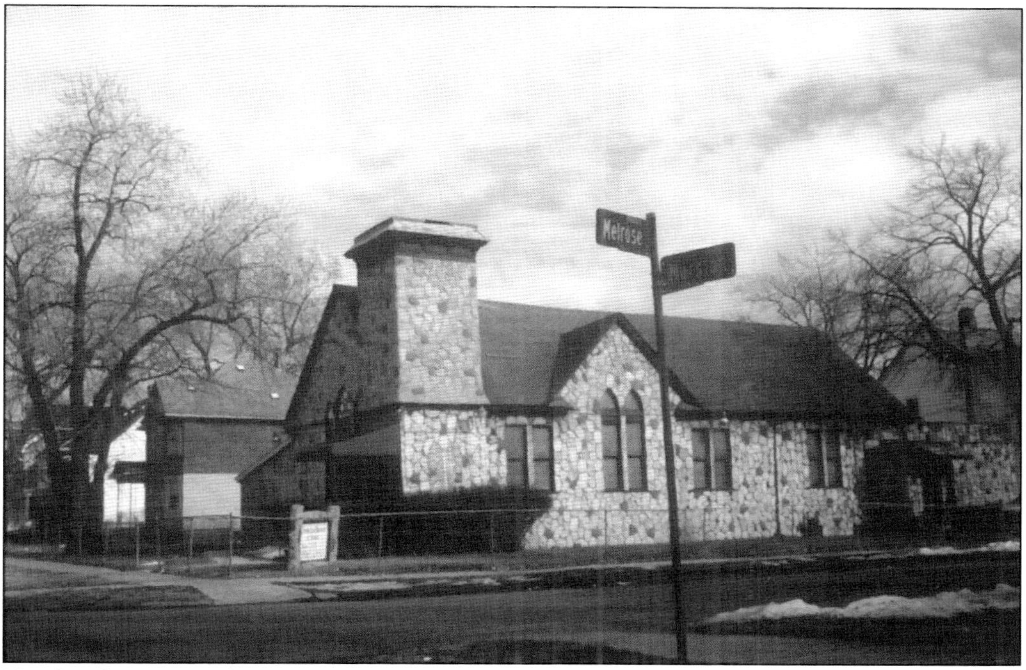

Nearby, the Ezras Achim Turover Synagogue opened on Marston and Melrose in 1935.

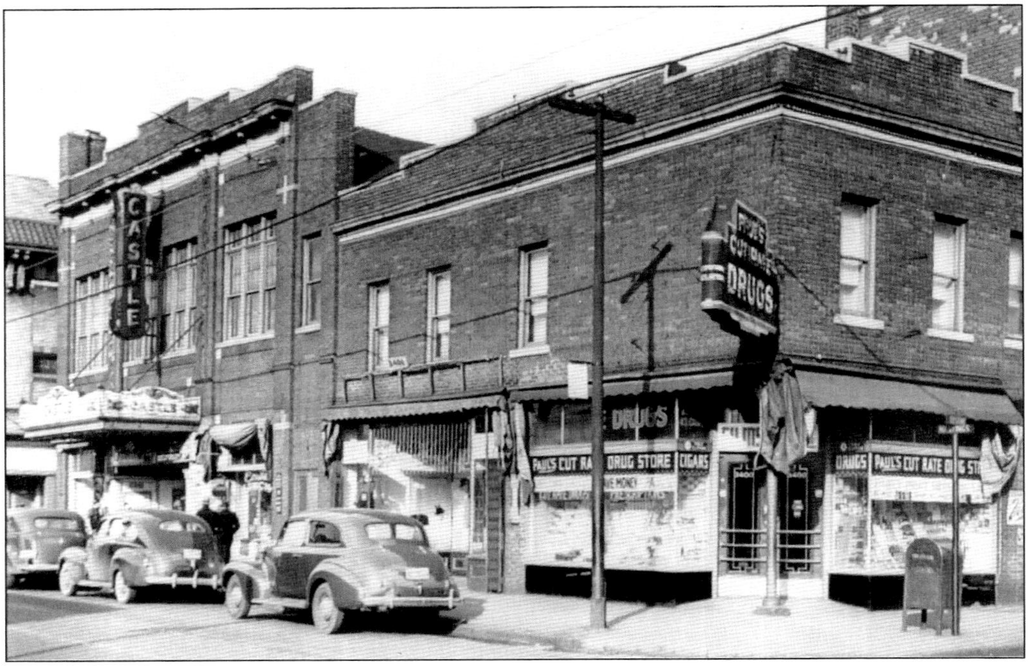

South of the Oakland district on Hastings Street, most remaining Jewish families were leaving the area and the landmarks such as the Castle Theater and Paul's Cut Rate Drugs. (Courtesy Manning Brothers Historic Photographic Collection.)

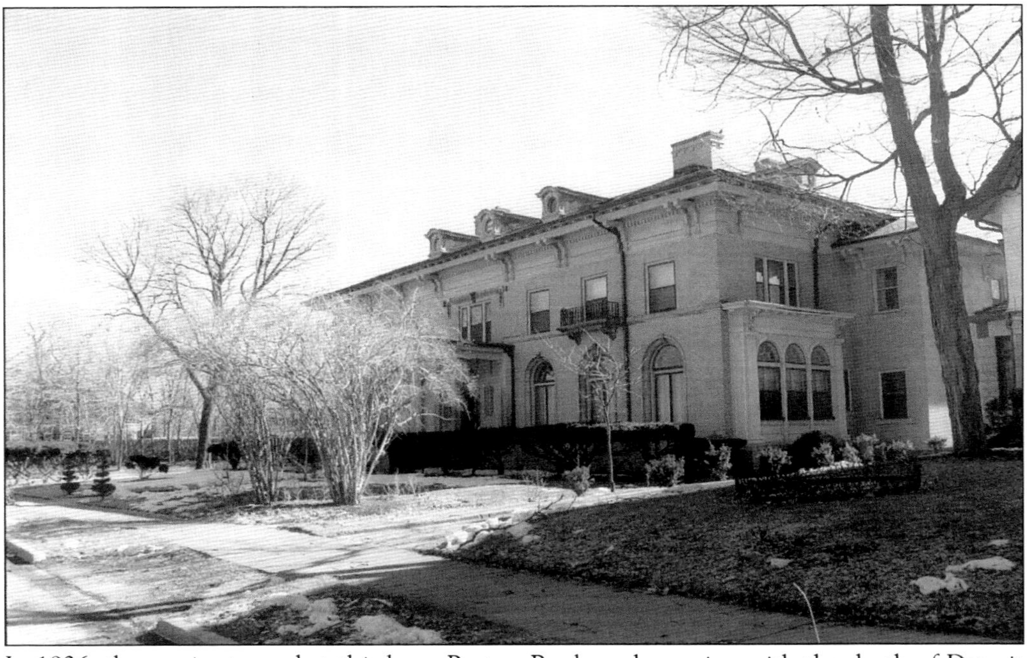

In 1936, the music stopped at this huge Boston Boulevard mansion with the death of Detroit Symphony Orchestra conductor Ossip Gabrilowitsch. In his last years, the famous conductor had lent his name to Jewish causes.

The Beth Abraham moved to Linwood at Fullerton, its fourth location since its founding a half century ago.

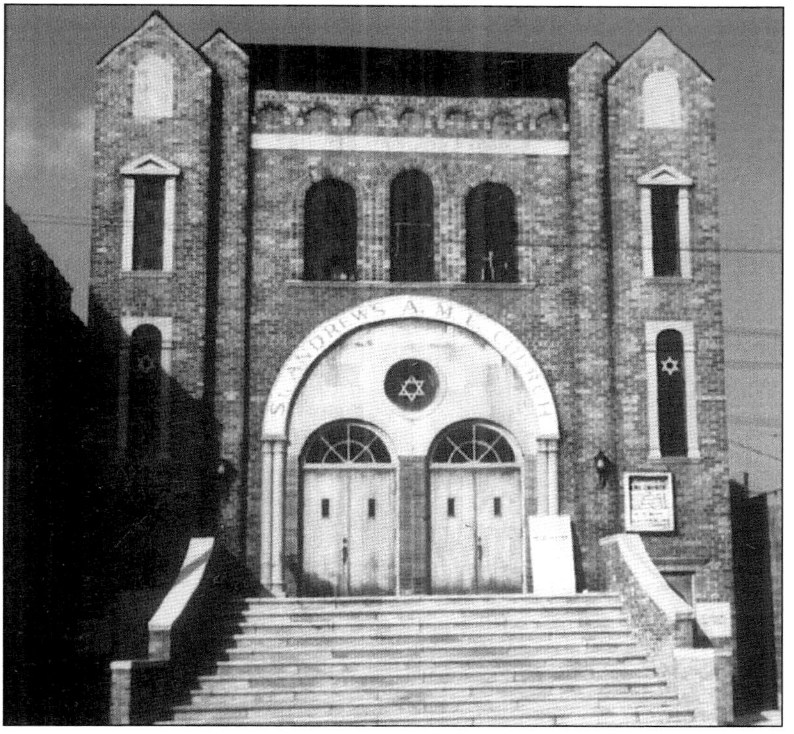

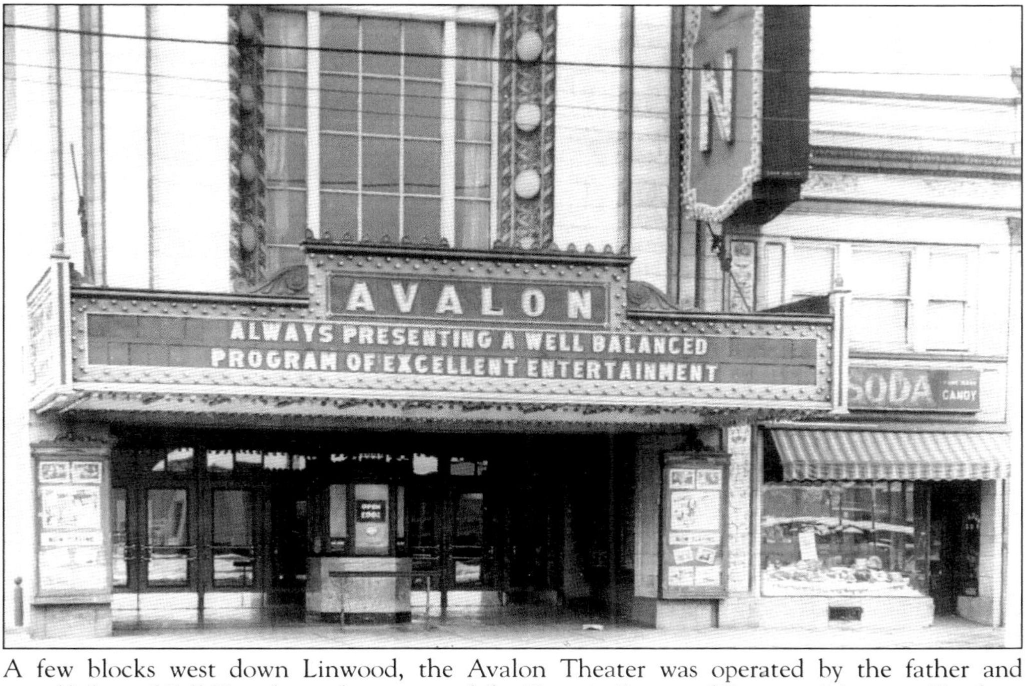

A few blocks west down Linwood, the Avalon Theater was operated by the father and grandfather of Bill Davidson, the owner of the Detroit Pistons. (Courtesy Manning Brothers Historic Photographic Collection.)

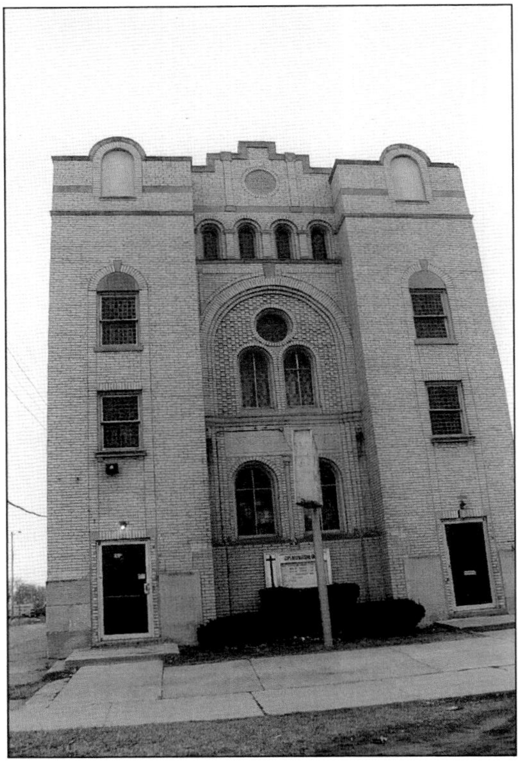

The Mishkan Israel was on Blaine and Linwood closer to the Twelfth Street section.

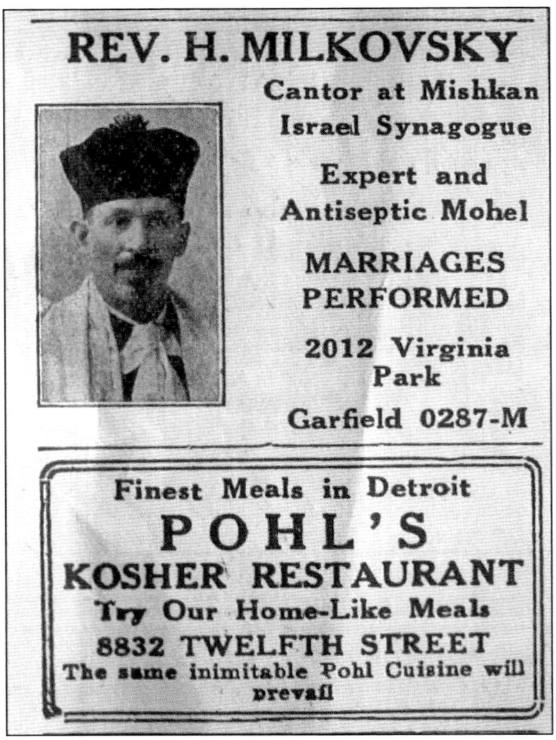

The synagogue's cantor often advertised in the weekly *Jewish Chronicle* that he performed marriages and circumcisions.

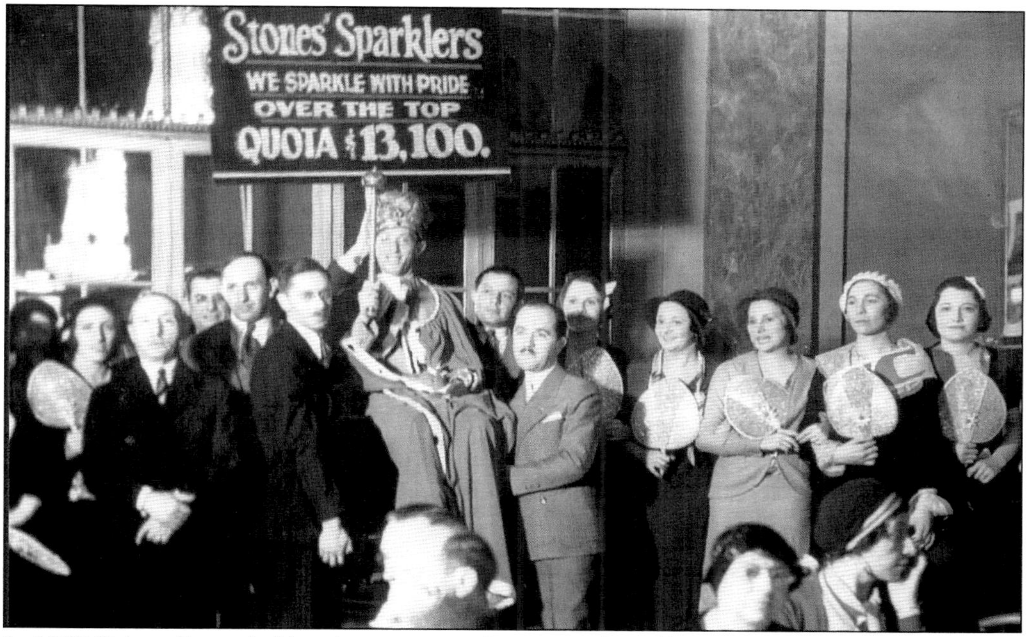

In 1937 Sidney Stone led his division over the top in the Allied Jewish Campaign. (Courtesy Leonard N. Simons Jewish Community Archives.)

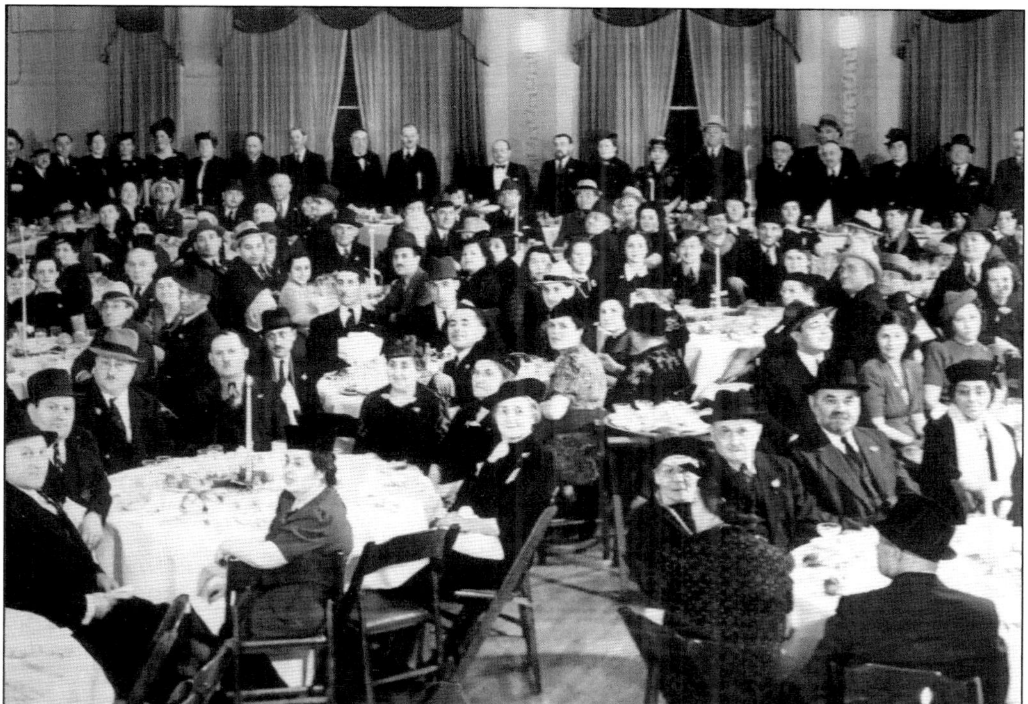

The Detroit branch of the Mizrachi Organization of America had their dinners at the Statler Hotel on Washington Boulevard.

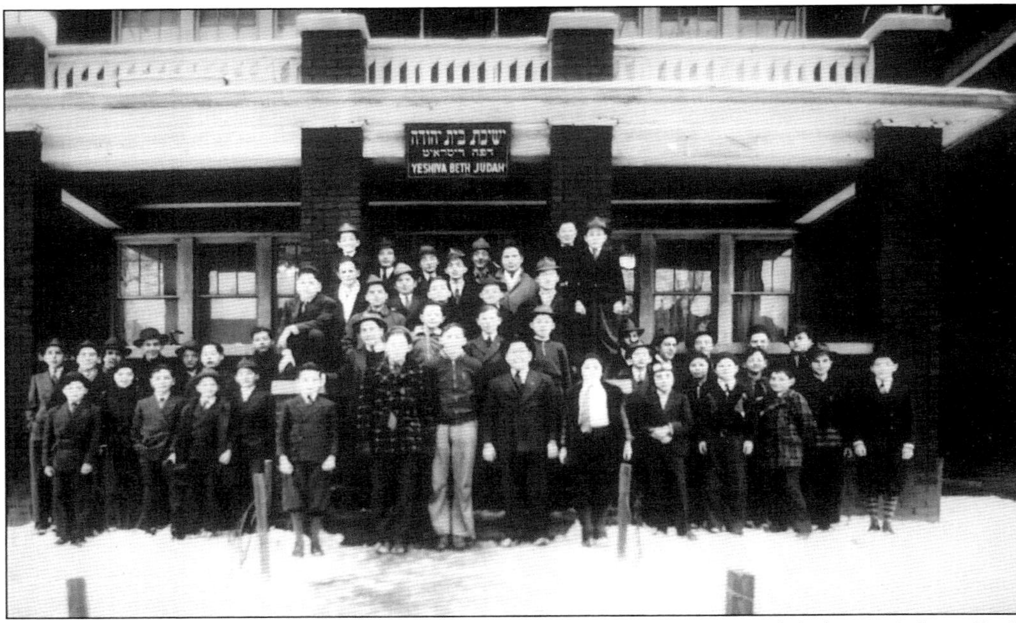

The Sunday and weekday afternoon Hebrew school—Yeshiva Beth Judah (now Yeshiva Beth Yehudah)—named after Rabbi Judah Levin, was located in a four-family flat on Elmhurst near Linwood. (Courtesy Yeshiva Beth Yehudah.)

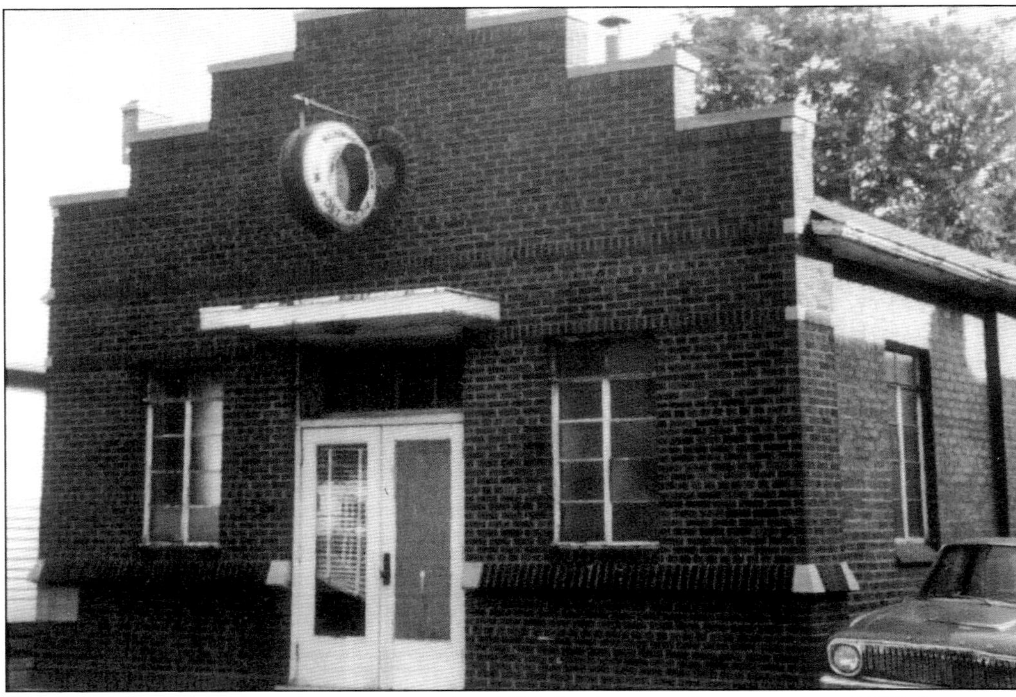

The River Rouge Congregation, organized in 1929, built its small synagogue in 1938. It was two miles south of the River Rouge Ford Plant. The small congregation employed visiting rabbis and rabbinical students on a part-time basis.

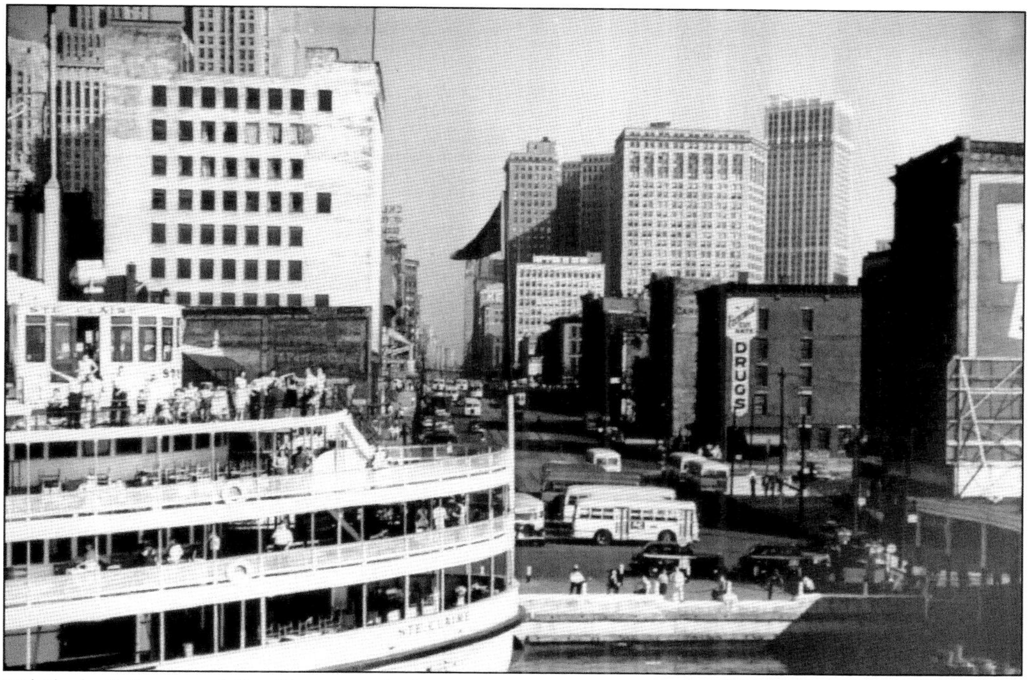

While buildings and families were being torn apart in war-ravaged Europe, Detroit prospered as many families moved to the Motor City in search of a better economic life. Because of the Depression, Detroit had only grown by 3.5 percent in the previous ten years. Black residents numbered 149,119, or 9.2 percent of Detroit's 1940 population of 1,623,452. The summer of 1940 was a tranquil time in Detroit. Families took leisurely boat rides on the Detroit River. They had no idea that many fathers soon would be overseas in the military and some would never return. (Courtesy Burton Historical Collection of the Detroit Public Library.)

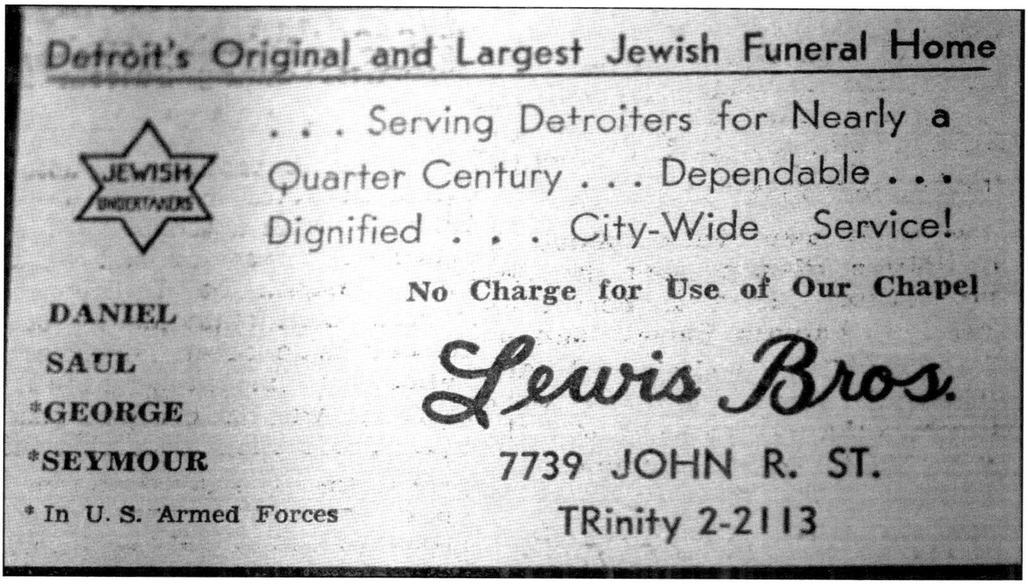

Two of the Lewis brothers served in the U.S. Armed Forces.

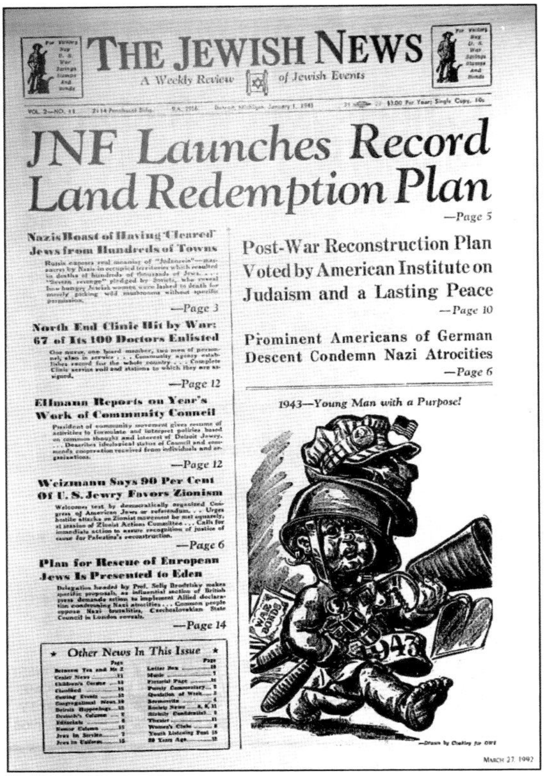

THE JEWISH NEWS

A Weekly Review of Jewish Events

JNF Launches Record Land Redemption Plan

—Page 5

Nazis Boast of Having "Cleared" Jews from Hundreds of Towns

—Page 3

North End Clinic Hit by War: 67 of Its 100 Doctors Enlisted

—Page 12

Ellmann Reports on Year's Work of Community Council

—Page 12

Weizmann Says 90 Per Cent Of U. S. Jewry Favors Zionism

—Page 6

Plan for Rescue of European Jews Is Presented to Eden

—Page 14

Other News In This Issue

Post-War Reconstruction Plan Voted by American Institute on Judaism and a Lasting Peace

—Page 10

Prominent Americans of German Descent Condemn Nazi Atrocities

—Page 6

1943—Young Man with a Purpose!

Many Jewish Detroiters followed local, national and international news through the weekly *Jewish News*, which was founded in March 1942. (Courtesy Detroit Jewish News.)

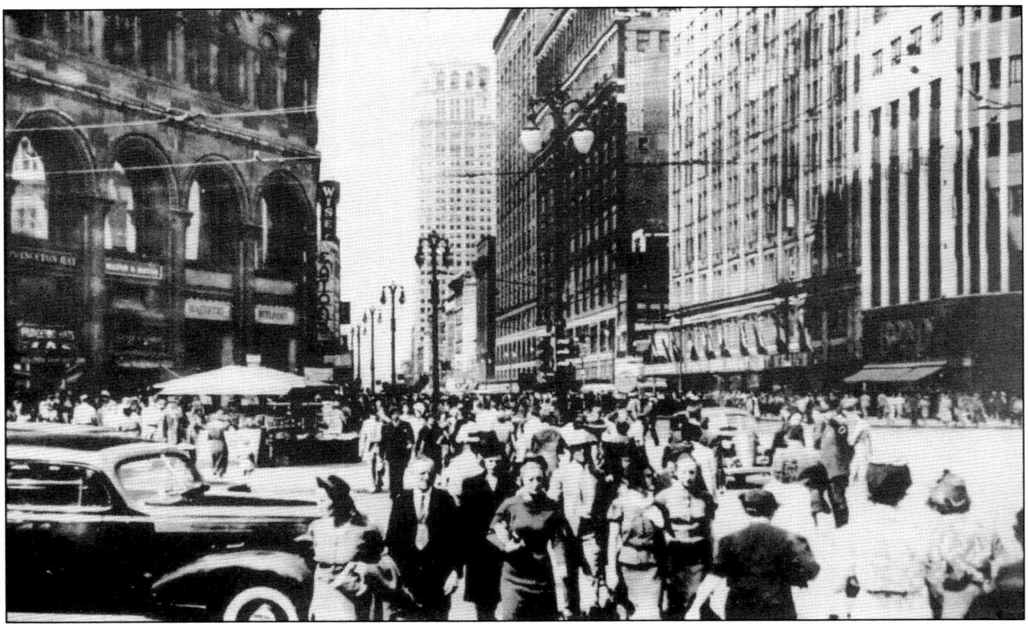

With the war over in 1945, most families were reunited and the Woodward shopping district had more shoppers on the streets.

After the war, the Jewish population was shifting as new establishments were relocating closer to Dexter, as this ad in the *Jewish News* showed. (Courtesy Detroit Jewish News.)

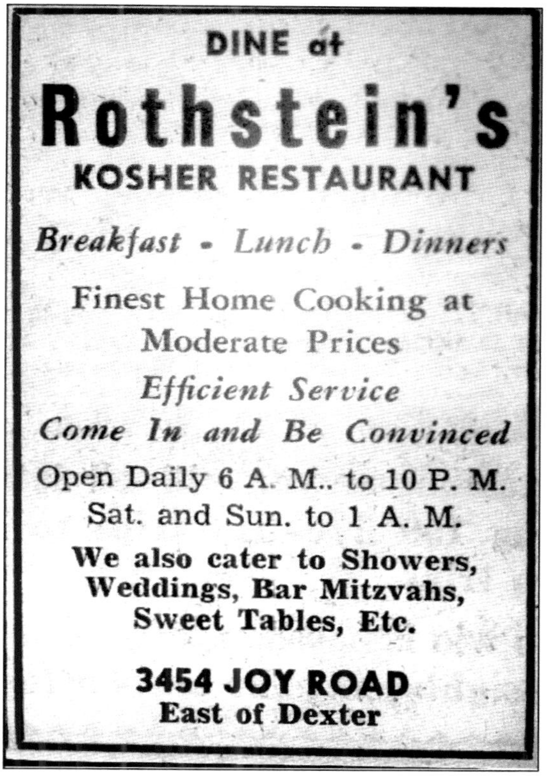

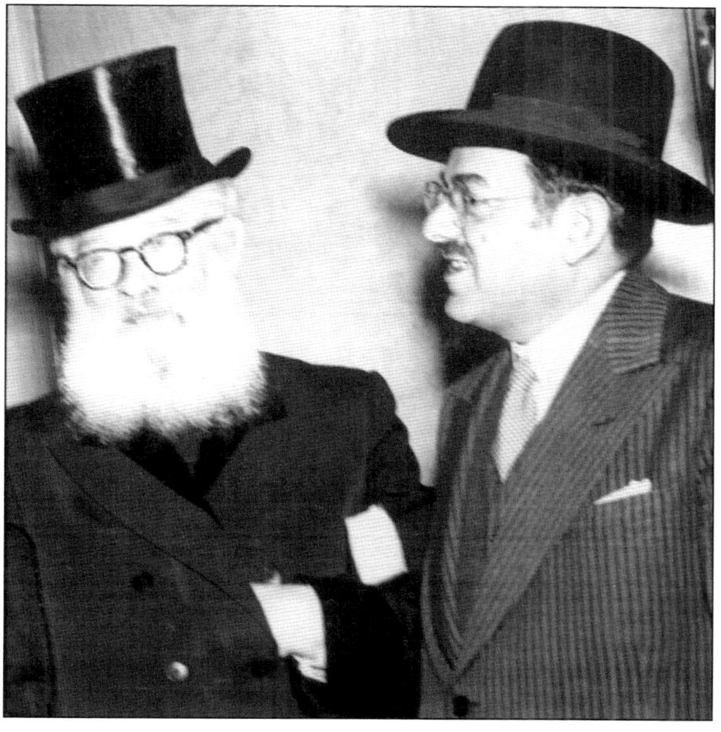

Rabbi Joshua Sperka greets Rabbi Isaac Halevy Herzog, chief rabbi of Israel. (Courtesy Judge S. Sperka.)

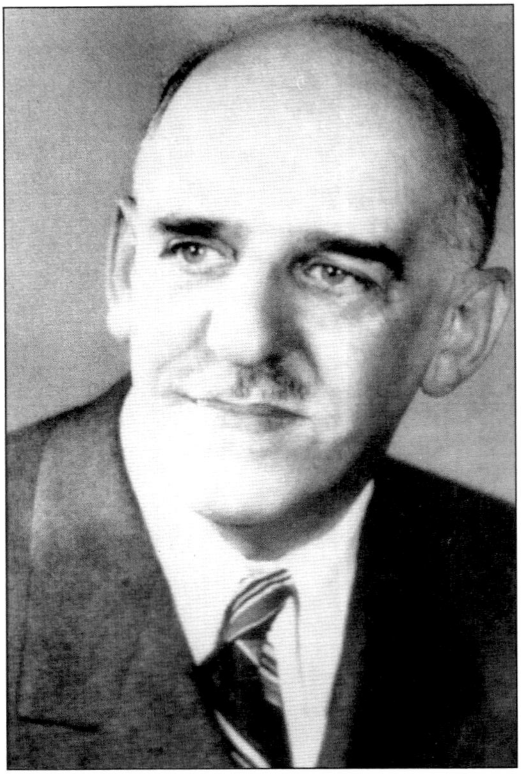

Fred Butzel was loved, admired, respected, and held numerous offices in Jewish and humanitarian causes. After his death in 1948, the building on Madison recently purchased for the offices of the Jewish Welfare Federation was named the Fred Butzel Building. (Courtesy Archives of Jewish Welfare Federation.)

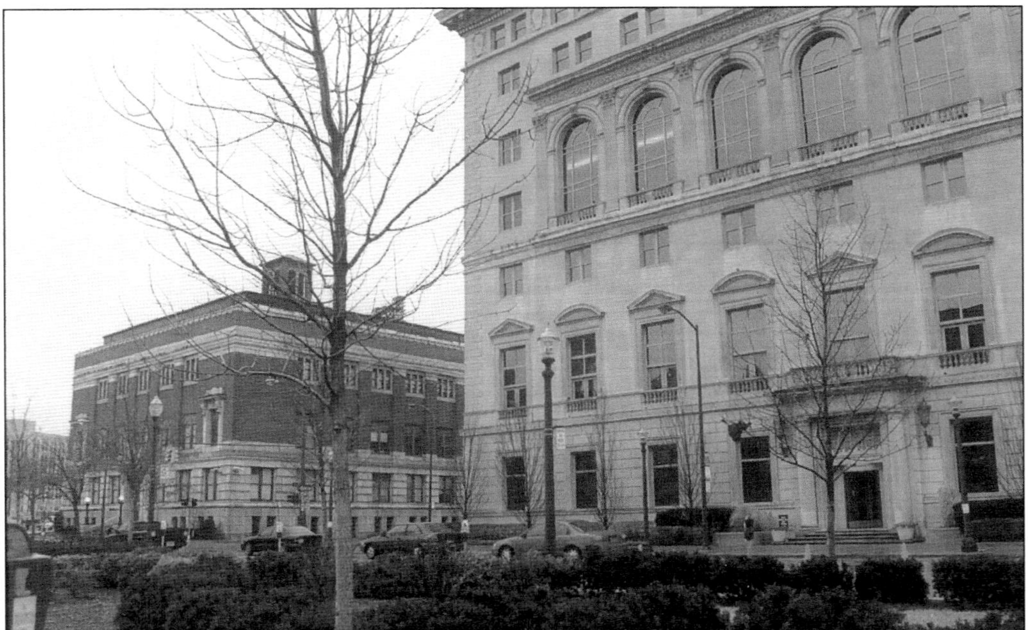

The Jewish Welfare Federation would stay at that location until 1992. The elegant Detroit Athletic Club, designed by Albert Kahn, also fronted on Madison.

Five

1950 AND ONWARD

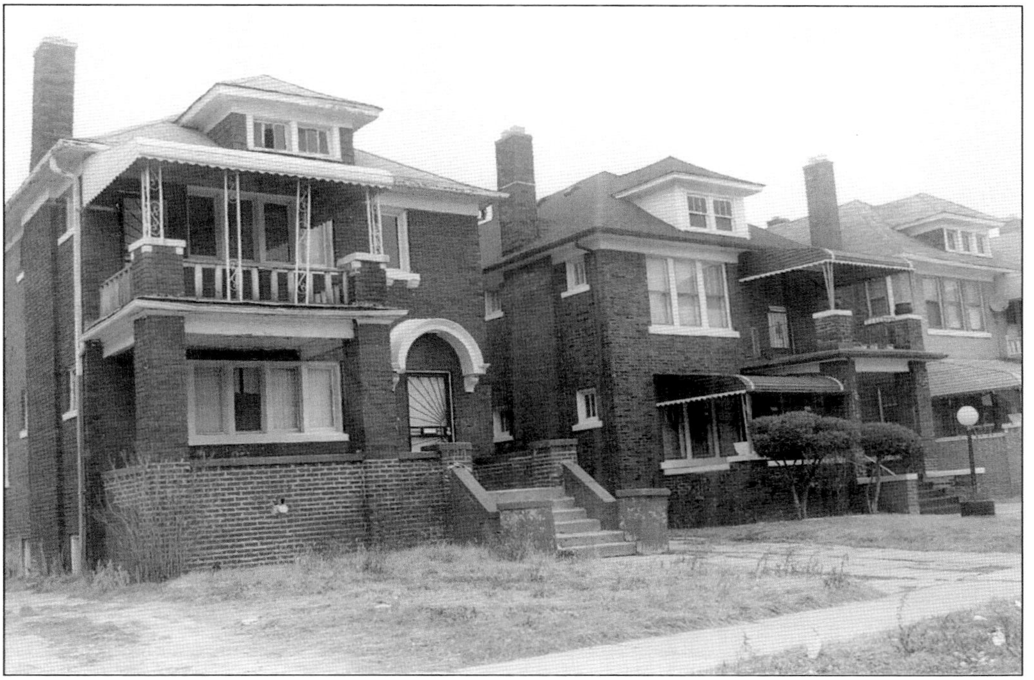

Detroit was still a growing city in 1950 with 1,849,568 residents, a gain of 246,116 over the previous decade. The bulk of the Jewish population could be found along the Dexter and Linwood corridor from Joy Road north to Davison. Many Jewish families lived upstairs or downstairs in homes such as these on Tuxedo, between Dexter and Linwood.

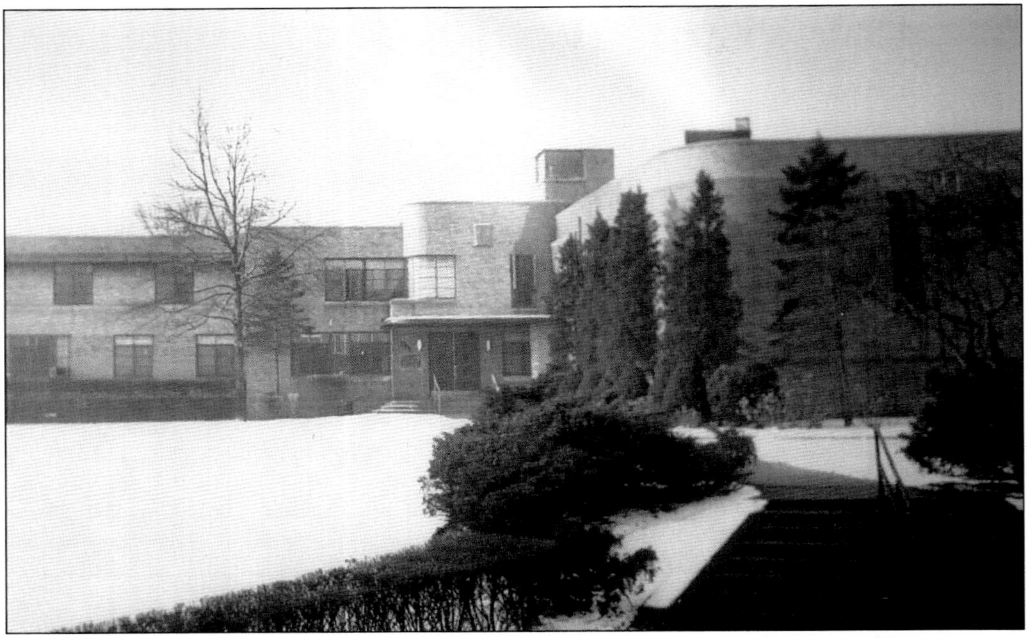

The Jewish Home for the Aged—the Old Folks Home—was on Petoskey west of Dexter.

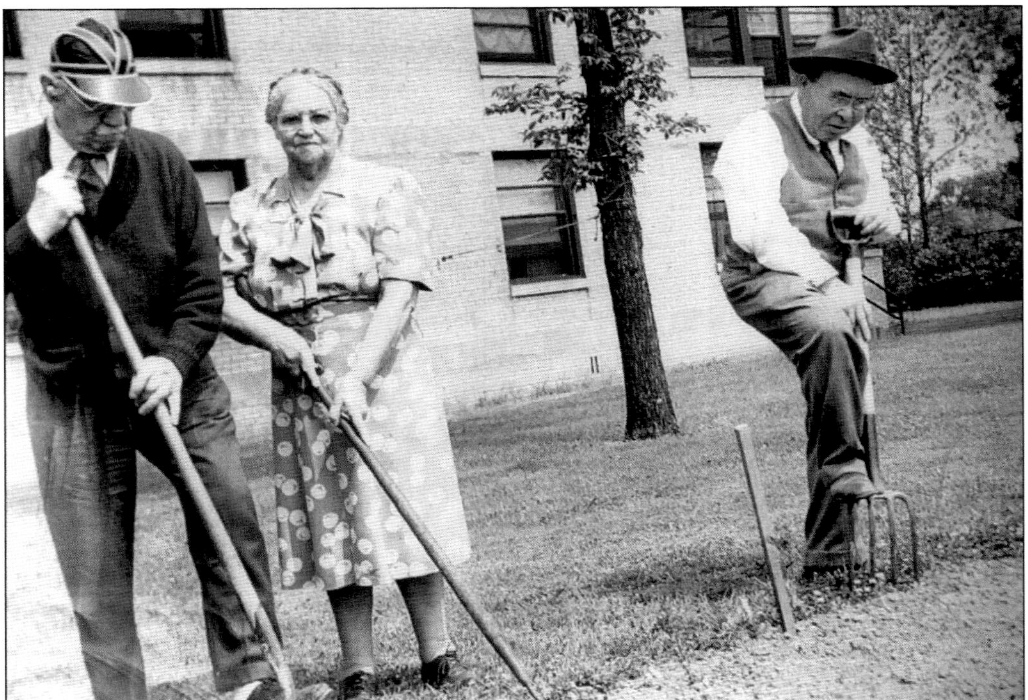

Residents had plenty of gardening area on the grounds. (Courtesy Leonard N. Simons Jewish Community Archives.)

Most residents preferred reading Yiddish newspapers to those printed in English.

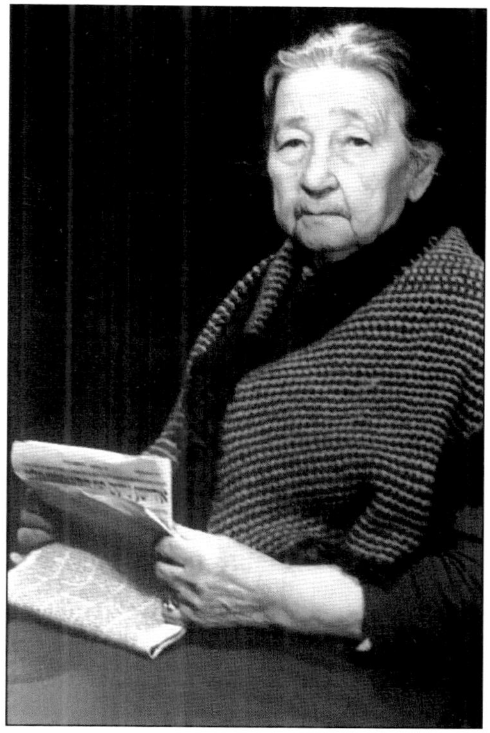

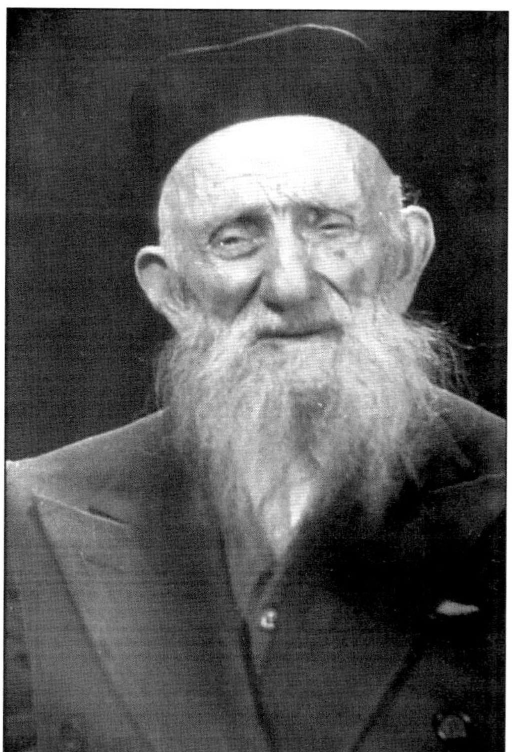

Cheerful Isaac Nagel celebrated his 105th birthday in 1952. (Courtesy Leonard N. Simons Jewish Community Archives.)

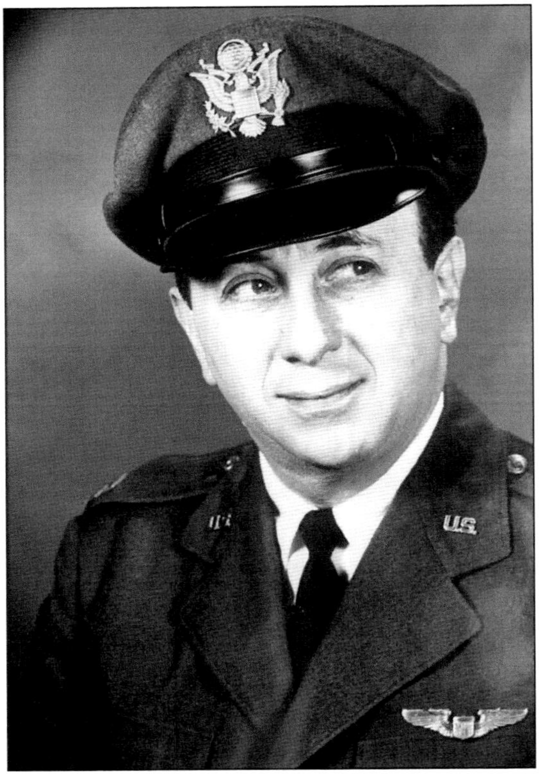

World War II hero Marvin Schlossberg became a radio and television celebrity known to generations of Detroiters as Sonny Eliot. (Courtesy Sonny Eliot.)

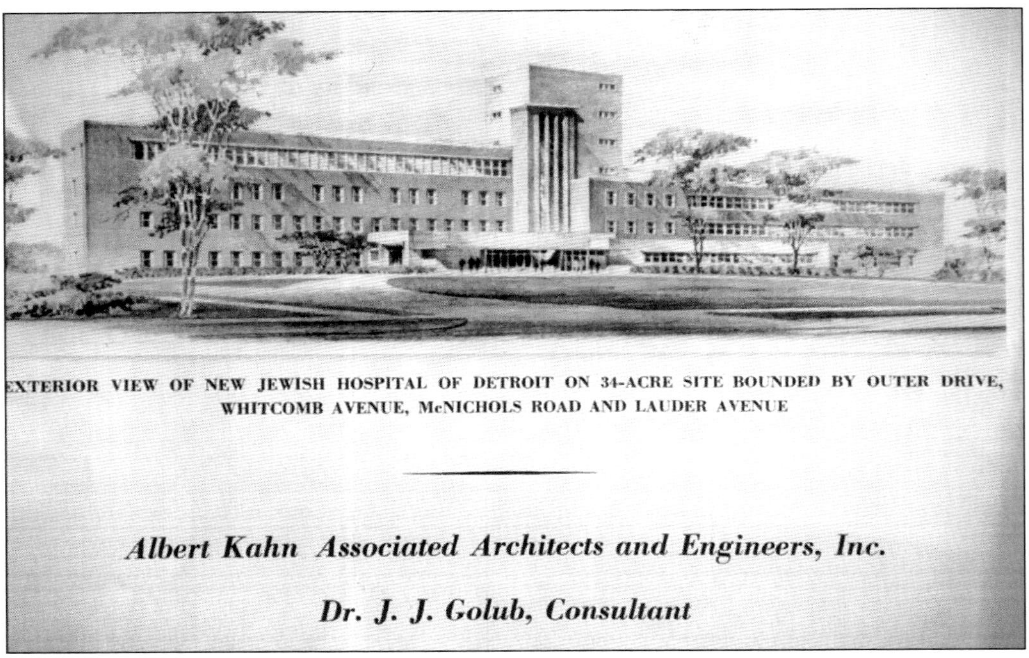

After decades of community involvement, Sinai Hospital opened in 1953. (Courtesy Leonard N. Simons Jewish Community Archives.)

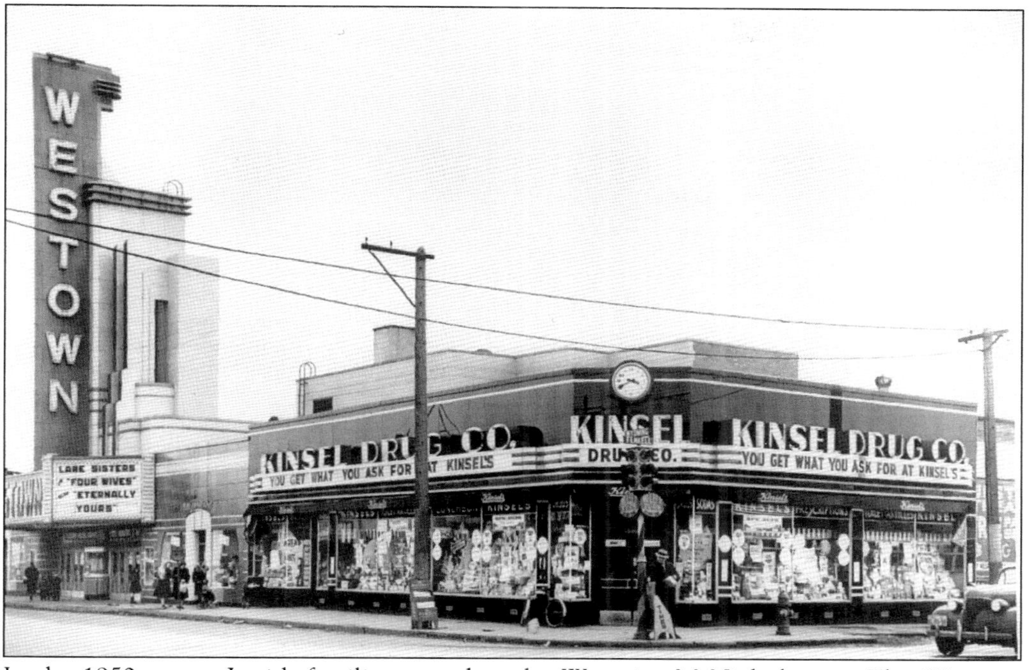

In the 1950s, more Jewish families moved to the Wyoming-McNichols area. The Westown Theater and Kinsel Drug Store, south of the Jewish population on Wyoming, were popular destinations. (Courtesy Manning Brothers Historic Photographic Collection.)

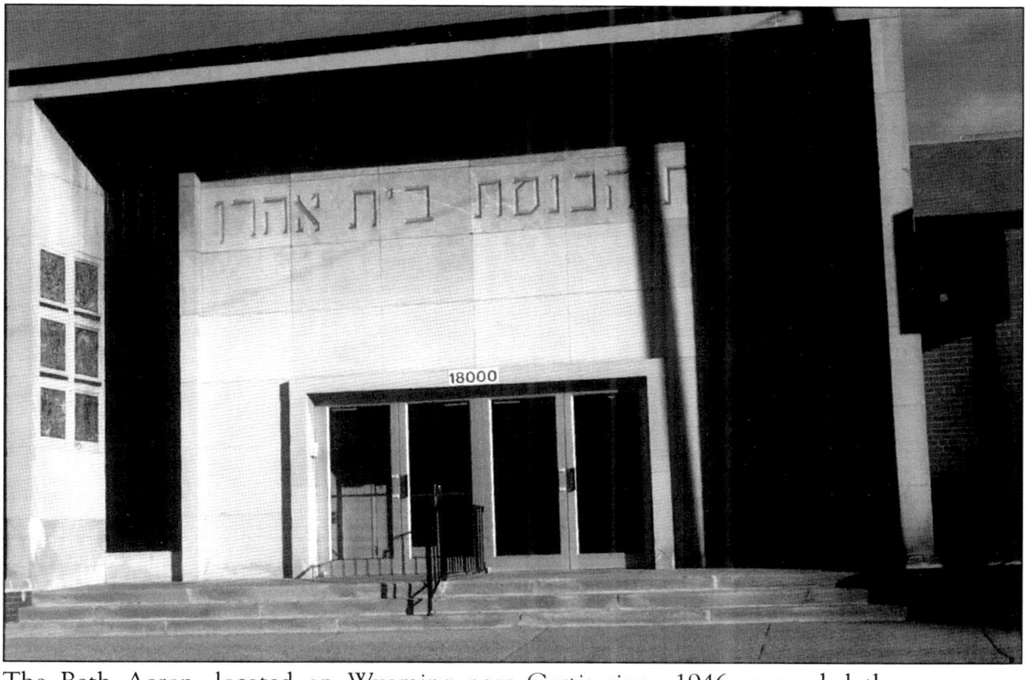

The Beth Aaron, located on Wyoming near Curtis since 1946, expanded the synagogue building in 1955 and 1959.

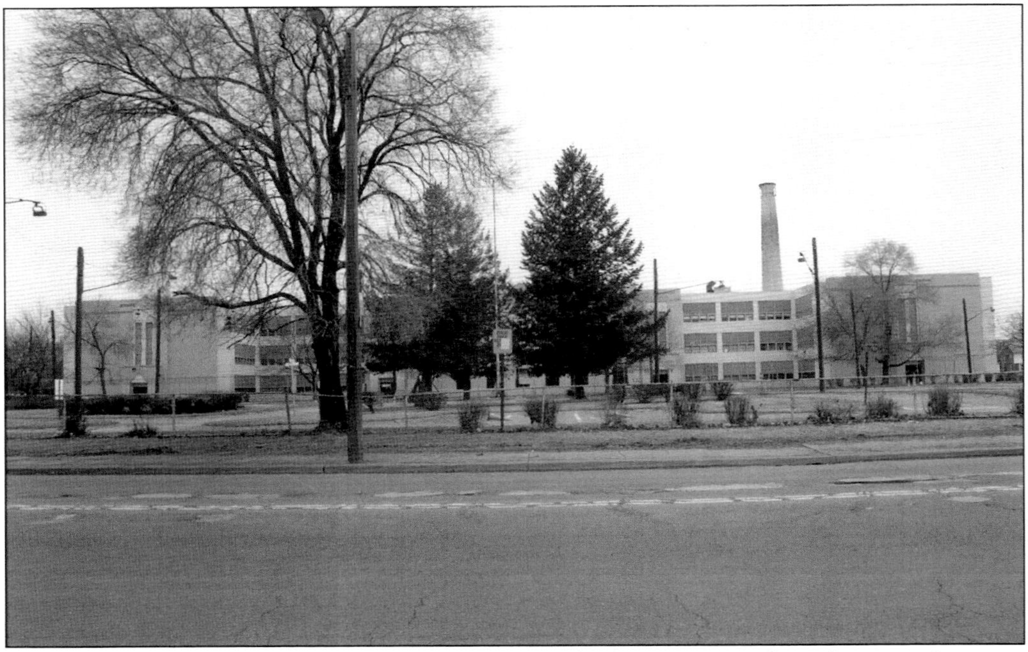

Mumford High School on Wyoming south of Curtis had a major Jewish student population in the 1950s.

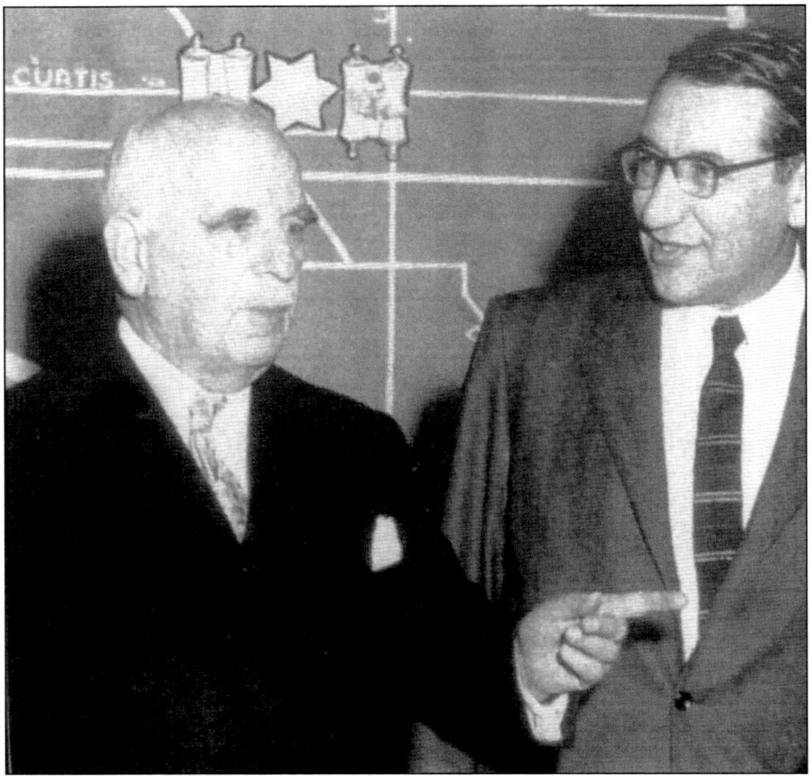

Justice Henry Butzel makes a point to community leader Max Fisher at the annual meeting of the Jewish Welfare Federation in 1956. (Courtesy Jewish Welfare Federation.)

Two decades after many Jewish establishments left Twelfth Street, African-American businesses populated the area.

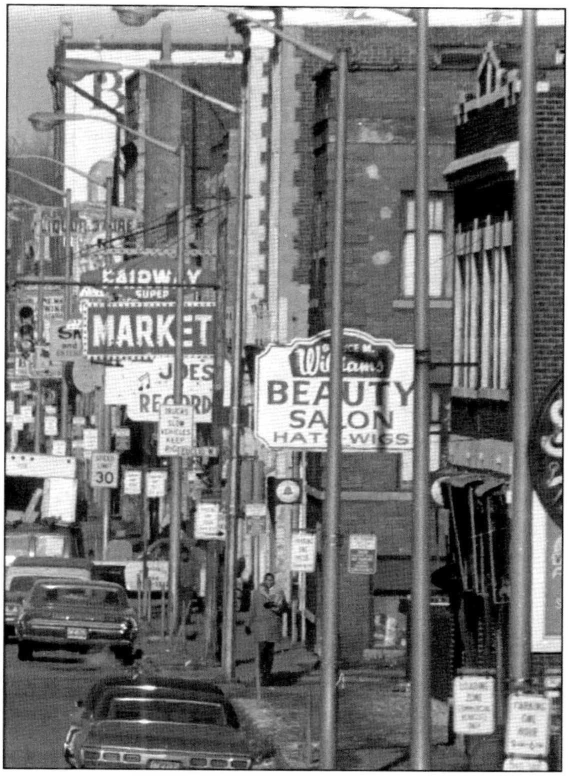

The July 1967 riots destroyed much of the commercial area along Twelfth Street. When the smoke from 1,300 fires cleared, 2,700 businesses in Detroit had been looted. (Courtesy Walter Reuther Library of Wayne State University.)

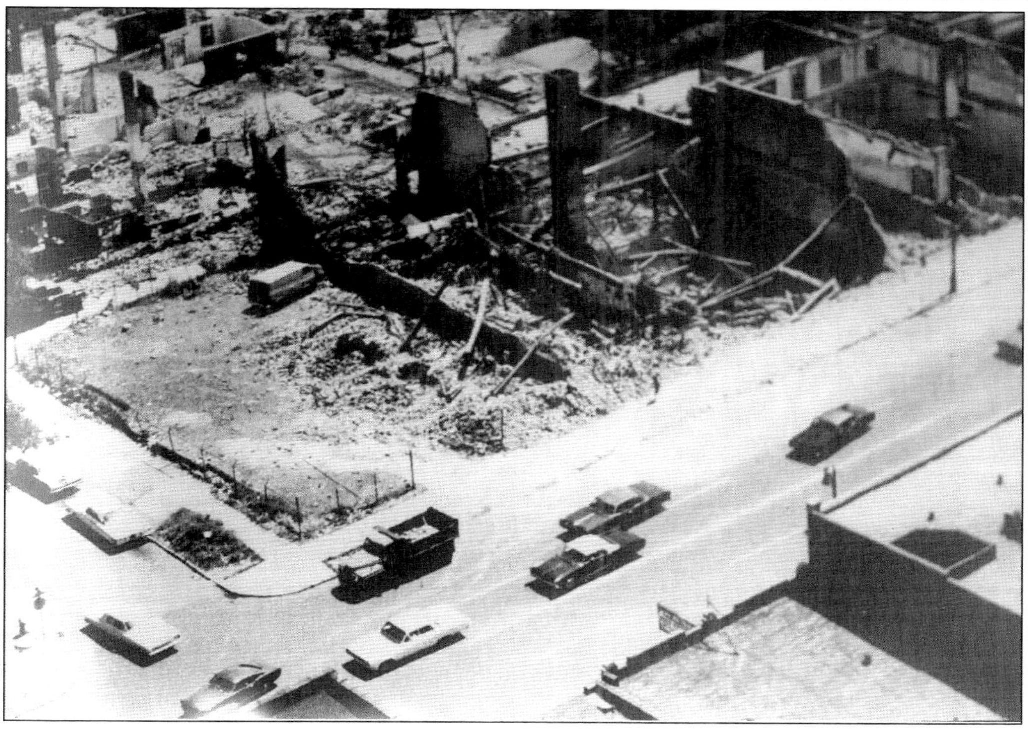

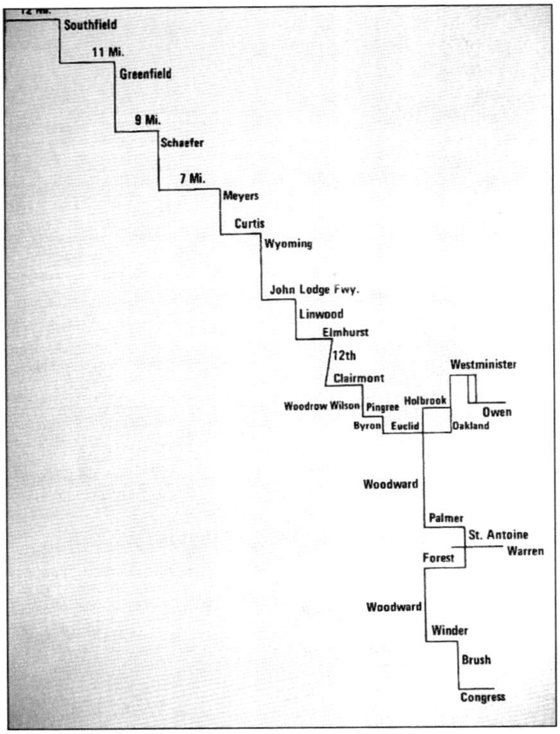

The riots quickened the pace of Jewish migration to the suburbs. The Jewish neighborhoods of previous generations had become almost totally African-American.

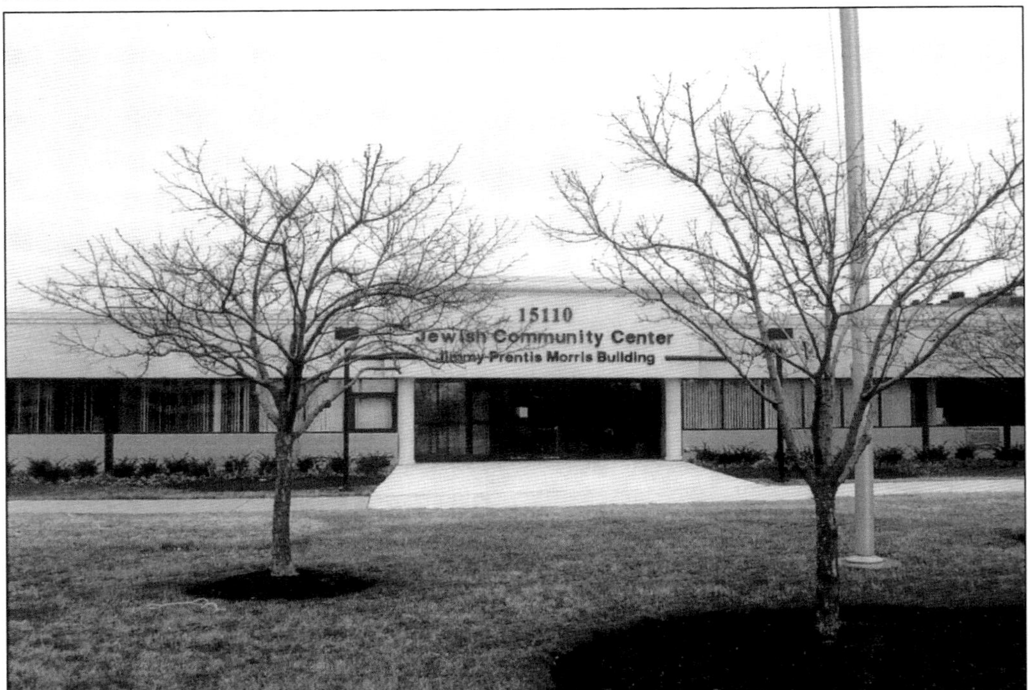

Many families moved from northwest Detroit to the Oak Park area near the Jewish Community Center on Ten Mile Road east of Greenfield.

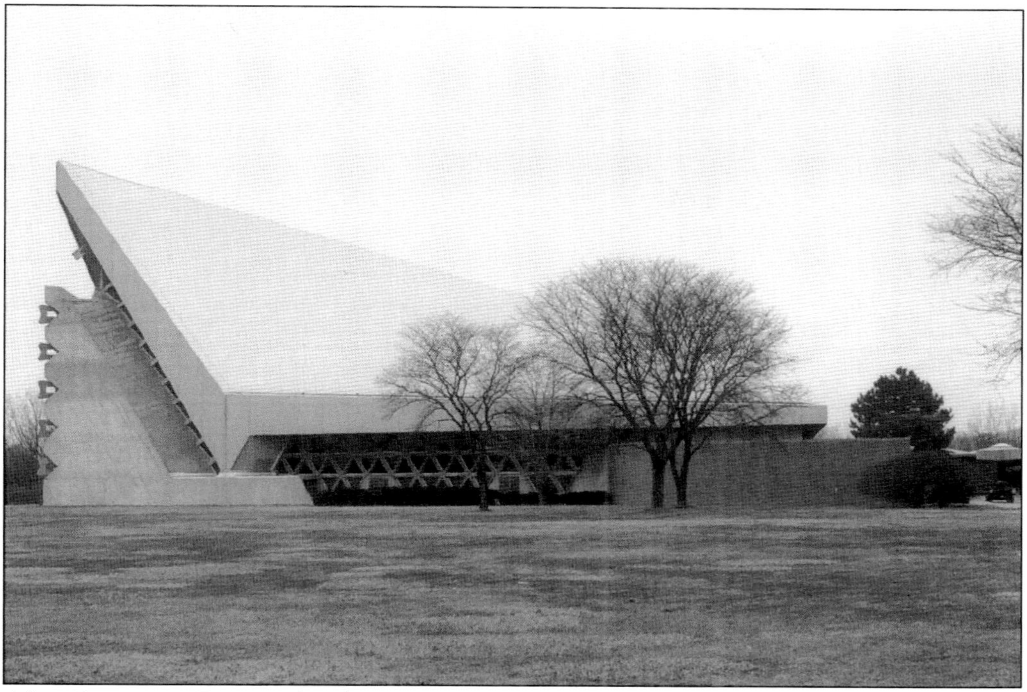

After 101 years in Detroit, the Shaarey Zedek Synagogue opened in the Northwestern Highway, Bell Road and Eleven Mile area in December 1962.

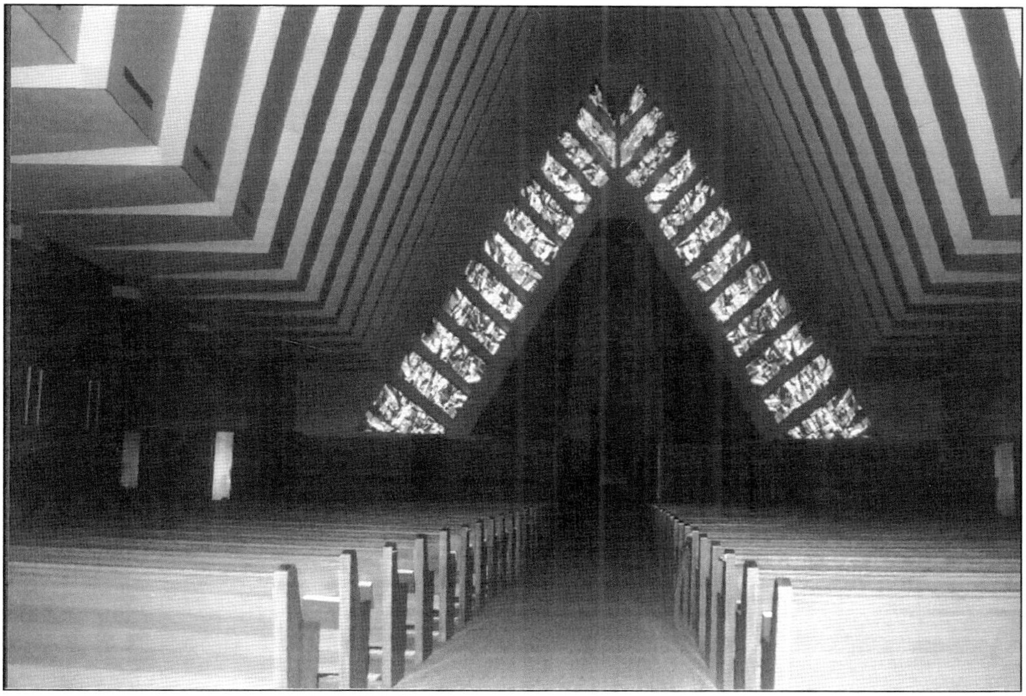

The Shaarey Zedek sanctuary became somewhat of a Jewish tourist attraction in the 1960s.

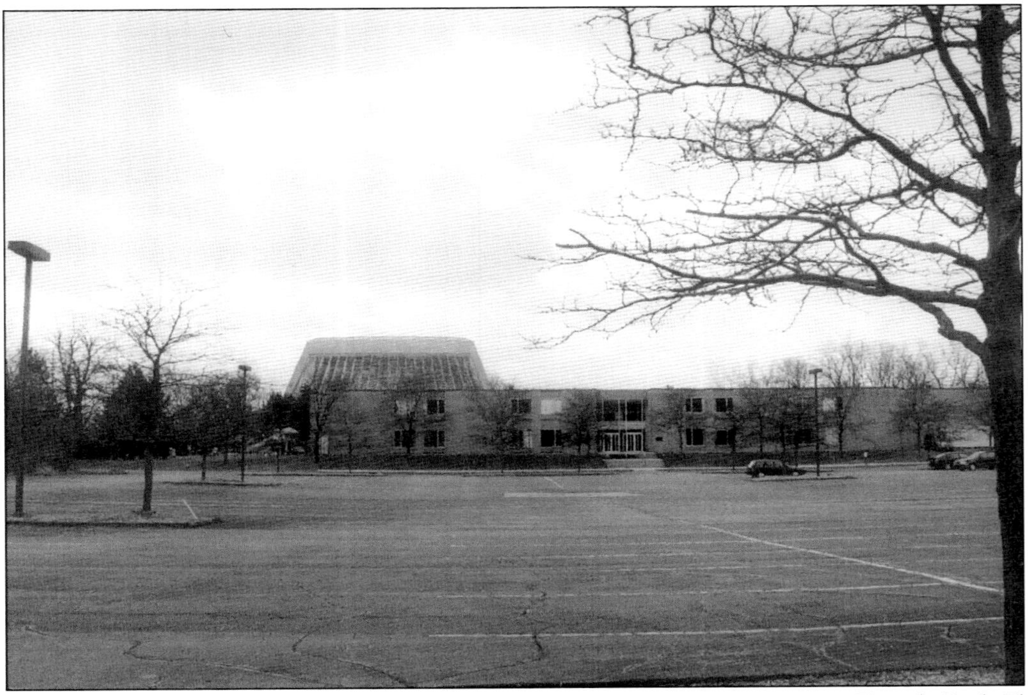

In 1974, after 52 years on Woodward and Gladstone and 124 years in Detroit, Temple Beth El opened its huge complex on Telegraph north of 14 Mile Road.

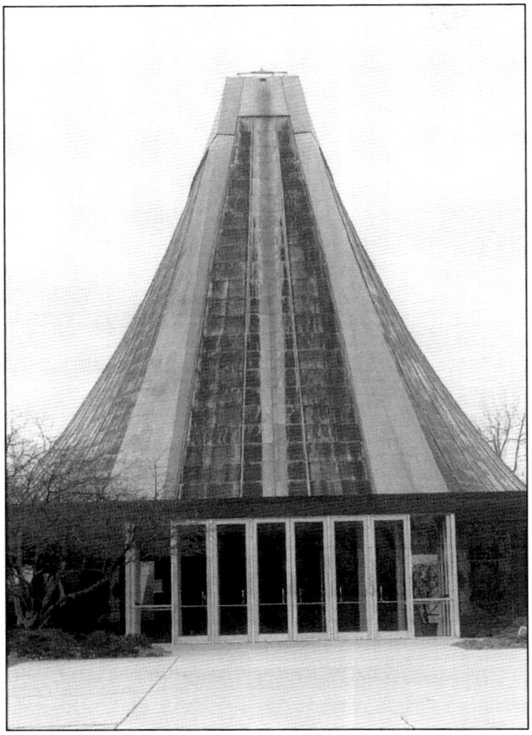

Seen here is the entrance to the sanctuary.

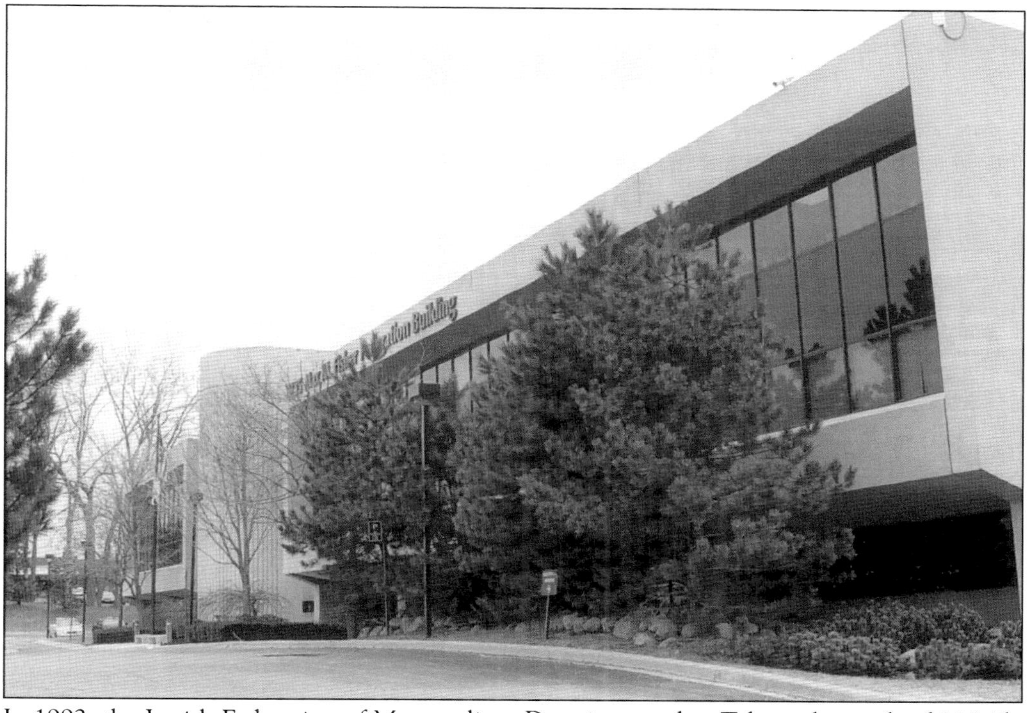

In 1992, the Jewish Federation of Metropolitan Detroit moved to Telegraph, north of 14 Mile Road, and honored Max Fisher by naming the building after the longtime community leader and philanthropist.

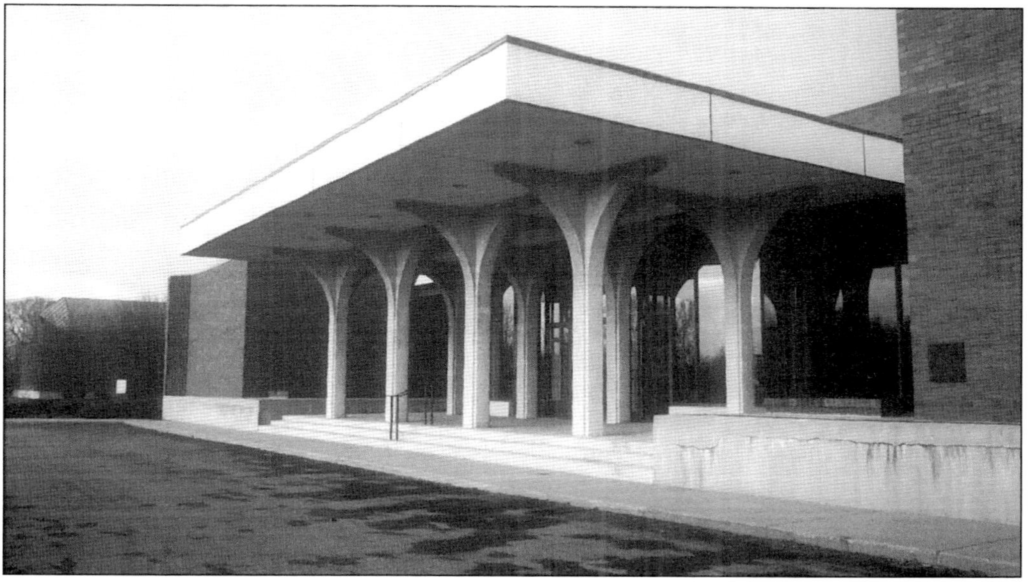

Beth Achim's congregants consisted of a merger between Beth Aaron and Beth Achim. Dwindling membership forced it to merge with Adat Shalom on Middlebelt Road. The Beth Achim Synagogue building on Twelve Mile Road east of Lahser became the new home of Akiva Hebrew Day School in 1999.

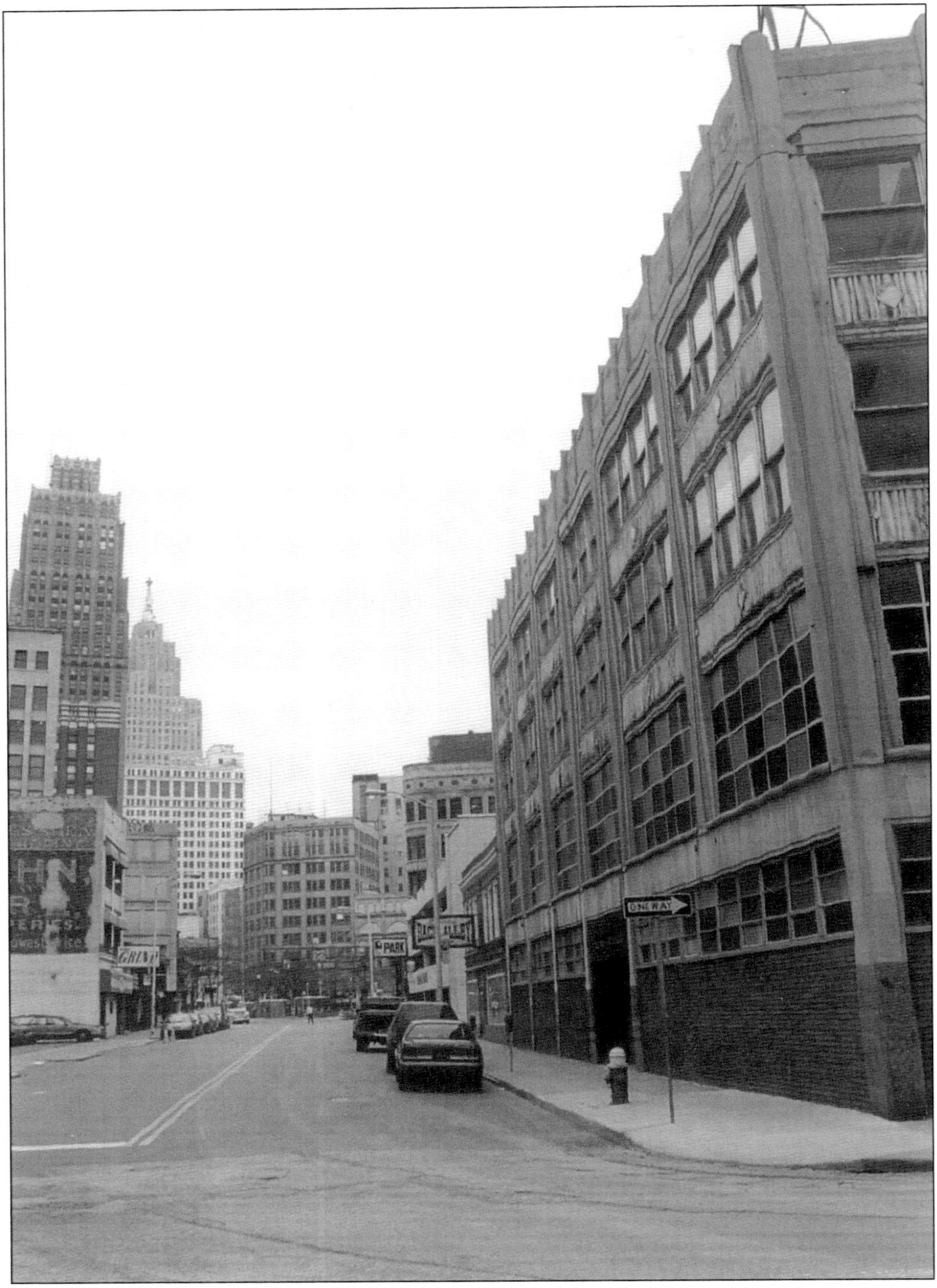

The Downtown Synagogue (right) at the end of Griswold was a fixture for over half a century. However, a deteriorating building and dwindling membership gives the only synagogue in the city of Detroit an uncertain future.